Faith, Pride & Works

MEDIEVAL
CHURCH
BUILDING

Faith, Pride & Works

MEDIEVAL CHURCH BUILDING

TOM McNEILL

TEMPUS

In memory of my mother, G.H. McNeill (née Fox), 1904-2005, who from an early age encouraged me to study the past.

First published 2006

Tempus Publishing Limited
The Mill, Brimscombe Port,
Stroud, Gloucestershire, GL5 2QG
www.tempus-publishing.com

© Tom McNeill, 2006

The right of Tom McNeill to be identified as the Author
of this work has been asserted in accordance with the
Copyrights, Designs and Patents Act 1988.

British Library Cataloguing in Publication Data.
A catalogue record for this book is available from the British Library.

ISBN 0 7524 3643 0

Typesetting and origination by Tempus Publishing Limited
Printed in Great Britain

CONTENTS

PREFACE AND ACKNOWLEDGEMENTS

A book on medieval church building may be many things, although no one could write one which gives a comprehensive guide to the whole subject in a single volume. This one is simply a commentary on the buildings themselves. It is based on visiting the standing remains of churches, not on the results of excavations, nor on the historical documentation, although it takes note of both. It began with Professor Martyn Jope in that he gave me my first experience of research on churches. More importantly it takes from him the starting point that churches may be approached like any other artefacts from the past in that they are the product of human choice and dialogue, based on the needs and the technological possibilities of the time. However, it concentrates on the design rather than the technology which Martyn so liked; in effect on the styles. In doing this, it tries to follow a course between the ideas that the church builders were following a pre-ordained path, a typology, or that the buildings were the creation primarily of the talents of the controlling individual masters. Given the rejection of the teleological impetus as 'the story', it is perhaps surprising to construct the book chronologically. The point is not, however, to reject the idea of cumulative development, gradually adding to the stock of ideas over time, but to explain it differently. I wish to place the stress on the choices available to the builders at any point and to note that they made these choices not as individuals but as groups. The churches of the Middle Ages were the product of the community of those involved in their construction, from the patrons through the craftsmen, but also the wider community of society beyond the builders.

This is not the product of the sort of single-minded research programme beloved of university directors (nor, even more to their chagrin, of large research grants) but of two other processes. One is a steady habit of visiting churches and the other is of trying to explain them to others, notably students. The first has required the indulgence of my family on numerous occasions, and I am glad to acknowledge it first. The Queen's University of Belfast has provided the students and the means to make the visits, culminating in granting leave of absence to gather the material for this book. I would also like to acknowledge the sources of the following illustrations; *1*: John Rylands library, University of Manchester; *20*: Winchester Archaeological Unit; *6, 8* and *29*: K. Blockley and Canterbury Archaeological Trust; *8* and *29*: R.D.H. Gem and *42* and *64*: C. Wilson.

I

INTRODUCTION

One of the main features of modern Europe is the legacy of the Middle Ages. We do not have to argue that this legacy should dictate the future of the European Union to appreciate that failing to understand the medieval period greatly weakens our knowledge of our present condition. It was a period when the Roman tradition of law and organisation was joined to the Barbarian idea of personal responsibility. It was, contrary to the modern image of the medieval as backward, a time of great competition and innovation when many of our institutions (the nation State, parliaments) or mechanical inventions (mills and clocks) originated. Our landscape, its fields, villages and towns, has its origins in the period, and a part of that landscape is made up of the major medieval buildings. Above all, it is impossible to imagine a European village or town without its medieval churches, or more recent imitation of them.

The study of these buildings has been active for a long time; one of the main routes both into the study of the medieval period and also the use of physical remains for this. Rickman's publication (in 1817) of the classification of the styles of medieval architecture in England arranged in chronological sequence was one of the first works of archaeological classification, the systematic ordering of physical remains from the past. Throughout the nineteenth century medieval church building was a major area of research, either as a topic of controversy over contemporary style and religion or as a subject in its own right. As the religious controversies died down in the twentieth century, the pace of academic interest grew. It tended to focus on two areas. One was the organisation of the building industry and the means by which the churches were constructed. The other was the attribution of individual buildings to particular masters which was linked to the search for the origins of their styles and the movements of ideas among them. In the first of these the emphasis has been more on the written documentation, which has become increasingly available as the originals are edited and gives information about the costs and organisation. The second is based firmly on the analysis on individual buildings or elements of them which are held to betray the hand of the master and the sources of his training. The drive for research and publication has therefore been away from general books of explanation of church building in the Middle Ages.

While this may seem to be a good reason to write one, it also acts as a warning. The subject is so dauntingly vast that to try to compress an account into a single volume is rash. It is a very specialised subject area, somewhere angels should fear to tread. The colleague who mentioned the scheme of writing such a book to me first, when I was holding forth to students outside the west front of Norwich cathedral, has a lot to answer for. In this activity of explaining medieval churches to students lies the basic justification for the book. This book is not aimed at giving a descriptive account of the churches of Europe but is a commentary on them. It needs a minimum of description to explain the topic, but description of the individual buildings is better sought in the specialised literature on them: the same applies to the general accounts of means of their construction. It is largely based on places I have visited and the world I have tried to study. This excludes the Mediterranean and thus the buildings of the Roman Empire, either in its Classical or Byzantine forms; Spain and Italy are not part of the medieval world with which I am acquainted. Secondly it concentrates on the larger churches: while I do not subscribe to the idea that it was only in the centres of political power that new inventions occurred, it remains true that it was in the great churches that they were most obviously displayed.

They astonish us by their size (either height or length), by their technological skill and by the beauty of their overall design and their detail. I find it extraordinary that anyone can visit them and remain unimpressed, although the members of my family are constant reminders that my enthusiasm is not universally shared! This said, I should like to avoid the use of personal value judgements in discussing the churches. This is partly because I find it obtrusive but also because it is irrelevant, for we do not know either whether we are seeing the same thing as the original (many have lost their paint, for example) and we do not necessarily appreciate the same things as past generations. It also inevitably sets up connections in the reader's mind (how can a great design belong with a poor one?) and thus can distort the pattern of their creation. On the other hand it is disingenuous to deny any preferences and to do so would result in a flat and boring account so, inevitably, some have crept in.

The study of churches has always been different from the study of those other major medieval buildings of the period, the castles. The study of them was much less well-developed in the nineteenth century and took off only slowly during the first part of the twentieth. This is a response to the way that they have become the subject of an academic debate, rejecting the idea of them as purely military structures and seeing them in their wider landscape and cultural context as buildings which had many functions and which tell us about many aspects of medieval life. By contrast, the purpose of churches has not really been disputed: they are obviously centres of the Christian faith (1).

1 The Virgin oversees the construction of a church. *John Rylands Library, University of Manchester, Latin ms 39*

This is what caused the nineteenth-century ecclesiologists to turn to the medieval ones, because they wished to connect their own religion to what they saw as an age of faith and this is why the academic study became embroiled in contemporary disputes. To the barbarians who inherited the lands of the Western Roman Empire, Christianity and Roman traditions were inextricably intertwined; throughout the earlier Middle Ages, literacy, the Christian Church and the ideal of the united Roman Empire were basic to the idea of culture in the West. Faith required the men of the West to build churches; without it there would have been none. It did not, however, prescribe the size or form of the churches. Perhaps surprisingly the actual ritual of the Church has not been identified as a great influence on the architecture of the medieval churches. The love of processions, the increasing demand for private chapels as well as the main space in the building are two such influences, but they are not seen as driving the main developments.

Faith inspired the act of building the churches, but it was pride which dictated the pattern of their construction. The monopoly of faith held by the Church ensured that the institutions of the Church were both rich and powerful. Medieval lordship, like all elite systems, demanded display and building was one of the preferred means of this. Pride in the institution – whether monastery or cathedral – and pride in craftsmanship led to the competition which fuelled the developments of churches. The resources put into the churches show how

2 Chartres cathedral: air view

contemporaries valued them. These were buildings erected by paid craftsmen and one way to estimate their value would be to give a costing of some churches in money terms. It is easier to quote castle costs than church ones, a position which is, perhaps, surprising given that they were constructed for Church institutions, abbeys and cathedrals, which were both literate and accustomed both to making and keeping records. Partly the problem is caused by the upheavals of the Reformation and revolutions which targeted these very institutions. The main reason, however, is the very nature of the works. They were very slow projects to be completed only after work for more than a generation, while the great churches seem to have had almost continuous building work on them. Castles, by contrast, were often put up quickly, to meet the need of an impatient lord, and once finished might be left alone for a time. They therefore had records opened specially for the work, rather than merged into continuous expenditure.

One of the best-known campaigns is the work to replace Westminster abbey, paid for by King Henry III from 1245-72. The annual expenditure here averaged about £2100 over the 27 years. To put this in perspective, we may compare it with taxation figures. The seven exceptional taxes levied by Henry between 1220 and 1237 raised a total of about £112,000 between them. This is about twice as much as the costs of the abbey, but these were large sums to meet specific crises in government. Another comparison would be with the castles built by Henry's son, Edward I, in Wales. The annual expenditure of a little over £2000 compares well with the costs of each of the castles of Rhuddlan, Harlech and Conwy, but with two differences. Firstly the latter two were going up together, so that the king had to cover both at a time when he was also building elsewhere. However, and crucially, the castles each took less than 10 years to build: Rhuddlan nine (but mostly done in four), Harlech six and Conwy four. They were cases where speed was achieved by throwing money at them, different from the long process of a church. At the end of Henry's reign, in fact, the new church was still hardly half finished. The £40-50,000 spent on half of Westminster would have finished the castles of Flint, Rhuddlan, Harlech and Conwy. The difference is in the difference of the workforces: building castles needed many more unskilled (but cheaper men) than churches.

Another measure of the expense of a church is provided by the exercise carried out by James in 1972, when he attempted to give a costing for the construction of Chartres cathedral (2) by modern methods over the 30 years of its main period of construction. In two areas modern construction saved considerable sums of money: on moving material to the church and moving it around the site, especially lifting it. In this way his figures are therefore cheaper than with medieval construction but the wages he paid were greater (even allowing for the change in the value of money) especially for the unskilled. As a guide, therefore, the exercise is valuable but not precise. He estimated the annual costs to average about £707,150 in 1972 values; in today's terms (multiplying by 26) a little under £18,386,000 a year.

Both Westminster and Chartres were very large projects; even for greater churches we cannot treat them as typical, where perhaps half the yearly expenditure would be nearer the mark. Morris has calculated that among the 85 largest churches in England, large-scale projects were being carried out at about 30 at any one time during the thirteenth century. If we add in the rest of the work, on smaller projects at other large churches and the building of the lesser ones such as parish churches, we may easily double this volume. This would give, in thirteenth-century terms, an expenditure of some £60,000 in a year on all church building, the annual investment of the yields of four major taxations. The population of thirteenth-century England was steadily increasing through the century, but an average of some 6 million people or 1.2 million households might be a reasonable figure. Following James' calculations from Chartres, in modern figures the total expenditure would be about £600 million per year being spent on churches across England. This would work out nowadays as a yearly levy of about £500 per household for church building as the number of thirteenth-century households is smaller than now; £500 per household is half a Milton Keynes Band C council tax. In terms of royal income, compared to tax yields or in relation to the population, the costs of church building for England were high.

They were highest in the thirteenth century because that is when the population was highest, but the slackened effort of the later fourteenth and fifteenth centuries had to be met by a smaller population. The investment of money in churches was formidable in its economic impact. Donations from pilgrims and other benefactors provided some of this, but the core source of the money was in the landed estates of the churches. These produced goods, corn grown or rents and services often levied in goods not cash. Much of the produce was transmitted back to feed the clergy of the church, but a great quantity was sold. The proceeds from this provided the money for the building, to pay the craftsmen, labourers and suppliers employed on the projects. In this way the landed resources were cycled into the general economy rather than being locked up in the internal expenses of the church communities.

The men who had this money and used it in the works constituted the community of builders, falling into four groups. Perhaps the most important, certainly in their own eyes, were the patrons who paid for the work. These were not all churchmen, although the great majority of them were. Kings and great lords patronised church building projects from a mixture of motives. Building churches, like building castles, was part of the equipment of power; both left a permanent legacy on the landscape to contribute to the prestige of the builder. Henry III's investment in the rebuilding of Westminster abbey came partly from his personal piety, but much more from motives of pride and politics. It was a response to the building by Louis IX, king of France, of a new chapel (the Ste Chapelle) at his palace in Paris to house relics recovered from the Holy Land. Henry was drawing attention to Westminster because it was founded by his predecessor, Edward the Confessor, for whom he tried to obtain saintly status to enhance his lineage and royalty. It was a help that Edward was Anglo-Saxon, not Norman and French,

3 Lavenham parish church from the south-west. The Spring chapel lies beside the chancel

4 The plinth of Lavenham church tower. The De Vere star (right) and the merchant's mark of Thomas Spring (in the shield on the left) commemorate the principal benefactors of the project

and he named his son after him. Kings from Ireland to Austria sought to have their kingship enhanced by cathedrals at their centres of power. There were more personal reasons of individual piety to the carrying out of vows, which happened throughout the Middle Ages from William the Conqueror at Caen in the eleventh century, to Margaret of Austria at Brou in the sixteenth. All the motives can be seen in the parish church of Lavenham (3).

The two richest men of the area, the Earl of Oxford and Thomas Spring, contributed to the building of the tower, while Spring later celebrated his wealth and the grant of the right to bear arms in a private chapel (4). At the same time, the parish community of this rich cloth town rebuilt the nave in a display of their communal pride.

When churchmen or church institutions embarked on new building projects it was from the same motives. The honour of the institution and the saint to whom the church was dedicated demanded that services should be held in a proper setting befitting their status. Saints were ever present where their relics were held and they would express their views through miracles and disasters. Pilgrims also expected that the relics which they had come to venerate should be displayed appropriately, and pilgrims might bring gifts to further the process. Rivalry with other institutions also played a part as did the ambitions of individuals. Bishops and abbots, as much as kings and lords, liked to leave behind a building as a legacy of their lives; after all, as celibates, they could not found a dynasty to uphold their name.

Faith and pride still required work, from the skilled and the unskilled, to translate the aspirations into reality. Apart from the patrons, there were three other groups who built the churches. The top one of these was made up of the masters of their crafts. A church required a whole variety of these, the main ones of mason and carpenter (responsible for the scaffolding and cranes perhaps as well as the roofing) and then the plumbers for the lead roof and guttering, the glaziers, plasterers and smiths, to service the iron tools, etc. Each trade would be responsible to its master and each of them would have a part to play in the design of the church. At the same time there was a clerk to control the finances, often detached from the household of the patron and acting as his or her representative. If the master mason had a pre-eminent position, he did not have a free hand. It would have been rash not to consult the experts in the other fields about the demands he was to make on their skill and resources, while it would be important to keep the patron on side. It is therefore likely that the major decisions and problems would have gone forward for discussion to a group of the relevant masters and the patron. This group may not have been a formally constituted committee, and its composition may have varied according to the nature of the business to be discussed, but behind every master must have existed some such group.

Below this we may identify groups of sub-contractors who had little input into the general design but were responsible for carrying out parts of it. The accounts often record the payment for elements, sometimes large ones such as a porch, by task work when a man has been given the contract for it. It is likely that individual features, arches or windows with their tracery, could be treated in the same way by being given to specialist teams. What we do not know is how far these teams or individuals might be responsible for aesthetic decisions as well as for the carrying out of the master design. Clearly in some things such as the carving of a capital on a pier or the glass painting of a figure, the precise form of the work must have been left to the individual craftsman. On the other hand, the individual figure or carving was often part of a series, perhaps reflecting a view or message for the church as a whole, scenes from the saint's life or the like. Here again we see the need for co-operation between the master, the patron who will have devised the programme or story and the individual who would give expression to it in the actual work.

It would be the same with suppliers. With the stones from the quarry, it makes obvious sense if these are cut before they are sent to the site; it would be silly to load carts with stones which were too big. Again we can see in the records that the quarrymen frequently supplied lengths of cut stone such as string courses as well as large items like columns ready-cut. It is more efficient if all the stones in one course, or layer, are of the same height; this is best done in the quarry but how well it is done will affect the building at the end. Timber needed to be cut to the right lengths at least, again work to be done in the forest to save carting. On the one hand, there are accounts of the difficulty of supplying the right size of timbers holding up work, while on the other we find accounts of roof timbers cut and pre-fabricated in the forest and sent to the site for assembly. Out of this arose the practice, from the fourteenth century onwards, of having a single building contractor who looked after both the design and the supplies. He was paid a single figure for the whole works, or else a figure each year, replacing the more direct employment of the workforce which gave us our accounts of the earlier period. Allied to these were the men who provided transport to the site and around it. The first were the carters while the efficiency of the latter was greatly improved by the thirteenth-century invention of the wheelbarrow which allowed one man to convey a load which previously had taken two to carry in a stretcher. In all this we see the need for co-ordination and consultation.

All these men had been trained in a skill which required personal investment. The fundamental part of this was the apprenticeship system, whereby a boy was engaged to help and be instructed by a master. By the fourteenth century it had become normal that this would take seven years, usually starting at the age of about 14. To get a position as an apprentice, with the opportunities it might provide to become a master, was not easy. It required contacts and someone had to support the apprentice during his training. An apprentice was often recruited from a family of another craftsman and, when he became a master, he would not be content with a basic wage. In the thirteenth-century accounts we can see a craftsman being paid two or three times the rate of a labourer, and being employed for longer in the year. After this the sub-contracting system would allow the new master to take on supervision of gangs and so gain experience in solving practical problems and in the management of men. This would form the pool from which

5 Canterbury cathedral choir from the west. In the foreground the work of William of Sens with alternating single columns in the arcade and twin openings in the triforium; beyond is the work of William the Englishman with paired arcade columns and four equal openings in the triforium

the master of the craft on the site would choose his key assistants, who would then be eligible to take control of a project elsewhere. The masters were important men who achieved considerable position in a society normally dominated by birth. Famously William Wynford, master mason, and Hugh Herland, master carpenter, dined in 1391 with William of Wyckham the bishop of Winchester at his new foundation of New College, Oxford; their servants dined with the college fellows. These were the king's masters and the royal works provided such men with high wages and administrative responsibility. More commonly, masters were absorbed into the freemen and burgesse of the towns in which they lived. The losers in this system were the men with skill but no capital or contacts to be formally trained, the journeymen who remained without contracts and just paid by the day, who made up the bulk of the workforce at the sub-contracting level.

The final group was that of the unskilled. Building work was seasonal because of short days in winter and because the mortar could not be laid if there was danger of frost. The slack of the winter also allowed the more skilled men to stockpile cut stone or timber and the other components so that they could be put in place next summer. The result was that the workforce fluctuated greatly in numbers through the year. At Westminster in 1253 it went from a high of 426 men employed in total in June to a low of 100 in November; the great bulk of the fluctuation was in the labourers, whose numbers went from 220 in June to 30 in November. A dip in their numbers employed at the end of August and the beginning of September, when 100 fewer were employed, tells another part of the story. This was harvest time, when men would be needed back in their home villages returning to the building site after it. Again, if we perform similar estimates as with the money, we can see how the church building industry permeated through society. Westminster was a big enterprise, we should not take its figure of 400 as typical but cut it to, say, 250 for an average large project; as we have seen, we should think of the equivalent of some 60 such projects as happening at any time in thirteenth-century England. To this we may add some 50 employed in the supplying of materials to the site and their transport. This means that we may think in terms of perhaps 18–20,000 men employed at some time during the year on church building. Perhaps one household in 600 received some income from the projects.

A community of interest pervaded this community of builders. The patrons were concerned to build ever greater structures, the craftsmen and labourers to be employed to do so. Again there was usually a broad agreement on the aims of the building, that it should be as large and as innovative as could be achieved within the limits of the resources available. Just as the greatest pressure within the workforce was towards co-operation, so it was between the patrons and the masters.

To stress the force of the whole community of builders is to run somewhat counter to one of the strands of twentieth-century writing on medieval churches. After the Romantic nineteenth-century enthusiasts for the Gothic revival and all things medieval, who produced the remarkable idea that it was amateur churchmen who built the churches, there was a reaction. One of the strengths of research in the last three generations has been to concentrate on the names and identities of the masters of the works. This arose in part from the art-historical concern with attribution, but it was needed to establish that these were the result of professionals who applied hard technological ideas to the problems of churches and to dispel the vagaries of the earlier thoughts. The focus on attribution to an individual has created other problems in turn. At times it has been in danger of distorting our view of an individual, as in the way that the career of Henry Yevele during later fourteenth-century England has grown larger and larger.

It is often based on the idea that the one master will not change his motifs during his career: match the motifs and that is proof of the work of the same person; conversely if the features differ the master was different. There are cases where this can be proven, just as there are cases where documentary evidence can also show the reverse. Gervase of Canterbury records the precise point at which one master of the works at Canterbury, William of Sens, was replaced by a second, William the Englishman; the design of the church changes at that point (5).

The considerable changes in design visible at Boyle in Ireland or Selby in Yorkshire, both in the thirteenth century, do seem so drastic as to be the work of different masters and gangs. On the other hand, the bay designs of Romsey abbey differ but the details of the construction of the arcade and triforium arches show that the arch for each bay was predicted in the bay before and it is most likely that work was continuous but that changes were continuous too. At Rouen cathedral each bay of the nave has minor differences; although these have been attributed to different masters, it is more likely that they were just the result of continual experiment. The continuous building of cathedrals such as Wells, Lincoln or Salisbury over decades is likely to have involved many changes in personnel at the top, yet the group ethos held either to the original plan as at Salisbury or developed it steadily as at Lincoln and Wells. The axiom that masters were reluctant to change mouldings as they went through their career is not a proven law and should be used with caution. In the attribution of the design solely to the master mason, there is more than a hint of Carlyle's myth of the Great Man. It links up with the assumption that all changes are to be sought in the centres of power (provincial is often a pejorative term) and that ideas flow from the top down. Again it may be true at times but is not a universal law and it is to be used carefully.

A second general approach has been to focus on the question of the origins of ideas. This links to the stress on the individual master because it is natural to ask about his training and background before he undertook the work. This may be natural but it has three drawbacks. The first is that the focus on origins picks out a trail of ideas culminating in the one under consideration. Inevitably the other ideas around at the time are ignored if they do not play a part in the trail and it stresses the typological approach which often appears to imply that there was a clear, single path of progress which was followed by all. This underplays the level of choice confronting the designer of a building and also the importance of the history of the idea after its invention, which is of at least as much interest as its origin. The third problem is the myth of the single origin of a style. Few ideas, if any, occur out of the blue; there is always a source and then a source for the source, and so *ad infinitum*. It is impossible to fix on a single point. This is made much more difficult if the style is a complex one, involving a number of strands. There is a temptation to argue that one is pre-eminent and concentrate on that. In fact the crucial issue is neither the sources nor the elements of a style but how and when they came together and were accepted as a whole by the majority of builders afterwards. What we can usually see is a style emerging from a debate about competing ideas. For it to be successful the new style must be accepted by the rest of the building community. This may happen as a result of them seeing the finished prototype and being converted. It is more likely that it happens because the other builders were part of the original debate.

This leads to the final problem at the heart of much of this discourse; what should we mean by 'style', a word much bandied about in this subject but one least often defined as a concept? It can be used on a number of levels which are quite different things but which are all described by the same word. The first is the whole concept of a building, extending to the overall organisation of the space, most clearly defined in the plan of its internal divisions, to the structure which makes the building possible and to the decorative scheme inside and out. Within the story of medieval churches in this sense the Romanesque produces a number of individual regional styles; the early Gothic produces at least two and the late Gothic one. Below this meaning in the hierarchy of effect is what we might call the manner of the building. This concerns not the total concept of the building and its space but its decoration alone. As such, it will almost certainly involve a number of individual elements used together and the aesthetic judgement on which it is based may well affect other parts, such as the plan; if simplicity be the overriding aim, as in English Perpendicular Gothic, we will see aesthetics and plan combined. Finally there is the work of the individual artist or craftsman, what we might call the signature.

This last is not the subject of this book, for it is concerned more with the wider movements or processes as befits an archaeologist rather than an art historian. The distinction between what is here termed style and manner is more than just a matter of semantics. The style is a complex thing. The vision of the whole church is a matter which will bring in the concerns of the patron and the craftsmen. More importantly, by involving plan and structure, a change at this level of style will require not just the ideas of the master in control but changes to other crafts as well. A high vault will require not only the ideas to solve the engineering difficulties but new foundations and ways to cut the stones of the piers and the buttresses, new schemes of scaffolding and centring for the carpenters and a response from the glaziers to the higher windows. A whole new way of moving material around the site may be needed. To carry the new idea out will need a re-training of a number of sections of the workforce. This will not be done overnight but will take a long period of training and experiment; again it is where and when all these come together that is the crucial question, not the origin of one or more element. A new decorative manner will depend on new means of carving and new shapes, but not wholesale differences in the basic skills. It is much easier to envisage its introduction as a single point and its spread as being quicker than that of a new style. The community of builders is the key: a style requires the input of all the key masters, a manner perhaps only a part of them. The distinction between style and manner and the involvement of the other crafts and patrons in a style provides a microcosm of the whole process of construction. Building a medieval church needed the whole community, from patron to labourer, inspired by faith, driven on by pride in their institutions and culminating in their work.

2

THE FIRST ROMANESQUE

BEGINNINGS: THE CASE OF ENGLAND BEFORE 800

Converting pagan societies presented the Western Christian Church in the fifth
to seventh centuries with real difficulties. The Church in Europe, apart from the
British Isles, was deeply rooted in the late Roman Empire; it represented continuity
with it in Gaul and elsewhere even if the secular Imperial power and institutions
had gone. It demanded a dominant place in the new world; neither tolerance
nor humility was on the agenda. Socially and institutionally this required the
establishment of a new elite (with suitable resources) in appropriate central places,
to be in the Roman model, towns. They needed large buildings; again if they were
to follow the Roman model they would have to be of mortared stone or brick.
England was lost to paganism in the fifth century. In Ireland and the other 'Celtic'
lands, the missionaries from Britain and northern Gaul compromised, abandoning
the Roman institutional framework (especially the bishopric based on a town)
and building structures in the native technology of wood.

England presents us with an interesting case history in the problems of
conversion and compromise between the Barbarian and the Classical ties. St
Augustine's mission in 596 came from Rome and he had a Roman agenda not a
'Celtic' one, intending to revive institutions such as urban bishoprics and to build
in the more durable medium of mortared stone or brick. With his enterprise we
can see a classic case of the communication of ideas, with the immigration of at
least the nucleus of the new Church: a new elite and the community of craftsmen
they needed to serve their building aspirations. The grand Roman church was
based on the basilica, the public Roman judgement hall. It was a long rectangular
building, with lines of arches (arcades) dividing the central nave from the two
side aisles, and decorated inside with different-coloured marbles or mosaics.
Outside, their size was expressed in length not height, just as the decoration was

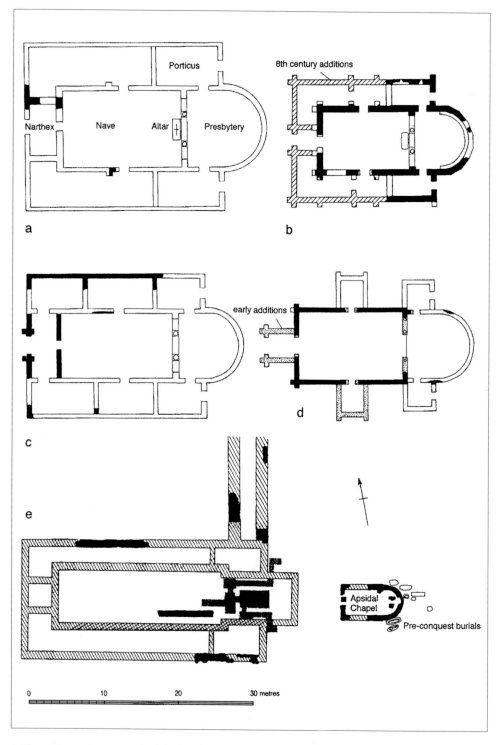

6 Plans of seventh-century English churches: a. Canterbury cathedral; b. Reculver; c. St Augustine's, Canterbury; d. St Pancras, Canterbury; e. Hexham. The short proportions and apses at the east of the four Kentish churches contrast with the plan of Hexham from the North. *After K. Blockley & Canterbury Archaeological Trust*

concentrated on the interior. The plan could be made to express the symbolism of the cross by the addition of a cross-space, the transept, at one end of the nave and aisles.

The study of early churches across the British Isles is not easy, particularly when it comes to chronology. Local patriotism, whether for the country or the parish, demands an early date for any structures found. The well-known fallacy of 'crude = early' is allowed full rein and simple structures abound. The few documentary references are exploited beyond their weight, particularly in the practice of arguing that when there is a documentary reference to the existence of a church in a given place, the existing remains should be equated with this and cannot be a later replacement. Much of what we know was uncovered in excavations conducted in the late nineteenth century or first decades of the twentieth, so the quality of the evidence is poor.

All these pressures combine to make it highly contentious to isolate a distinctive group of buildings and therefore building practice for the seventh or eighth centuries. We can, however, accept with confidence some early churches of the south-east of England, the so-called 'Kentish' churches. Their dating must rest on 'external' evidence, essentially good reasons to accept that the existing remains should be equated with a church mentioned in a contemporary account. The key building is the one excavated beneath the later church of the great abbey of Saints Peter and Paul, usually known as St Augustine's, in Canterbury. When the earlier church was demolished to build the new one in the eleventh century, the monk Goscelin gave a list, with positions of the tombs, of the burials of the early archbishops buried there and it is possible to identify them with the graves uncovered when the early church was excavated about 100 years ago. Goscelin is likely to have had access to reliable information so that the equation of his tombs with the surviving physical remains makes the identification of the building as being that built in the seventh century reasonably secure. Shared features of design and technique link it to others in the area, in Kent and Essex, as detailed by Clapham, writing in 1930, who also makes the strongest case for linking these buildings to a contemporary Mediterranean context.

These were quite consciously Mediterranean buildings, in their concept (expressed mostly in the plan) and in their technology. In plan they appear unambitious in size, particularly notable in the churches of Canterbury where we might expect to see grandeur (6). St Augustine's was c.18m wide and less than 30m long overall, including side rooms (porticus) and a western narthex (or entrance hall) to the nave; this compares to the fifth-century church of Orleans at c.85m long. They are not so simple, however, in their features; the chancel, which was normally in an apse, could be marked off with a triple arcade reusing Roman columns. Rather than aisles, they have one or more side rooms, porticus, reached from the nave. They are all built, unlike those of 'Celtic' Britain, in materials associated with Roman tradition, with a strong emphasis on brick, at least for quoins and dressings; some, suh as the church of St Pancras in Canterbury were entirely made of brick (7). The masons have either selected and cleaned the individual bricks from old Roman

structures in the city very carefully (for there are no broken ones, let alone signs of two or more still joined by their original mortar) when they reused them, or else they set up a brick kiln to produce new ones. The clearest exception to this dominant use of brick, at Bradwell in Essex, is explained by its situation within an abandoned Roman fort which provided a ready supply of stone to hand. The origins of this building technology lie in the overtly late Roman culture of the Mediterranean.

Other seventh-century churches in England differ from the Kentish group. In the south of England, there is the first church on the site of the cathedral of the Old Minster at Winchester, built apparently of stone and initially with a square chancel not an apse. In the north of England, we have the western part of the nave and the west porch at Monkwearmouth (7), reasonably attributable to the seventh century because of the (un-Roman) animal art of the carvings on its door as well as the reference to the existence of a western porch by 686. The church at Monkwearmouth, to which the west porch was attached, appears to have a much longer, narrower plan, but the early buildings employ the Roman technology of poured concrete foundations and were decorated with painted plaster and coloured glass; there were brick floors. The plan of Hexham church (6) may be in part recovered from the scrappy notes of nineteenth-century discoveries; also a long, narrow nave, possibly with aisles and a square east end, though with a detached apsidal chapel further to the east. Both Hexham and Ripon have

Above and left: 7 Brick and stone in seventh-century Anglo-Saxon churches: A. St Pancras, Canterbury (opposite) and B. Monkwearmouth (above)

the remains of early crypts built of good ashlar blocks, presumably reused from Roman buildings, and perhaps the churches built over them were too.

Three buildings in particular have been uncovered, or emerged from detailed study, to widen our knowledge of eighth/ninth century Anglo-Saxon churches (*8*): Cirencester, Canterbury cathedral and Repton. The first two have been excavated and have no remains surviving above the original ground level. Even the plan is incomplete, destroyed at least in part by later building; at Cirencester only a little over a half of the area of the church was available for excavation. The new Canterbury cathedral, replacing one of brick, probably of the early seventh century, has been tentatively dated to the ninth century, perhaps to around the middle of it. There is no independent dating for Cirencester. The crypt at Repton with a church added to it has been dated to the eighth and ninth centuries. This is a complex structure, starting as a relatively simple free-standing burial crypt. This was later joined to a church built to the west at an unknown period. The crypt had then a vault inserted and was raised up; it is suggested that this was done in the earlier ninth century before a grave was dug against it in the later ninth century. Significantly this last phase saw the outer walls decorated by projecting stone pilaster strips, a feature of ninth-century building in Germany or France.

Cirencester and Canterbury have quite different plans from the seventh-century 'Kentish' churches, stressing length over breadth; more than twice the length but little wider (*8*). The nave at Cirencester was flanked, not by aisles, but by at least three individual spaces or porticus; there appears to have been a semicircular apse at the east end. Even more interesting is the possibility that they had towers. The west end at Cirencester seems to have had three north–south walls at the west with only some 3.5m between them overall; these look more like strengthening measures for a single structure than the foundations of walls of two individual spaces. The Canterbury nave appears to have been closed at the east by a wall about 2.5m thick, too strong for the foundations of a screen or arcade; it defined a square space between the nave and the east end. Both of these may have been the foundations of towers, western at Cirencester, central at Canterbury. The east end of Cirencester was probably marked by an apse with an inner semicircular crypt. Centrally planned Repton shows the ability to construct groin vaults and have some architectural pretensions with its strips and columns. There are some churches which may connect the earlier Kentish churches and those of Canterbury and Cirencester but are poorly dated. The church of Brixworth has a plan of a long nave flanked by lines of porticus and a ring crypt to the east, which may link it to Cirencester, while it shares the chancel arches and the use of brick with the Kentish group. Apses are apparently absent at Winchester, Hexham (although found in the small eastern church there) and Monkwearmouth. If these may be eighth century or earlier, churches such as Wareham or Deerhurst, which seem to be associated by their plans, may be later.

The key problem is dating. In particular, for reasons which will be discussed later, there is a real problem in the north of England, where a number of churches have been attributed to an early period because of a mixture of references to a

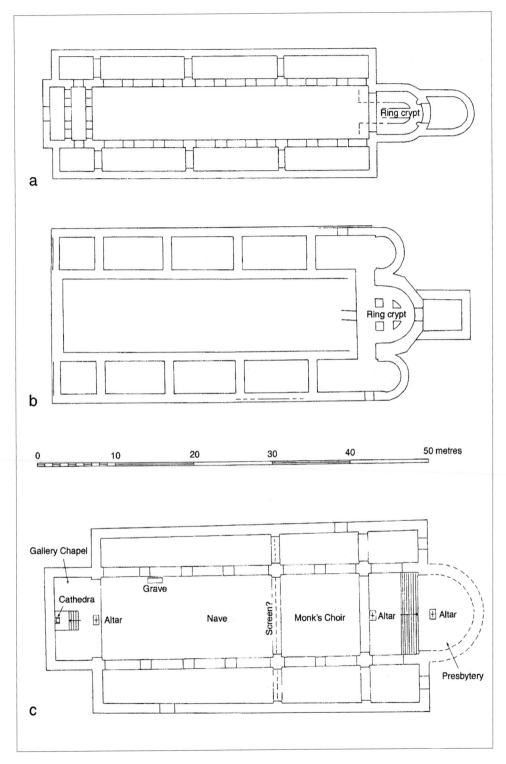

8 Plans of possible ninth-century churches: a. Cirencester; b. Werden; c. Canterbury cathedral. Note the greater length compared with the seventh century seen in *Figure 6. After Gem 1993 & British Archaeological Association*

church on the site noted by Bede and an absence of recognised later features. If we try to make a case that links the Kentish group of churches with the later Canterbury, Cirencester or Repton, then we are arguing that either they were built to serve a similar view of what a church should look like, and how it should function, or that the building tradition had a single line of training and tradition. This is likely to be wrong on both counts. If we consider the plan as illustrating the concept of the church and the provision for its use then the contrast between the shorter Kentish churches and the other, longer ones should be significant, especially if we think that the later ones were equipped with aisles, permitting processions rather than porticus which provided space for altars and burials. The complex triple arch at the east end, which would lend itself to the provision of a screen, contrasts with a single opening to the chancel in the focus of ritual.

The abandonment of brick in favour of stone is interesting and demands consideration. Timber was attractive as a medium for its speed, adaptability and ready availability. It was fatally non-Roman in its connotations, however, and was always considered inferior to stone or brick for churches where display and durability were paramount. The working of stone is no easier than that of brick and it is not a question that suitable stone for building was more available than the clay, water and fuel needed to make brick. Both are equally durable and carried the same prestige of Roman associations. Stone has one key advantage, however; it is much more suitable for carving than brick. Carving was important at the time with the production of high crosses of the Insular tradition uniting the whole of the British Isles, from Northumbria through Iona to Ireland. Certain motifs derive from Classical art, notably vine scrolls, but the carvers develop away from them. Stone crosses allowed sites to acquire the prestige of stone without the complex infrastructure of laying out, production of mortar, scaffolding, windows etc. which were involved in the building of a stone church. Stone acquired a prestige which it was never to lose throughout the Middle Ages north of the Alps.

THE IMPACT OF CHARLEMAGNE

English churches such as Canterbury or Cirencester represent a trend, drifting away from the Mediterranean tradition, which may also be paralleled in France or Germany in the eighth and ninth centuries. This happened just as Charlemagne transformed the idea of a Frankish kingdom into that of a Western Empire, in part a revival of the Roman one. He ruled from 768–814, being crowned emperor in 800. Church renewal and reform was a central part of his programme for government, and it was continued vigorously by his successor, Louis the Pious. This work was to be based on a managerial reform of the upper echelons of the church, providing more effective bishops and more powerful monasteries, better organised from the top down and closely connected to the power of the emperor. These reforms were associated with new buildings to express the new ideals. The greatest physical symbol of this renewed Roman ideology was the showpiece of the chapel of his palace of Aachen. This was a self-conscious assertion of the Roman tradition and has often been seen as typical of the Carolingian ideal. It was octagonal in plan, derived from the churches of Saints Sergius and Bacchus in Constantinople and San Vitale in Ravenna, which was especially chosen because it is distinguished by mosaic portraits of the Emperor Justinian and Theodora in the chancel, representing just the sort of Christian and Roman Empire to which Charlemagne aspired. The internal decoration of Aachen, like that of Roman buildings, far exceeded the external, with a lavish display of reused Roman marbles and columns; the western gallery is derived from the one at the Exarch's palace at Ravenna. However, Aachen is not a slavish copy of the Byzantine model. The plan was simplified to give a single line of symmetry from west to east, leading from a single western door (San Vitale has two doors leading via an indirect route through a narthex into the body of the church) under the Imperial gallery on the outside at first-floor level up to the Imperial throne at the east. The vaults of the side aisles of San Vitale were complex groins: at Aachen they were simpler barrels. The vaulting changes may be the result of a lack of skill, but the plan was probably changed to give more impact to the position of the emperor.

Aachen, for all its Imperial prestige, was never going to be typical because it was pre-eminently a palace chapel, not a church for general use like the great majority. Neither the patrons nor the craftsmen followed the Aachen path either in detail or in the idea of imitating Byzantine building. Instead, as in England, they looked back to the longer naves of Gaul, the basilica but with modifications, placing an emphasis on length in contrast to the central plan of Aachen or the short naves of Kent and some Byzantine churches, continuing the traditional idea of the basilica, but with additions. The most dramatic addition was that of towers; in origin they may have been a late Roman motif, but now they transformed the visual impact of a church in two crucial ways. Towers were placed either at the west end or at the crossing points of the transepts, making the division of the church into its parts obvious from the outside and encouraging the viewer to see it as the sum of those parts. With these new church towers men were building higher than trees for the first time in Europe.

On occasions ninth-century builders appreciated the combination of the towers and transepts so much that they repeated it at both ends of the church, giving a western block, the so-called westwork. The progress of this can be seen from the church of St Riquier of the 790s to Corvey of the 870s (9). This was more than just a visual feature. The westwork provided a gallery overlooking the church from the west. This was primarily a ritual space for a second choir or extra altars, but it might also provide a secular purpose for the display of power. Like the western gallery at Aachen (which faced outwards, however) this gallery could give space for the emperor when he visited the church or the bishop or abbot; if the east end celebrated the dominion of Christ, the west end could serve the dominion of the earthly lord. At the east, crypts to display the relics of saints to pilgrims grew in prominence.

9 Corvey: the Carolingian westwork

The Carolingian age gave Western Christianity the crucial feature of the square monastic cloister, set against one of the nave walls of the church (which gave more impetus for the length of the nave) as seen in late eighth-century Lorsch. This became the distinctive feature of Western monasticism as opposed to Byzantine monasteries, which were constructed with a church central to the courtyard and living space for the monks around the perimeter. It imposed the sense of uniformity at the heart of the Carolingian Church reform of monasteries, best seen in the scheme, dating from *c*.810, for a model monastery (probably never built) preserved at St Gall. Here the church with its attendant cloister is set within a complex of other buildings which serve the great landed estate which supported the monastic community and their visitors.

These major features of Carolingian plans are matched by some decorative motifs. The large expanses of blank walling (for windows and doors were kept small) were relieved by having raised vertical bands of stonework, pilasters, on occasions linked at the top by a row of arches, blank arcading. The church at Lorsch is approached through a formal three-arched gateway, which perfectly displays the way Carolingian building looked both ways, to the Roman past and the medieval future. The Classical arches are framed by attached columns (both Classical features) which support, not the arches, but a horizontal string course. The horizontal course in turn supports the pattern of pilasters linked by triangular 'arches' at the first-floor level. In spite of the Classical elements of arches and attached columns and a varied and Byzantine wall surface, the ensemble is far from Classical canons of taste.

This is the sum of the Carolingian 'style'. The plan features are not consistently present. Werden, for example, appears not to have had a tower (although it received a massive westwork later) and to have had a row of porticus on each side rather than a continuous aisle, while the east end shows a lack of any true transept. East ends matter, for they are crucial to the ritual use of a Christian church, at least until the Reformation; similarly, the westwork reflected ritual use, with two choirs singing in turn from either end of the church. Transepts were often hesitantly deployed. Some were side spaces reached through doors in walls north and south of the crossing space, rather than through arches of the same size as those to the east and west. Others were the reverse, wide spaces which cut right across the junction of the nave and chancel. The popularity of length in churches also probably reflected their use for processions, but this would have been impeded by the lines of individual porticus; central plan, porticus or aisle is a choice which is important to the ritual use of the whole building, so the variety of practice must reflect an uncertainty in the ideal of a church, among the patrons who commanded them.

AFTER THE CAROLINGIAN EMPIRE: LATER NINTH CENTURY TO c.1000

After Louis the Pious, the Carolingian Empire collapsed in a long drawn-out process of disintegration. It fell into an eastern and a western part, the origins of modern Germany and France. While the central authority in the west dissolved, in the east the Ottonian dynasty restored Imperial power in the second quarter of the tenth century. During the later ninth and tenth centuries, the invasions of Saracens, Magyars and Vikings crossed Europe and the British Isles. It is important to see these in perspective. On the one hand, it is right to point out that the invasions cannot have affected everyone in the area concerned; that large areas were unaffected for periods; that the Vikings in particular also acted to stimulate town formation, in Ireland for example: the story is not one of unmitigated slaughter and pillage. On the other hand, the disruption affected those with most to lose and those least able to protect themselves most severely, and this meant that the Church was particularly hurt, in its income and in its organisation. This inevitably must have had a disproportionate effect on the building industry: disruption in supplies and, above all, in training.

There is a contrast between the records of the West and the East of the former Empire in this respect, however. In the West, the part which is now France, the record shows many churches as destroyed with a long interval before there is a recorded phase of reconstruction. By contrast the number of recorded destructions in the area of Germany is smaller, while the interval before reconstruction is shorter. There is only a very short gap around 900 when there is no recorded building activity. This has great significance for the history of the building industry. A gap in construction of a generation would have meant a gap in the training of new craftsmen. If this is prolonged to longer than that, there will simply be no one left trained in building skills to pick up the industry when order is restored; this seems to have been what happened in what is now France, but not in Germany. From the second quarter of the tenth century, church building under the Ottonian emperors of Germany was continued from the earlier century, proof of the continuity of tradition, and therefore of building through the years of turmoil, which may not have been as disturbed as the popular image suggests. England also saw great political turmoil and the Church suffered severely during the ninth century, but it also saw a revival in its fortunes under the kings of the House of Wessex during the late tenth century. The result was that it was in these two countries (rather than in France) that we see the main developments up to the millennium, in the production of great churches and in the proliferation of stone church building on a lesser scale.

One of the latest surviving churches of the late Carolingian period is the westwork at Corvey, dating to the 870s; as already noted this provided a façade flanked by two towers on the exterior and a large western first-floor chapel with a gallery to the interior; the ground floor has groin vaults. There are a number of documentary references to buildings in Germany between the end of Corvey and the middle of the tenth century, notably the church of St John at Mainz on either side of 900 and St Servatius at Quedlinburg from the 930s. None, however, survive and our earliest remains date from after 950. At St Pantaleon, Köln, the only parts surviving from the late tenth century are the westwork, with circular towers at the outer angles. The interior had a large first-floor gallery in the Carolingian tradition, with the main arch towards the body of the church made from voussoirs of alternate red and white stone imitating Roman brick. The exterior wall surfaces were articulated with vertical and horizontal stripwork which also picked out the pilasters and arcading in red sandstone contrasting with the white ashlar of the main walling. Gernrode, to the east in Saxony, was founded about 960 by one of the new families of Counts who arose to serve the dynasty of the Ottos (10).

In plan it is now a double-ended basilica with western and eastern blocks. The eastern crossing is markedly skew from the line of the nave; the actual crossing was only made a true square in the nineteenth-century restoration. The eastern apse, less restored than other parts, is built of quite rough masonry of sandstone rubble, but vertical pilaster strips divide the exterior up. The masonry improves for the nave and it might appear that the church was constructed in stages: eastern block, nave and then the westwork. The nave is a double square in plan, with piers at the corners; the north and south walls of the squares are divided into a pair of arches separated by a column, forming the arcade between nave and aisles. Over each pair of arches is a 'triforium' of six small arches, breaking up the blank wall. These reflect the divisions of the arcade, but the clerestory at the top forms a continuous band with the windows unrelated to either arcade or gallery. The western end is complex. At present there is a screen wall with two three-quarter round turrets at either end, not free-standing like those of the St Gall plan but prominent. Originally there was a square tower between the angle turrets and the nave: the present apse is a later addition after the tower was removed, both in the twelfth century.

Shared Carolingian features such as westworks and pilasters, should not mislead us into seeing the Ottonian period as having a coherent idea of a large church, for the plans of many vary quite remarkably. There are churches built on the basis of an octagonal, or oval, plan. The original church of Deutz, across the Rhine from Köln and started in 1002, had an oval plan, evoking surviving Roman remains such as the church of St Gereon in Köln, or even possibly the Pantheon of Rome. At Essen, a half octagon with a gallery screened by arches overtly imitating the palace chapel of Aachen was added to the earlier nave in the mid-tenth century. At Paderborn, in the palace chapel and the cathedral, there are two churches to illustrate the theme of variety. St Bartholomew's chapel about 1017 is built with columns, domes and capitals which are so close to Byzantine work that they must have been built by men from the Mediterranean. South of the palace is the cathedral on the top of the hill, now dominated by a massive single west tower, rebuilt in the 1220s probably along the lines of the early eleventh-century one. As odd as anything is the complex of buildings excavated beneath the cathedral of Eichstatt, where the builders added two free-standing structures west of the

10 Gernrode: the north side of the nave

surviving rectangular Carolingian church. The western of these was D-shaped in plan, while between it and the basilica was a circular building with two circular turrets attached north and south. All these were built under the patronage of major figures, ecclesiastics close to the Imperial court. This gives a clue to an important explanation of the variety of designs from the Germany of the tenth century. They were very political structures, giving out messages as to the connections of their patrons. Overwhelmingly these were references to past Imperial glories, either of Late Antique Rome, or to Charlemagne: the octagonal and circular plans were always connected to these models. The designs were, therefore, inherently eclectic, relying on the individual preferences and knowledge of their patron.

On the other hand it is interesting to note that geology and different traditions of building came together to make a difference between buildings in the north-west of the German Empire, in the Rhineland, and the north-east, Saxony. St Pantaleon at Köln is built mostly out of well-cut white limestone ashlar; the string courses, interior arches and other details are picked out in red sandstone, like the brick courses of a Roman building (11). By contrast, Gernrode and Paderborn are constructed of coursed rubble blocks of the local brown sandstone with no colour effect. At Essen, at the eastern edge of the Rhineland, the exterior of the westwork is built of coursed sandstone rubble, but the interior has its grand arches picked out in alternating red and white stone. An atrium was added later, surrounded by a colonnade; while the bulk of the walling is in sandstone rubble, the columns are of red sandstone. At the boundaries of the two traditions, both are in evidence, showing the self-conscious coherence of the two.

CHURCHES IN BRITAIN IN THE TENTH AND EARLIER ELEVENTH CENTURIES

The tenth century saw dramatic change in England. In the south, the house of Wessex succeeded in uniting (or conquering) the country, including eventually the north as well, to create the single kingdom of England. Hand-in-hand with this went a reform of the Church on Carolingian lines, with a strong set of bishops and abbots, appointed by the kings and linked closely to them, who set out to transform the management of the Church. The monasteries were reformed on Continental lines, bringing in a more uniform and rigorously observed Benedictine regime. Below the bishops, the parishes were developed in the countryside, built with the systematic levying of tithes.

The church building in England during the period, which must extend here to 1066 rather than 1000, provides information on two important issues: the pattern of the large church projects and their designs, and the evidence of the proliferation of stone church building in the lesser churches around the countryside. The story of the large churches built in England in the century before 1066 shows that their builders appear to have been strongly influenced by the churches of Germany.

11 St Pantaleon, Köln: the interior of the westwork

We have three cathedral plans, at Canterbury, Sherborne and Winchester (20A) and at least one major abbey plan, St Augustine's, Canterbury; although all these major churches are unfortunately known from their ground plan alone. A typical Ottonian westwork, an apse with a transept and crossing tower, flanked by two prominent stair turrets was added to Canterbury cathedral possibly best dated to after 1011 to make it into a double-ended basilica like Gernrode or Hildesheim. The excavations at Winchester cathedral showed that after the mid-tenth century, a series of additions, including a massive westwork, were made to the original small seventh-century cathedral (20B). The eleventh-century additions to Sherborne resulted in a church with eastern and western transepts; the western built against an earlier central tower. The Ottonian links are all they have in common, however; Canterbury's orthodoxy in sharp contrast to the eclecticism of Winchester or the modest scale of Sherborne. The abbey of St Augustine saw a remarkable experiment about 1050 when the abbot Wulfric decided to join the old main church to a smaller one to the east with a rotunda. The idea almost certainly came from the church of Dijon to be discussed later. The scale of these churches is large but the striking thing about these English churches of the early eleventh century is their variety, the lack of a clear pattern of what a major church should look like.

England also has a large number of surviving lesser churches, many of them built for the expansion of parish churches at the time. Identifying a church of this period (900/950 to 1050/1100) is a contentious process. There are two kinds of structural evidence we can bring to bear. The first is the presence of towers (12) and stripwork around doors, windows or belfries. The arguments for identifying the presence of a tower as indicating a ninth century or later date have been well rehearsed since the 1930s: towers at such early churches as Monkwearmouth or Brixworth are later additions built over a porch; some such as St Mary-le-Wigford in Lincoln are known to have been built during the period from independent evidence. The stripwork also links up to parallels from the Continent, as does the general dating of the towers. Many towers are also associated strongly with the second kind of evidence; certain features found on buildings known to be of tenth century or later date, such as Odda's chapel at Deerhurst or the chapel at Winchester castle, both dated independently to the eleventh century. These features are pilaster strips, double-splay windows and 'long-and-short' quoins, which form a package, occurring frequently together in the same church. The result is what is sometimes seen as 'typical late Anglo-Saxon' style, even though buildings with these features were certainly built anything up to 50 years after the end of the Anglo-Saxon political State in 1066. The most curious thing about this package of features is their geographical distribution, which is firmly southern English (13).

Only one pilaster strip is found north of the Wash; only one long-and-short quoin and two double-splay windows are found north of the Humber. This is in contrast with the distribution of towers (14) or stripwork which covers all of England east of the Pennines, Severn and Devon. The buildings in the north have obviously

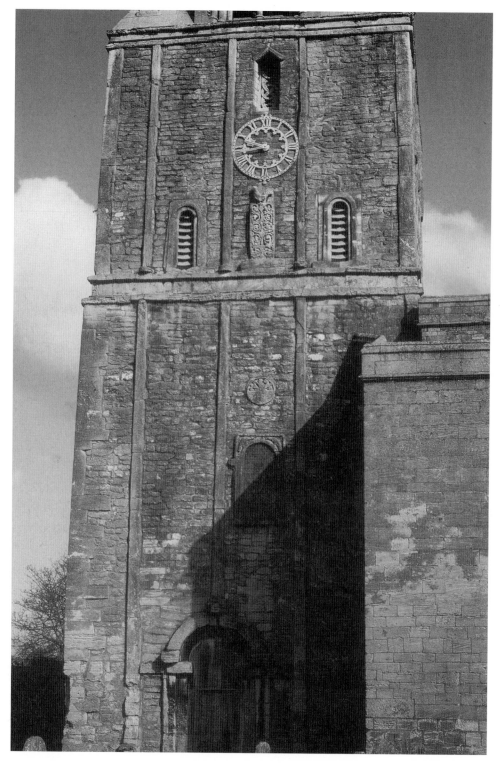

Above and opposite: 12   Church towers in A. southern (Barnack, above) and B. northern England (Bywell, opposite)

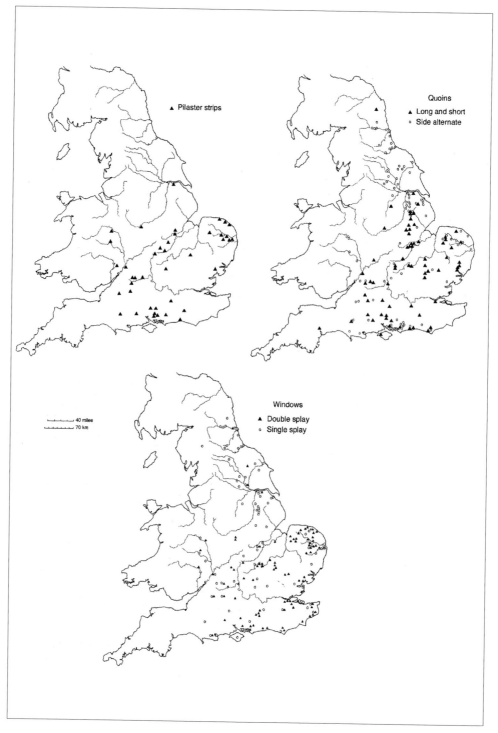

13 Maps of late Anglo–Saxon building features: pilaster strips, quoin types and window types

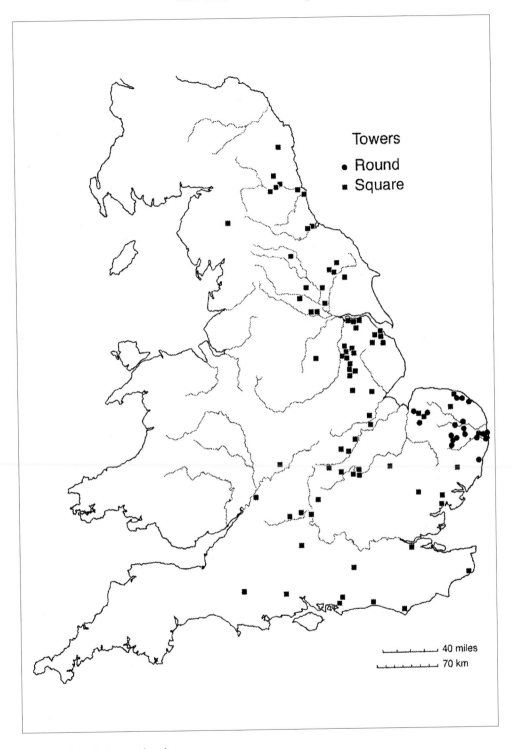

Towers
● Round
■ Square

_____ 40 miles
_____ 70 km

14 Map of Anglo-Saxon church towers

for long been recognised as different from the southern late type. The northern type has been typified by the widespread use of masonry of squared blocks laid in courses with wide mortar joints and different quoining ('side alternate' rather than the southern 'long-and-short'). Also recognised as typical of the north are the towers with the same masonry and double belfries over a string course (*12*). The difference between north and south has long been recognised, and the northern towers have also long been dated to the tenth or eleventh centuries like those of the south.

However, the problem comes with those northern churches which happen not to have towers, but which share the other features of masonry type, etc. with them. These have been separated and mostly been ascribed to the seventh or eighth centuries and not associated with the towers or the churches of southern style. The most famous of these are the church at Escomb and the present chancel at Jarrow; Ledsham, Corbridge and Seaham churches are also seen as belonging to the group of seventh-century northern churches. The result is that we have a picture of the south of England with two groups, a few early churches (the Kentish ones with others such as Cirencester, Canterbury cathedral or Repton) dating to the seventh to ninth centuries, and then a much larger number dated to the tenth to eleventh centuries. In the north there is a picture of much greater continuity with the churches much more evenly spread over time. The difference is explained much more in terms of date than of geographical distribution, in spite of the clear regional nature of the late southern features. This picture needs to be reassessed. Two of the northern churches, Ledsham and Corbridge, have towers which have been explained as additions built over an earlier porch like Monkwearmouth. There are problems with this. The evidence for the porch at Corbridge is that the stones are smaller higher up the tower, but this is better explained as evidence that the builders avoided straining the lower masonry and their backs by putting the lighter stones higher. The tower at Ledsham is an addition to the nave; it is clearly built over the west gable, which means that the ascription of the chancel to the seventh to eighth century does not therefore affect the date of the tower. It has a decorated doorway which has been shown not to be a restoration as is sometimes said but which must date the tower. Neither Seaham nor Escomb have any dating evidence independent of the others apart from the fact that they are simple structures (the fallacy of simple equals early).

The crux of the issue comes with the present chancel at Jarrow. There were three structures at Jarrow built before 1100: a tower (usually presumed to be of the eleventh century although a spirited attempt has been made to have the lower part earlier on the basis of doors being of a 'primitive' type) which links a larger building to the west with the standing 'chancel' to the east. The way that the tower links the other two shows that it was later. The present chancel was originally free-standing, although whether it could ever have stood only 3m from the end of the western one is questionable but possible. The original seventh-century stone buildings at Jarrow and Monkwearmouth were recorded by Bede specifically as being built one after the other in the 680s, surely by the same masons, but the masonry of the present chancel at Jarrow is quite different from the Monkwearmouth work. The arches of openings at Monkwearmouth are made of a number of well-shaped voussoirs; those at Jarrow of very few stones, even (for small windows) an arch carved from a single block. The Monkwearmouth masonry is of small stones with large quoins rising through some four courses; at Jarrow the masonry is of the northern English type, as at Escomb or Ledsham, with large stones and side-alternate quoins. It seems quite unlikely that Monkwearmouth and the present Jarrow chancel were built by the same masons; Monkwearmouth should be accepted as of the seventh century, but Jarrow chancel should be rejected as such. It was, however, clearly in existence (and probably old to be venerated) in the eleventh century when the church was restored and the tower built. The simplest explanation is that it dates, like others of its type, to the tenth century and was joined to an existing nave to the west in the eleventh century. The date of the nave, now destroyed and only known from eighteenth-century descriptions, is unknown; its plan resembles that of Cirencester or Wareham, themselves undated. The present chancel at Jarrow, however, cannot be used as evidence that the northern churches which it resembles date from the seventh century.

I would conclude that there were in tenth- to eleventh-century England two traditions of building, north and south (13). It is important to note how the two traditions share features as much as differences. The most obvious is that of towers, but also other features, such as the belfry openings; with both regions using stripwork around openings, particularly doors and chancel arches. The openings are often constructed clumsily with voussoirs not cut radially or with the arch cut from a single block of stone. Significantly, the towers of Lincolnshire can be seen to share the horizontal divisions and double belfries with the north while four were added to naves with long-and-short quoining of the southern tradition. The masons at the boundary of the two traditions drew from both. The point is that the masons of the two regions share in many ways similar images of a church and the features which it should have, especially the scale, the plan of a simple, unaisled nave with a square east end and the western towers for a significant number; other features found in a minority are the western gallery (evidenced by raised doors), the high, narrow doorways without rebates or the roughness of the walling.

At least as important as individual features or details is the basis of the industry. The source of the stone used is a crucial test of the industry; we have seen that brick was rejected early on as a significant part of the building. This left two sources available: reused Roman stone (with some brick) or freshly quarried stone. The case for widespread reuse of Roman material has recently been made by Eaton. However, quarrying was always an option. In eighth/ninth-century Ireland and Scotland, the stone High Crosses cannot have used Roman blocks for there were no Roman buildings there in the first place. The consistent use of Bunter and Keuper stone in the various phases of Repton church argues strongly for quarrying there in the ninth century. In southern England, the buildings of the tenth and eleventh century show the wide distribution of stone from the Oolite belt of the Cotswolds to the south and east; some may have used Roman material but not the majority. On the other hand, the characteristic masonry of the north during the same period may be based on the reuse of Roman stone, particularly the military structures such as Hadrian's Wall. Parallel to this is the exploitation of limestone for the mortar; a map of tenth- to eleventh-century churches follows limestone sources closely. Rarely preserved are the results of plasterer's work or the paint we know of from descriptions, while glass is seldom found now and may have been rare in the past. Less tangible, in terms of traces left now, are the scaffolding systems required especially to build towers, along with the framing for openings, arches, doors or windows. Roofing materials, timber framing, thatch, shingles or slates relied on traditional crafts, but they needed to be adapted to stone building. These were all essential steps to take before the building industry could flourish.

FRANCE AND IRELAND

France during the tenth and early eleventh centuries had suffered from the invasions of the preceding century and was also divided into smaller political units than either Germany or England. The power and patronage of the combined secular and church authorities was missing there. The individual regions had different experiences, both in the establishing of secular authority and in the restoration of church building. One area, Normandy, saw a coherent programme of building, to which we will return. Another region, where later building was supreme, was Burgundy, where we have at least three major buildings of the period. The church of Tournus was built in stages: an eastern apse with radiating chapels of around 950 and a nave with experimental vaulting in the aisles and over the main nave, followed by a large westwork of the early eleventh century (15).

The rubble masonry of the westwork is decorated with pilasters and arcading and the whole is flanked by two towers, a straightforward piece of work in contrast to the enterprise of the east end and the experimental vaulting. The church of St Benigne at Dijon (started in 1101, dedicated in 1018) comprised two major parts. The first was a large nave with double aisles: a large rotunda (whose crypt survives) was crudely joined on to the east end of this nave. Not only was the resulting plan quite eccentric, but the standard of carving in the crypt is surprisingly low for an area which saw some of the finest carving in twelfth-century Europe. In modern scholarship, and during the eleventh and twelfth century, Burgundy was made famous by the presence of the great monastery of Cluny. Founded in 911, its second church (Cluny II) was started after 950; all we know of it is the plan partially recovered from below the remains of the later buildings. The church plan was plain compared to the extravagance of Dijon, an aisled basilica with an east end of projecting chapels, the apse echelon plan which proved very popular later, but not in Burgundy.

Out of these three we can make no coherent pattern of building. One real development was an interest in the eastern end (28). The apses at the east end

15 Tournus abbey church from the
south-west

of Cluny II are one model used in tenth-century France. Before 1000 at least, the church of St Martin at Tours was built with another design; a semicircular ambulatory around which were arranged chapels. By the 1020s at Bernay in Normandy followed the apse echelon plan of Cluny II where the central apse projected further east than the two which flanked it; two apses off the transepts projected less far again. The ideas were not only being developed but were being communicated across the regions of France.

Church building in Ireland may be seen in the light of the processes found in England. The practice of building in stone probably appears in the eighth century although we cannot identify any of the products on the ground with any certainty. From the tenth century onwards came the round towers, detached structures found in the more prosperous monasteries. They were objects of prestige, secondarily used for storage of relics or books or even as refuges, as the towers were elsewhere in Europe. They were not sophisticated structures; by building in a round plan something like half the volume of the structure was stone work and openings are few. However, in a society which had largely built in wood before this, they are significant. The round towers became a symbol of Irish monasteries; partly used for storage and display of relics but primarily buildings which proclaimed (they would have been visible from afar) the existence and wealth of the monastery which built them. In form they reflect the stair turrets of a Carolingian or Ottonian church such as St Gall or Gernrode, but in Ireland they were free-standing. The occasional use of raised stripwork around openings and

16 Donzy parish church, Burgundy: tower, rubble walling and pilasters

triangular heads to doors and windows recalls tenth- or eleventh-century English practice. As elsewhere they marked the advent of an industry employing the skills of quarrying and cutting stone, producing lime and erecting scaffolding.

Towers were obviously a crucial feature (*16*), one which marked out the ambitious church from the humbler, purely functional one and making the link between the grand churches, the cathedrals and abbeys, and the parish churches. A common variety marks out the period, found in large and small churches sharing a basic similarity across Europe from the Pyrenees and north Italy to the North Sea. It had its various stages demarcated by horizontal string courses; the topmost with a belfry stage. The horizontal divisions were often decorated with pilasters and blank arcading so that the type has a certain inherent similarity right across Europe.

SUMMARY

The term the 'First Romanesque' has not been popular because it is difficult to define in terms of an architectural style, especially if style is to be defined in the terms of the Introduction to this book, through a consistency in plan, structure and elevation. The collected features of the First Romanesque do not meet these criteria. It is defined by a number of elements or features, such as the presence of towers or the use of pilaster strips and blank arcading to relieve the monotony of the rubble walls. The earlier Carolingian hesitancy about how to combine plan elements such as transepts or crypts into a church was overcome during the tenth and eleventh centuries. The result was an acceptance of major features such as the westwork and transept, articulated by decorative divisions of the blank walling, just as the better designs in Germany pick out the internal divisions of arcade and gallery. The mechanism for this relationship is not the straightforward one of a single tradition of training but instead was a looser form of communication. The thing that spread was the idea of having (for example) a western tower, with pilasters, etc. which was then translated locally into practice. The features which go to make up these First Romanesque towers are not technical, requiring a craftsman's knowledge to explain them, and they might be transmitted by anyone interested in noting features of churches. The communication is likely to have been descriptive ('the new church is terrific – it has towers at either side of the choir') rather than analytic ('the westwork has a groin vault carried on low piers with cushion capitals on the ground floor with a gallery opening through an arch with double mouldings into the nave on the first floor'). The first can be carried by the non-specialist, the churchman or patron, for example; the second is the language of the mason. Communication was proceeding through the first group but not the second during the First Romanesque; it was essentially informal and depended on local practice to carry it out. The importance of the Classical references to Ottonian political ambition to found a new Empire in Western Europe are the most obvious evidence of these links of patronage.

The parish church towers back up the point well. We find towers with pilasters and arcading, horizontal courses and stages, with a variety of ways of combining them, built right across Western Europe. There is neither a single model for the towers nor a normal way to make them or to combine the features, yet they are clearly all related, in the impressive additions to the church as a whole (towers) or to their decoration (pilasters). This is just the sort of thing we might expect a patron to be concerned about, the impressiveness and decoration of the church they had commissioned.

The building practice was irregular and imprecise. The idea of accurate plans was known at the time, as shown by the grid of squares within which the St Gall plan for a monastery was drawn, or the way a similar grid may be applied to the cathedral at Canterbury (17). The tenth-century *Life of St Oswald of Ramsey* describes him preparing his grand new church:

> he searched diligently for masons who would know how to set out the foundations of the monastery in the correct fashion using the straight-edge, triangulation and compasses.

Against this are the remarkably irregular plans of the churches at Gernrode (although here we may suspect the effect the problems of a long, drawn-out building campaign) or at Barton-on-Humber. The walling is also irregular, the result of the widespread use of rubble with wide mortar joints. Particularly in East

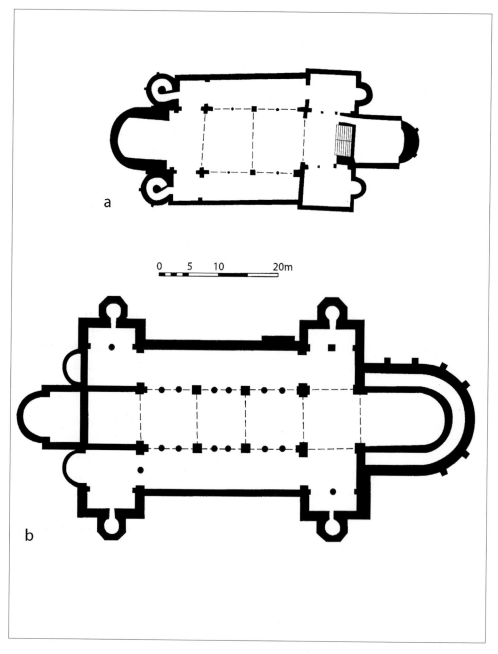

17 Plans of the churches of Gernrode (a) and St Michael's, Hildesheim (b); both are designed around squares but they are markedly irregular in the case of Gernrode. Note also the much greater size achieved by the start of the eleventh century at Hildesheim

Anglia, the masons were ready to use flint for the walling, which had to be laid in copious amounts of mortar within shuttering. It has been suggested that some of the forms for pilaster strips used in England, as at Barton-on-Humber, can be related to carpentry techniques better than stone ones; the same is true, of course, with the mortice and tenon joints derived from carpentry used on St John's High Cross at Iona.

If this sounds dismissive of the work of the First Romanesque, it is not meant to be. What the men of the tenth or eleventh centuries achieved was to make all the subsequent developments possible. The patrons might wish to build churches of overwhelming size and beauty, but their wishes would be pointless without the industry capable of realising them. What the men who wished to develop a full building industry had to do was to overcome an inherent block to progress. Without a steady stream of work, there was no mechanism to train up the workforce. Without the workforce to carry out the projects, there would be no steady stream of sites to train the men at. It is the eternal problem of the aspiring portrait painter whom no patron will commission until he has carried out a number of commissions. The most extreme case was, of course, the British Isles of 596 where there was no tradition of stone building at all. In these circumstances the normal solution is to import men with the skills and the aspirations from outside, which is what St Augustine did, but interestingly he and his successors failed in their attempt to connect the Kentish group of buildings with the Mediterranean ideas and craft. The cultural and geographical appeal of Gaul was stronger, along with the appeal of stone over brick. The Carolingian attempt to expand the building industry and to reintroduce a Mediterranean stream to North-Western Europe had a more complex history. The strictly Roman part of Charlemagne's revival was only a small part of the effort and it had little long-term impact on the forms and building techniques used. On the other hand, the aspirations that he provoked among the ninth-century churchmen lasted. The processional church, the monastic cloister, towers and the Imperial westwork were important ideas which took firm root, although they seem to have remained as individual ideas.

The organisation of the building industry, the building community, was essentially local or regionally based. Northern Germany combined the old Roman lands to the west of the Rhine with the plain to the east, then known as Saxony, conquered by the Franks under Charlemagne and now the core of the new Empire of Otto. Geology, as well as the Roman inheritance, produced their masons' different training. In England this is seen clearly in the north–south divide. The differences relate only slightly to natural distributions such as the difference of stone. They reflect much more the difference between the south, dominated by the House of Wessex and increasingly oriented towards what is now France, and the north which looked across the North Sea. The boundary between the two is ill-defined, in this as in other matters, but Lincolnshire significantly looks both ways.

This is why the proliferation of smaller churches is so significant. Until the later tenth century, well demonstrated in England, the main effort of stone building had gone into the great churches in a top-down approach. However, it was the multiplication of lesser jobs which meant a major growth in the training of men in the basic skills of the industry: quarrying, simple stone dressing, scaffolding, etc. Concentrating on the simpler skills but delivering them in quantity was the way to unblock the vicious circle. Hence the imprecision of much of the work; it was carried out by men who were working at the limits of their skill. It also linked the main area of economic growth in the tenth and eleventh centuries, which was in the expansion of the lesser estates, to the building industry. The industry had created a positive loop, from the larger buildings (inherited from the Carolingian programme of major abbeys and cathedrals) into training, leading to the ability to build more widely with lesser churches and so train more craftsmen to carry out more new work. The ability to carry out the work was not, however, enough; what they lacked was a clear model of what the new churches should look like; there was no consistent style. The recognition and application of such a model or style is what makes the difference between the First and Second Romanesque periods.

3

SECOND ROMANESQUE: THE GREAT CHURCH ACHIEVED

By the end of the first quarter of the eleventh century, the building industry of Western Europe was capable of delivering the trained craftsmen, the quarried stone, the timber, mortar, plaster and roofing needed to construct a great church for a patron with the power and ambition to build one. What was lacking was a vision as to how a great church should look and be built: a style. Germany under the Empire was the part of Western Europe most able to provide the resources and the peace to enable a series of connected projects to be undertaken which could develop one. The power of the emperor and the Church were even more closely connected than Charlemagne's had been and it remained so until the end of the eleventh century. Nothing symbolised this better than Otto I's founding of the new archbishopric of Magdeburg, from where the archbishop could play a dominant role in the westward expansion of the German Imperial secular and religious power against the Slav rulers. That was in the middle of the tenth century and Imperial court patronage had grown since.

While the German Empire recreated the power of traditional authority by combining Church and State, the Church began a major managerial reform from the middle of the eleventh century. It was driven by two principles: hierarchical clarity and uniformity. The hierarchy of bishop and priest was reinforced by a stronger papacy, backed initially by the power of the emperor. The main effort bore on the various communal churches, which were half monastic houses, half groups of secular priests. Priests closely connected to the local aristocracy often occupied these communal churches; one of the aims was to enforce a divide between the two, as well as to release Church estates and resources from lay control. Churchmen were to be clearly distinguished from laymen. Their situation had to be clarified, usually to bring them formally under monastic rules; in later tenth-century England monks often replaced traditional clergy even in cathedrals. The monks did not escape the attentions of the eleventh-century reformers; they were both the main engines and focus of the movement. Instead of individual houses with individual practices, they were to come closer together; by the end of the century the idea of the monastic order, uniting the houses into a single hierarchical organisation was emerging. Again, estates and resources were being focused, while communications were being reinforced.

Emperor Otto I founded the archbishopric and cathedral of Magdeburg in 968, shortly after Gernrode. It has been superseded by the present cathedral, as have other Imperial foundations. The earliest surviving project undertaken from the Imperial court is St Michael's church at Hildesheim, founded by the ex-tutor and friend of Otto III in about 1001 and finished by 1033. Hildesheim is a double-ended basilica; as such it is like Gernrode but both its scale and finish are much greater (17). It is a fully developed 'double-ended', wooden-roofed basilica, overwhelming on the outside, impressive in the interior, although what we see now has been heavily restored on the original lines after 1945. The towers, apses and transepts at either end of the nave dominate the exterior. The plan is composed of three squares to Gernrode's two. Inside, the nave is divided from the aisles by an arcade where two columns support the arches between the piers which demarcate the squares, creating from the basic square an alternating rhythm of column and pier which was to have a long future. Like Gernrode, the clerestory runs in an unbroken row of windows which ignores the divisions of the arcade below. The few original capitals to have survived later restoration are plain 'cushion' forms, quite unlike the elaborate Classical capitals found at other churches of the time. Hildesheim stands at the junction of the tenth-century churches and a series of great churches constructed under the direct orders of the emperors, just as its builders combined features of the Gernrode generation with ones found later.

The Emperor Henry II founded the cathedral at Bamberg shortly after his succession to the Empire in 1002, in a deliberate imitation of Otto I and Magdeburg. The cathedral, consecrated in 1012, is only known from excavation, its ground plan but not its elevation. It was a double-ended basilica with an eastern apse flanked by towers and a western transept and second apse; the nave was aisled with large, thick piers closely set in the arcade. Henry's successors, Conrad II and Henry III, were closely linked to the rebuilding of the cathedrals of Trier, Speyer and Mainz in particular from the 1030s to the end of the century (18).

The cathedral at Trier still consisted to a large extent of late Roman work, but after a repair of the eastern parts consecrated in 1037, the archbishop undertook to rebuild the western half completely. He and his masons provided a new front to the west with an apse, transeptal towers and round side turrets. The elevation was articulated with pilasters and blank arcading: significantly the upper windows of the apse were not aligned with the larger, lower ones.

The greatest of these buildings was the cathedral of Speyer (19), started in 1030 or just before and carried on in a series of campaigns which saw a number of changes until the whole was finished by 1061, only for further repairs to be needed before the end of the century. The church was therefore not a sudden conception but the result of developing ideas by those responsible. Its plan (the

18 Mainz cathedral; east end

19 Speyer cathedral from the east

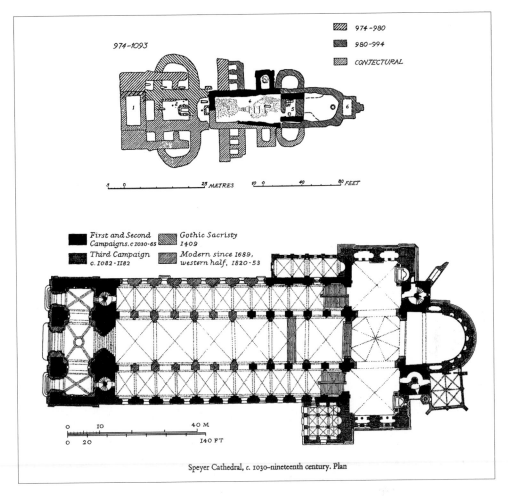

974-1093

974-980
980-994
CONJECTURAL

25 METRES   40   80 FEET

First and Second Campaigns. c 1030-65
Third Campaign c. 1082-1182
Gothic Sacristy 1409
Modern since 1689, western half, 1820-53

0   10   40 M
0   20   140 FT

Speyer Cathedral, c. 1030–nineteenth century. Plan

20A Plans of Speyer and Winchester cathedrals in the early eleventh century. The simple plan of Speyer contrasts with the many additions and changes of Winchester. *Winchester after the Winchester Excavation Trust; Speyer after Conant*

east end, the eastern part of the nave and the west end, because the western nave is a reconstruction of the nineteenth century) has a grand apse flanked by square towers; the nave is aisled. It is marked by its massive size: the whole church was *c.*130m long: the nave 13.85m wide with aisles 7.8m wide (20A, 20B).

The nave piers are 2.4m E–W and 1.90m N–S; this is the same as the width of the walls at their top, *c.*31m above the floor. The masonry has the two colours of the Rhenish tradition, especially the choir and crossing towers, but also the interior of the crypt. The size is emphasised by the articulation and organisation of the design. The exterior is divided into horizontal and vertical zones by pilasters and arches which enclose the crypt and choir windows. The windows of the nave clerestory and the aisles are aligned with arches of the arcade; the outside of the apse has an open gallery above the choir windows, with its openings aligned to the windows below. The proportions are reflected in the simplicity of the interior

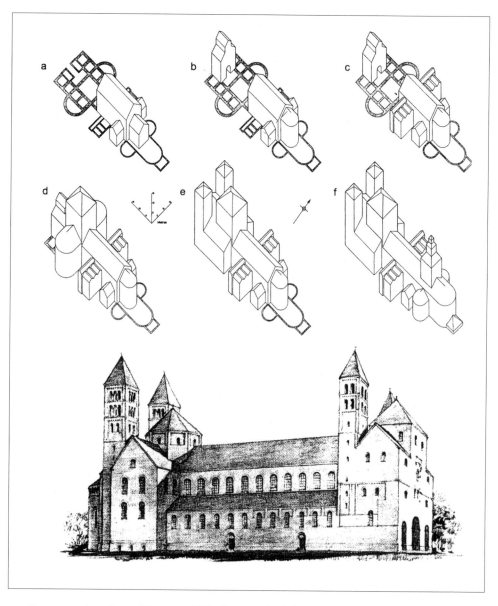

20B Reconstruction views of Speyer and Winchester cathedrals in the early eleventh century. Winchester shows changes and a confused design compared to the German one. *Winchester after the Winchester Excavation Trust; Speyer after Conant*

design: the nave has a two-storey elevation, arcade and clerestory only without any gallery, while the early capitals are of the plain cushion form. The church was meant to be vaulted from the start, at least at the east. The crypt has groin vaults, while the apse is also vaulted; the two bays of the choir have a reinforced barrel vault. The original form of the nave was of square piers, of alternating design, with every other one reinforced by a rectangular pilaster to the nave. Crucially, during the later work at the end of the twelfth century, the masons added semicircular shafts to the alternate piers with the pilasters, to carry high, groined vaults over the main space of the nave; the other piers had lighter shafts added.

The design of Speyer was picked up elsewhere. The cathedral of Mainz (*18*) saw two major building campaigns, one culminating in a fire in 1050 and the other after a second fire in 1081. The plan follows that of Bamberg and Speyer: the east end of a main apse flanked by towers. The eastern apse has the same gallery along with pilasters and arcades as Speyer. The internal elevation of the nave is similar with a groined vault over the nave and it too relies on size and proportion for its impact. The line of grand Imperial cathedrals continues with the building of Worms after 1120-30. Conrad II is said to have laid foundation stones in 1030 at both Speyer and Limburg an der Haardt on the same day. It is not on the same scale as Speyer, has a square eastern end and lacks any vault, but the proportions, simplicity and the western end with its towers are similar.

The various campaigns to bring the cathedral of Speyer to completion are important for how we look at the whole series of German buildings of the period. Clearly the designs were developed over a period of time longer than that of an individual master's working life. The relationships with the other churches were also part of a group activity. The designs, either overall, with plans and proportions, or of details such as pilasters, blank arcades or cushion capitals, all derive from the past. If the elements were traditional, and some were very much so, such as the continuing use of the 'Roman' transept cutting across nave and aisles in a single space at Hersfeld or Limburg an der Haardt, they were combined in a new way. The old variety had gone and there were new demands, notably for vaulting over aisles but then over the nave. The example of Speyer stood as the agreed, and long-lived, concept of a grand church for the Imperial court and the churchmen involved with it. The cathedral of Bonn whose eastern parts date to the 1160s, or (more strikingly) the rebuilt cathedral at Bamberg consecrated in 1237, all belong to the same tradition with eastern apses flanked by square towers and totally Romanesque detail.

In the century and a half after the completion of Speyer, until the beginning of the thirteenth century, the pattern of building in Germany maintained a balance between the overall concept expressed in the Imperial basilica and regional structures. The Rhineland saw churches constructed both traditionally and with new features. The novelty was in the plan of the east end. The church of St Maria im Kapitol in Köln was started in the 1040s and finished 20 years later; it had an east end composed of three apses arranged in trefoil plan with one ending either transept. This proved popular in the area, with other examples such as the church of the Holy Apostles (St Apostelen) also in Köln built to the same plan after 1192. The tradition of the masonry, however, goes back to the tenth century. The building of the great abbey church of Maria Laach, south of Köln occupied the first half of the eleventh century and resulted in one of the classic examples of mature German Romanesque (*21*). Its plan is double-ended with transepts and towers massed at both east and west along with apses at either end. The interior is straightforward, with a two-storey elevation and simple cushion capitals but the

21 Maria Laach abbey; the westwork of the church

nave is vaulted with groined vaults. The exterior is decorated or articulated with pilasters and blank arcades dividing up the various parts of the building. These are in either black lava or red sandstone to contrast with the good cream limestone ashlar of the basic walling, to give the same coloured effect as at St Pantaleon in Köln in the tenth century.

To the east in greater Saxony the churches have a somewhat different tradition, based on the same use of the local sandstone rubble as in the tenth century, contrasting with Rhenish ashlar. The emphasis on the westwork continues with churches such as Gandersheim or Freckenhorst of the later eleventh century being given what can only be described as screen fronts flanked by stair turrets. The enormous west tower at Paderborn cathedral was rebuilt in the late twelfth century along what must have been the tenth-century design. The west end of St Patroklus in Soest was also adorned with a similar massive square tower. The masons replacing Emperor Henry I's tenth-century church of St Servatius at Quedlinburg between 1070 and 1129, repeated the pattern of alternating pier and column with a flat ceiling found in Saxon churches of the tenth century. St Godehard at Hildesheim or the Liebfrauenkirche at Halberstadt are twelfth-century examples of the continuing Saxon tradition.

The German builders created a tradition out of two forces at the beginning of the eleventh century. On the one hand was the pressure, firstly from the emperors and then their aristocracy, for a certain type of church. It was to be very large and marked out on the outside by transepts and towers at either end of the long nave. This provided the setting both for Imperial galleries and chapels at either end, with space for processions and two opposing choirs. The masons pioneered the use of high vaults, organised the elevations into bays and worked to an aesthetic ideal of massive simplicity, represented by simple forms like the cushion capital. The detailed mason-craft continued to be regionally distinct, along lines established in the tenth century. The differences from that period and the eleventh and twelfth centuries lies in the use of the craft to work to the general, agreed concept of what constituted a great church across Germany.

INTER-REGIONAL INFLUENCES: FRANCE

The lands to the west of the Empire, which we now know as in France, were politically fragmented in the eleventh century. The power of the king was weak north of the Loire and virtually non-existent south of it. During the eleventh century the churchmen themselves were forced to take the initiative in carrying out the reforming programme without powerful Imperial or royal support. The Duke of Aquitaine founded a monastery in 910 in Burgundy, at the extreme north-east of his lands. The foundation was remarkable for the extent of the privileges he conveyed, particularly on the freedom from any regulation other than by the pope. By the middle of the tenth century the monastery was beginning to establish its own control over other, lesser houses, the start of the idea of the unified monastic

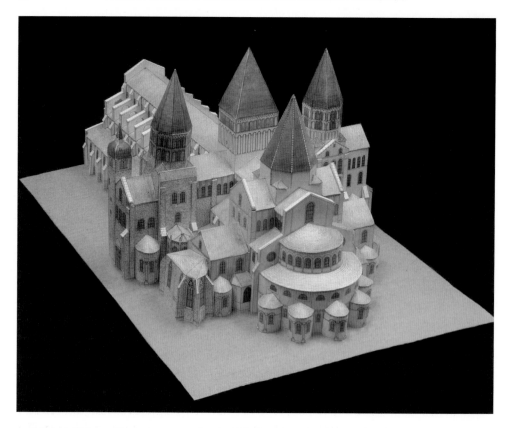

22 Model of Cluny abbey, reconstructed as it might have been in the twelfth century

order, and also a way of concentrating resources into the hands of the Abbot of Cluny. At the same time, the monks began a major building campaign, which saw the construction of a new church followed by a whole series of monastic buildings. The church was built to a plan (the so-called Cluny II, replacing the first church established after 910) which became one of the principal designs of France, an aisled basilica with an apse echelon at the east. It was not by later standards very large, some 30m long, but a lower narthex with two towers was added later to the west. Cluny's extension of control over other abbeys and the enormous prestige of its abbots during the late tenth and eleventh centuries has led modern scholars to seek examples where its architecture was followed elsewhere. During the first half of the eleventh century the church of Charlieu had an apse echelon east end, but so did others which cannot be linked to Cluny. Significantly it is in the western façade, the narthex and the decorated portal there that the strongest parallels lie.

In 1084-5 the church of Cluny was rebuilt on an enormous scale (Cluny III): only fragments survived the French Revolution but its main lines are known from eighteenth-century drawings and descriptions along with modern studies and excavation. It had a wide ambulatory at the east end surrounded by a necklace of radiating chapels to make a 'chevet' plan. West of this were two transepts, each with a crossing tower and the eastern one with two others at the ends, and then the double-aisled nave with an added narthex and towers like Cluny II. The whole building was some 140m from the apse to the first west end of the nave, with the narthex adding some 32m more to the length (22). The nave was c.40m wide and covered by a barrel vault with reinforcing arches at each bay 30m high; the arcade arches were pointed rather than semicircular and there was a triforium between the arcade and the clerestory. It was a match for Speyer in size but it was much more magnificently decorated. Not only were the architectural elements such as the arcade arches and the triforium pilasters given mouldings (the latter in imitation of Roman work) but the capitals of the apse at least were carved with figure scenes and the western portal had a major carving on the tympanum. Cluny III was vast and the monastic buildings were in scale with it (the eastern end of Cluny II was absorbed into them as a chapter house) so that, again, modern scholars have felt that it must have spawned imitations. Once more, however, direct imitations are few. The church of Paray-le-Monial was so close that it has been able to provide details to fill out our ideas of how Cluny III looked, but this is the only example where there are more than individual features taken, such as the painted apse of the chapel of the Abbot at Berzé-la-ville.

More to the point is to look at churches of the Cluniac Order of the decades around 1100. In the south-west of France a porch was added to the church of Moissac which has left us a superb series of high relief carvings of prophets, saints and animals. The church of Vézélay in Burgundy was rebuilt after a fire in 1120 when the church was under the control of Cluny. Two features stand out. The first is the series of groin vaults, not the arched barrel vaults of Cluny, over the nave. The second is the marvellous carving. There are powerful carvings on the tympana of the portals into the main church. Within the church are a set of capitals carved in a style that is not only impressive in its assurance and verve but also remarkable in its handling, even exploitation, of the difficult shape of the attached capital. Here the design has to overcome a space which goes from a semicircle at the base to a wider rectangle above, which means that figures have to expand with their height against any perspective (25). In England a little later, in the mid-twelfth century, masons at the Cluniac monastery church of Castle Acre built its west front with an elaborate display of the aniconic blank arcading and geometric patterns of the English style. In St Gilles near the Rhône delta there are three grand portals which are tours de force of the local style of carving of the late twelfth century. The Cluniac monks did have an effect on building in the monasteries of their Order but it was not in the form of a general pattern. Instead it was aimed at stimulating the most elaborate decoration in the masons from the region concerned. Technical features such as the means of vaulting were less important than the standards of art.

During the period of the rise and dominance of Cluny a second movement gave rise to international communications in building. In the eighth century the practice of making a pilgrimage to Santiago de Compostella became known outside its region of north-west Spain. By the eleventh century it had become one of the major shrines of Europe, benefiting from the danger and difficulty of the

23 Autun cathedral interior

route to Jerusalem and perhaps the overshadowing of the road to Rome by the increased traffic of Church bureaucrats. The pilgrims did not want to visit simply the shrine of St James but also other saints' shrines on the way; any church with important relics wished to attract them to their shrine. In the 1060s through to the end of the century four great churches, at Tours, Limoges, Conques and Toulouse, were built along the roads which led from northern France to the Pyrenees, as well as the cathedral church of Santiago itself. They shared the same plan of a grand ambulatory with radiating chevet of chapels at the east with a broad nave to the west; at Tours and Toulouse the naves had double aisles.

Between the naves and choirs of all were wide transepts with aisles. The aim was to provide a plan which would both accommodate great crowds of pilgrims and allow them to circulate from the west end up the nave aisles, across the transepts and around the main shrine in the choir apse. It must be stressed that the plan and the general scale of their height are what they had in common. Ecclesiastically, Tours and Conques were Benedictine monasteries, but not Cluniac; Limoges was Cluniac; Toulouse was the church of Augustinian Canons, while Santiago was a cathedral. Nor were they built to the same design except for the broad principles: St Sernin at Toulouse was built of brick in the Roman tradition not the stone of the others. All were splendidly carved, but in the local style. What united them was their plan, responding to the demands of their function as defined by the patrons who caused them to be built, communicating through church connections not those of the masons.

The foundation of the Cistercian Order at the end of the eleventh century introduced a new pressure for inter-regional contacts in building. Unlike the Cluniacs, the Cistercians quickly formed a self-conscious Order. It was tightly organised with a regular hierarchy of supervision of each member house; a new Cistercian house could only be founded by drawing monks from an existing one, which meant that the abbot of the 'mother' house was required to visit the daughter at least once a year. The abbots of all Cistercian abbeys met at Citeaux abbey each year to discuss the position of the Order. The principle behind this structure was to ensure uniformity of practice within the Order across Europe. Furthermore, the Cistercians came from the movement for monastic asceticism of the later eleventh century. As such, they defined themselves in part as being overtly in opposition to Cluny in that they set out to withdraw from pomp and display, and they specifically identified grand buildings as one of the things they rejected. Here, then, was an organised body with a coherent programme for building (24).

Bernard of Clairvaux had expressed his views on Cluniac building extravagance strongly in the 1130s and the Cistercians had by then developed a policy on building. In part this was purely negative; the prohibition of decorative carving which distracted the monks from ascetic contemplation or of towers which expressed earthly pride and expense. They also moved some way towards developing a specific plan for a standard church and monastery. This was based on squares; the choir was square ended and the transepts also square in plan. In some churches we can detect a proportional system whereby the plan is constructed around a larger square and a smaller one, with sides three quarters of the length of the larger one. There is always a problem in detecting metrical systems in medieval church plans. It is not clear whether we should measure walls from one face or along the centre line; we need to see the scheme repeated in a number of sites before we can be sure that it is not coincidence, but do not know how many or whether we are looking for the same scheme or the general idea; we do not know how far we should accept deviation from a theoretical scheme, how far we should apply modern precision of measurement. There is undoubtedly a modern fascination with applying metrological schemes (from the Pyramids onwards) to ancient structures which leads some to force the evidence into elaborate and largely bogus plans. However, right angles are essential to building and, from the tenth century, squares had been used as units for the layout of churches at Gernrode or Hildesheim (17). There are a considerable number of Cistercian churches constructed according to a plan whereby the larger square defines the dimensions of the choir and crossing as well as the width of the nave and two aisles; the length of the church equals the length of three sides of it. The smaller square gives us the width of the nave and one aisle or the east–west length of the transept and chapels; two of them the width of the whole crossing from north to south.

We must stress three points here. The first is that Cistercian churches by no means universally adopted this scheme even during the period of development

24 Pontigny
Cistercian abbey;
the church from the
south-west

in the middle of the twelfth century. The church of Mellifont in Ireland was a high-prestige venture; the first Cistercian abbey in Ireland, built with the co-operation of the local king and under the aegis of Malachi, friend and confidant of Bernard of Clairvaux himself: a French lay brother is recorded as coming to Ireland to help in the work. The builders of the first church at Mellifont did not follow the metrological scheme and they also introduced apsidal chapels into the design. Secondly this is a proportional scheme only; the size of the squares is not part of it, so that it gives a guide at best to the final plan. Thirdly this was purely a scheme for the plan of the church; it gave no help for the elevations. Even the specific prohibition of towers of 1157 might be flouted, as at the twelfth-century churches of Buildwas in England or Grey abbey in Ireland.

In fact Cistercian churches show a mixture of local and inter-regional features. The heart of the Order was in Burgundy and eastern France. From there came the use of the pointed arch and the pointed barrel vault into England or Ireland along with the men who spread the monastic and building practices of the Order. On the other hand a church such as Eberbach, built according to the proportional scheme of squares, had the square piers and groined vault of German practice. This said, the Cistercian churches were normally built by local men according to local styles. What distinguishes them from other contemporary buildings is not a specific feature or set of features but a general tone. In contrast to the idea of decoration and grandeur for the glory of God and the abbot responsible, the Cistercians built churches which were modest in scale and simple in decoration. Their fine proportions were their main aesthetic appeal, combined with the use of finely cut stone. The common factor was a tone set by the Order rather than any particular building practice of the masons.

France south of the Loire: regional strengths

The land here was a patchwork of counties or duchies west of the Empire, which stretched to the Rhône, an area where the power of the kings of France was very weak. North-east of this region lies Burgundy, which contained Cluny and inevitably the great churches there, particularly Cluny III, cast a strong shadow. In its plan and scale Cluny III related to the Pilgrimage type but there are local features too. The eastern apse of the surviving south transept is partly built in the brick-shaped rubble found at Tournus; it was steadily replaced with ashlar masonry, evidence surely of the learning curve of the local masons rather than of new men from outside. The building saw the wide use of pointed, rather than round arches in the arcades and a pointed barrel vault over the main vessel. Apart from its size, the main glory of Cluny III was in its carving, either the figure carving on the capitals of the main eastern apse, or of the great western portal, both of the first decades of the eleventh century. Compared to the standards of masonry and especially of carving to be seen at Tournus of the early eleventh century the change is immense. The carving of the capitals is lively and well balanced while the portal produced a new genre of monumental display.

These were features picked up in the neighbouring buildings to some extent. The cathedral of Autun, built in the 1120s and 1130s when the bishop was close to Cluny, is one of the closer followers of Cluny III. The internal elevation of the nave arcades has Cluny's pointed arches in the main arcade with a triforium and clerestory above it divided into bays by vertical shafts; the nave is covered also with a pointed barrel vault like Cluny (23). The plan, however, is far from Cluny with a simple transept and an aisled choir culminating in three apsidal chapels. The church of Vézelay was built at the same time, following a fire in 1120, when the abbey was directly under the control of Cluny. Its nave has only an arcade and clerestory with a strong horizontal string course in the place of a triforium; the bays are marked by shafts supporting groin vaults rather than a barrel vault, with the arches across the nave emphasised by building them in two colours of stone. Anzy-le-Duc has an octagonal crossing tower, a smaller version of Cluny's, but otherwise has no particular major feature in common. What distinguishes the churches of twelfth-century Burgundy above all else is their fine limestone and the magnificence of the carvings done in it. Autun and Vézelay have superb western portals (26). There are three portals at Vézelay, one to each aisle and a central one to the nave, all opening from a narthex. The three portray the life of Christ: his Nativity and Ascension to the sides, with his Majesty over the world in the central portal. His message is represented by showing the peoples of the world below Christ and the apostles, with miracles and the combating of sins in the arches over the tympanum. The narthex and the great western portals with their message are appropriate, not to an enclosed monastery but to one which was the centre of pilgrimage, in its own right as alleged holder of relics of the Virgin, and also as a starting point for the voyage to Santiago. At Autun the sculpture in the tympanum

25 Vézélay abbey: capital of David and Goliath

shows the Last Judgement dominated by the figure of Christ. Below his feet rise the dead whose souls are being weighed by St Michael and a devil (who tries, unsuccessfully to cheat by pulling down the scales); behind the devil is Hell, on Christ's right hand is Heaven. Both portals have superb sculpture in the sweep and energy of the figures, and in the delicate details of hands, feet or drapery.

The Autun portal is the work of a sculptor who was no shy or modest man; right below Christ's feet, at the crucial division between the rising dead and the hereafter, is the inscription: *Gislebertus hoc fecit.* Art historians have credited him with other carvings: a smiling, coquettish Eve who looks away as she picks the apple behind her back, asking the viewer to join her in pretending that she is not aware of what she is doing. The capitals of the nave are equally memorable in both churches. In Autun, Joseph is seen pulling the donkey carrying the Virgin and Christ on the flight to Egypt after the Nativity; he leans out of the capital to leave the central space to the others. At Vézélay the scenes on the capitals are dominated by ones from the Old Testament, with the same skill in composition and execution. Moses descends from the mountain with tablets of stone to find the sacrifice of the golden calf in progress; here represented as a well-grown bull with the arc of his neck and head framing the diagonal. David has killed Goliath and stands on a tree to cut off his head; David and the tree occupy the centre while Goliath (still miraculously on his feet) falls outwards out of the capital; the sword David uses links the two figures into a triangle (*25*).

26 Autun and Vézélay portal sculpture

To the south of Burgundy around the delta of the Rhône, the hand of the late Antique is stronger. Cathedrals such as Avignon, Arles or Fréjus are small, as befits the older Mediterranean pattern of small dioceses unlike the mighty ones of the north. They are dark inside because of the few windows, appropriate to the local sun; perhaps because of this there is little carving in the interior. Vaults are surprisingly unusual, with only four in the region, all barrel vaults. Aisles are also rare and ambulatories even rarer. The carving on the tympanum of the portal at Arles shows Christ in Majesty with the four apostles around him. Unlike the energy of the Burgundian figures, these are solemn and more naturalistically portrayed dignitaries. The cloister also has fine carving and Classical fluted pilasters. At Cluniac St Gilles there are three portals; the figures are still and upright in Roman cloaks while the ornament around them employs the vocabulary of Classical art: acanthus foliage, egg and dart, etc. It is probably significant that the largest of the churches, St Gilles, was Cluniac and may also be one of the earliest, the crypt begun after 1077; the above-ground church started around 1116; the façade is normally dated to after 1142 but seems to have been planned before this. Montmajour, a Cluniac abbey on the pilgrimage route, was also a building of the first half of the twelfth century but Arles and Avignon are both of the later twelfth century. The conservative Roman tradition was not eager to start on grandiose new projects.

The south-west of France, the Duchy of Aquitaine, stretched from the Loire to the Atlantic. The Counts of Poitou in the north gradually dominated politically the other counties of the old Visigothic and Carolingian Duchy of Aquitaine. They expanded into the lands towards Burgundy in the east and southwards to Périgord and the Saintonge bordering the Garonne; in 1052 they united these lands to those south of the Garonne although the County of Toulouse rose to absorb the regions east and south of this. Within Aquitaine we can see at least three traditions of church building. By 1100 the masons of Poitou had developed a scheme for a church with an ambulatory at the east, marked by three or five strongly projecting chapels. The nave was constructed with aisles but no triforium or clerestory; instead the arcade reached to the vault and all the light came from high windows in the aisles. A single roof covered nave and aisles, creating the so-called 'hall-church'. Typically the three spaces were covered by barrel vaults, the aisle vaults countering the pressure of that of the main nave. The church of St Savin-sur-Gartempe shows how the vault might be exploited for decoration with a vast painted sequence of Old Testament scenes. The main stone carving was reserved for the western screen fronts of the churches, usually framed by small turrets at the angles of the gable. The carving, seen at Notre Dame-la-Grande in Poitiers or Melle, consisted of tiers of blank arcades of deeply carved arches filled with figures. It is not delicate but it is dominant.

South-west of Poitou the churches of the Saintonge are more discreet. The eastern ends are apses of five or three canted bays. Around them the windows are framed in detailed and restrained carving, set off by the fine ashlar of the walls, often with attached columns and carved corbels at the roof line; the style is well seen at Rioux or Retaud, neither large churches but very fine. East of the Saintonge lies the Périgord. Here is the centre of a particular solution to the desire for vaulting in the churches. By 1100 at Cahors cathedral or St Etienne de la Cité at Périgueux the nave was composed of square bays, each covered by a dome. As a means of providing a vault it was simple but effective, especially as it left the side walls of the bays (and therefore the church) free of load, which was carried on the piers of the bays; they could therefore have any size or design of window. The design also worked well if there was an ambulatory

27 The church of Fontevraud abbey; although in Anjou, the builders chose to use domes of the technique found usually south in the Périgord to vault the nave

with semicircular chapels at the east, for the half domes over them built up well to the dome over the crossing. It had the drawback, however, of being very rigid in the planning of spaces within the church, which had to be built up of a series of squares and no other shapes. Although the practice is commonest in the Périgord, it is not unique to there; about half of the known domes are found outside it.

This brings us to the point of the interchange of ideas within Aquitaine. The cathedral of Angouleme lies between Poitiers and Périgueux (27). When it was built in the first half of the twelfth century it had an ambulatory with strongly projecting chapels and a western façade, both of Poitevin type. The nave and crossing, however, are built in the Périgord fashion as a set of square-domed bays. Aulnay, between Poitou and the Saintonge but belonging to the canons of the cathedral of Poitiers, has the apse of canted bays and windows of Saintonge style, but it is a hall-church and much of the carving of the portals relates to Poitou. The church of St Hilaire at Poitiers was a famous wooden-roofed basilica built in the eleventh century; some time around 1130 it was rebuilt with piers inserted to produce square bays to take a series of domes. The most northerly use of domes is north of Poitou at the abbey of Fontevrault in Anjou (27); its great, and surviving, kitchen is covered with a roof and turrets in Poitevin style.

Although it straddles the Loire rather than lying south of it, it is convenient to mention the churches of Anjou here. The church of St Martin in Angers had a dome over the crossing erected in the eleventh century and the Angevin masons continued to experiment with domical forms. By the middle of the twelfth century they had developed, as at the cathedral of Angers a system of ribbed domes which was able to span in three bays a nave 48m long, 15m wide and as high as the nave of Santiago. An odd variant of the idea is found at Loches, where the church nave is divided into square bays covered not with domes but with octagonal spires or pyramids.

One further point should be made about these southern French churches, and that is the evidence for literacy. Many of the portal sculptures and some of the capitals have inscriptions in Latin of the subject matter. Even more striking is the use of letters, rather than the symbols of the northern masons as masons' marks in the south-west.

Normandy and England: church building and politics to 1100

The period of the Viking invasions left the church in Normandy in a bad shape by 950. Bishops had been forced to evacuate their cathedral sees and most, if not all, major monasteries had been abandoned. During the later tenth century the situation began to be restored but surviving buildings are few. The church of St Peter at Jumièges shows the existence of a building industry in the First Romanesque tradition with circular double-splay windows almost in a tenth-century English style. In 1101 William of Volpiano came from Dijon to instruct the newly restored monasteries of Normandy in the practices of Cluniac monasticism. Dijon was the contemporary site of the major rotunda added to a double-aisled basilica; this left no mark in Normandy but his institutional reforms and links to Cluny (this was the time of Cluny II) did, and so may the idea of large buildings. The first of these that we can see is at Bernay, founded c.1036. The church has the apse echelon east end with transepts of Cluny II; the nave arcade has piers with attached half-round shafts while the soffits of the arches are embellished with broad, half-round rolls and roughly carved capitals.

The church of Notre Dame at Jumièges of 1037–65 shows a whole new standard of building. The church has lost its east end so we do not know its plan but the nave has a fine composition of three storeys clearly divided into double bays with alternate piers and columns; the shafts on the piers continue to the base of the clerestory. The triforium gallery has two groups of smaller arches, one for each of the lesser bays corresponding to the columns below. The stone is well-cut ashlar and the capitals are simple volutes, probably to be painted. The west end has a design of two towers flanking the gable of the nave which has a first floor gallery under a fine arch to the interior. The alternating bays, lack of carving and the western gallery all recall German churches of the preceding decades. Duke William and his wife Matilda were too closely related to marry according to the rules of the Church; in order to compensate for the sin, they founded two monasteries at Caen in whose churches are excellent examples of the virtues of Norman Romanesque. They take up the themes of Notre Dame at Jumièges: the fine but plain masonry with little carving, the three-stage elevation with a large triforium gallery, the bays delineated by half-round shafts. The east end of the church of La Trinité there, like that of Cérisy-le-Foret, had the apse echelon arrangement; St Etienne at Caen, like Jumièges, has lost its east-end plan.

Under the rule of the Danish King Cnut and his successor, Edward the Confessor took refuge in Normandy before returning as king of England in 1040. He founded a grand new monastery at Westminster the plan of whose church, a more or less exact contemporary of Jumièges, has been recovered from beneath the later rebuildings; the elevation has, of course, gone. This plan is basically like those of the Norman churches of the time, with apse echelon at the east and broad transepts and nave. England was a richer country than the Duchy of Normandy, but in 1066 they were united on the field of battle at Hastings. Not only did Duke William become king but there was a revolution in the aristocracy as well. In the Church the Anglo-Saxon bishops and abbots of the larger abbeys were replaced by men from the Continent; at the same time some of the seats of the dioceses were reorganised. Not all the newcomers were Normans, of course, but the dominant figures came from there, especially among the lay patrons. We might expect to see the seizure of power by the new men resulting in a spread of the same style of building developed in Normandy during the years following 1066.

The result was not, however, either the widespread importation into England of the idea of a church embodied at Jumièges, Westminster and Caen, or the development of a compromise between these ideas and the Carolingian and Anglo-Saxon tradition of the earlier eleventh century, as seen at Canterbury cathedral. In a number of ways the churches of the first generation after the

28 Contrasts in the design of the east ends of Romanesque churches: the chevet of Conques (above), and the apse echelon of Cérisy-le-Foret (below)

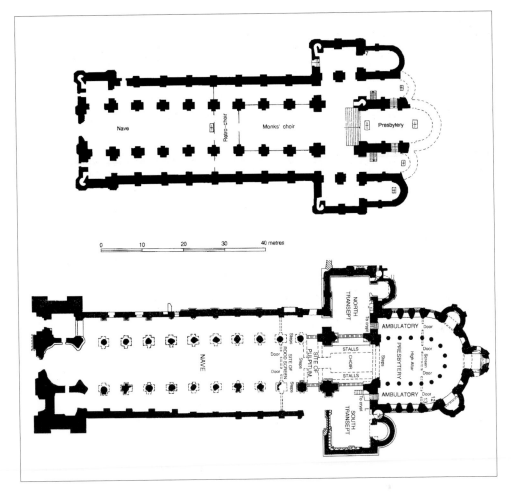

29 Contrast in the plans of Canterbury churches: the cathedral and St Augustine's

Norman Conquest, from 1066 to the end of the eleventh century show that the masons and patrons had a whole variety of ideas about quite major elements of the design of a big church. One of the most basic parts of a church is the plan of the east end, the heart of the ritual for which it is designed. Here there were two models available to the builders (28).

The first was the chevet, a semicircular ambulatory around the apse at the east, usually with projecting chapels around it, and the second was the apse echelon, with overlapping apses projecting further to the east in the central part and flanked by others down to the least projecting ones opening off the transepts. Canterbury cathedral, rebuilt soon after the Conquest because of a disastrous fire in 1067, was modelled closely on Caen with an apse echelon. Neighbouring St Augustine's, Canterbury, in keeping with their long rivalry with the cathedral rebuilt their church a decade or so later with an ambulatory (29). The apse echelon plan was chosen at Lincoln, St Alban's and Sarum; the ambulatory one at Chichester, Gloucester, Tewkesbury and Norwich.

The size of the new churches related to a balance of resources available and the urgency of the need, as when it was replacing a destroyed church, or perhaps when the see was moved to a new site, but it also reflected the ambition and confidence of the patrons. Here we may contrast the 10 bays of St Alban's abbey's nave with the seven bays of Battle abbey (built under the direct patronage of King William in memory of his victory) or Sarum cathedral. The 14 bays of Norwich cathedral are a little later (after 1096) and so perhaps attributable to the confidence of a second generation. Transepts were also rather surprisingly varied. Winchester cathedral transepts had an aisle around the three walls, other than those facing the central crossing, which carried a gallery around the outer sides. At Canterbury cathedral a pier in the middle of the opening between each transept and the crossing seems to have supported a two-storied transept with apsidal chapels to the east at each level. By contrast, St Augustine's at Canterbury, Chichester and others seem to have had transepts which were simple spaces open to the roof or vault. Sarum's transepts took the form of towers; how far they were open from the crossing is unclear from the fragmentary remains we have of the plan. The purpose of the galleries at triforium level over the nave aisles and sometimes linking into the transepts has been much debated. They may have been used to provide more altars (perhaps their earlier, tenth-century use) but are far too elaborate for this later. They look processional in their long spaces, but they are usually accessed awkwardly and by narrow and inconvenient stairs and wall passages. Most of the churches were conceived with strong vertical divisions between the bays as well as the horizontal divisions. However, this was very slight in the eastern apse of the choir at Norwich and omitted in the straight choir bays. The greatest contrast is found at Gloucester and Tewkesbury where the nave elevations were dominated by giant columns rising through the arcade to the triforium arches and supporting a low clerestory.

These cases omit two unique designs of the period. The cathedral Minster of York was rebuilt in the 1080s to replace the one destroyed in the wars on a new site north of the earlier cathedral. We know it only from the partial excavation of its foundations and lower courses of masonry below the later Minster. It had an aisleless nave with a strong central crossing tower. The transepts appear to have been almost self-contained square spaces with an eastern apse each. The choir is marked by wide foundations for the north and south walls which may be either combined for two narrow aisles or else to support a barrel vault over the central choir; it terminated in a single apse. The second unique design is that of the block built at the western end of the nave at Lincoln. It was part Carolingian westwork and partly a fortification confronting the royal castle to the west. All this said, the Anglo-Norman Romanesque buildings, even of the 1180s, had a few features in common. The outside was usually built around a clear eastern transept and crossing tower with something of a twin tower plan at the west. The internal elevations also varied, not just in details but in overall design. Inside, all had a three-storied elevation of arcade, triforium and clerestory, emphasised by relatively few strong arcade and triforium arches with little ornamentation.

Traditionally Durham cathedral, started in 1093 and finished by 1133, has been seen as the epitome of Anglo-Norman Romanesque and the starting point of its mature style. The implication has sometimes been that the master mason at Durham brought together the ideas of the generation before and created a building which was the source of most later ideals; the masterwork or pace-setter. The master at Durham is said to have done this in both the aesthetics of his design and in the technology of using rib vaults over the main vessel of the church for the first time in Europe: 'Durham made Cluny obsolete' (Conant). We must judge this view by looking at the two areas, aesthetics and vaulting, in context: how they arose and how far they were copied afterwards.

The plan of Durham is large but direct and straightforward: an east end of three apses, the outer two set in square ends, big transepts with eastern chapels but no gallery and a nave of alternating piers and columns. It is reasonable to see this as the result of a conscious design decision, to concentrate on the simplest versions around, rejecting the elaboration of the ambulatory plan, for example. As such it was not universally copied afterwards: ambulatories were built in the new choir at Canterbury cathedral finished c.1130 and at Leominster abbey, started after 1123, for example, but there were few and no more of the unique experiments such as Winchester. The square end linked well to its popularity with the Cistercians after the 1140s and became a consistent element in English Romanesque design.

The original exterior of Durham had five towers: two at the west, one over the crossing and two at the east end, over the side apses. In this it had a silhouette related to the German churches, but this display of towers was not much imitated later. The internal elevation of Durham reflected the earlier Norman pattern with its emphasis on the three stages and bay divisions, giving a strong proportional rhythm to the design (30). At Durham, however, the importance of the galleries was downplayed: instead of the wide openings towards the nave of Caen, at Durham the master gave them double openings which screened them off more. When the transepts were built (before the nave) doors from first floor passages were left to link up with the galleries over the nave aisles, but these were never unblocked when the nave was built; the galleries were not used as they were first conceived. Again this was reflected in later work, when the triforium of English buildings made a vital contribution to the general effect by repeating the arches of the arcade below to give the feel of a Roman aqueduct, but tending to be without the galleries behind.

In ornament, Durham continued the Norman love of architectural proportions and decoration confined to architectural elements such as the arches rather than carved capitals. One particular motif, the chevron, was first used prominently at Durham and became one of the hallmarks of Anglo-Norman Romanesque. It was in the area of design that churches in England and Normandy present a steady stream of development, so that we can arrange them typologically, dating ornament style by reference to churches of known date. It was based on an increasingly high standard of stone cutting, developed according to William of Malmesbury writing

30 Durham cathedral interior

in the 1130s to a decade earlier and the patronage of Roger, bishop of Sarum. The overwhelming impression is of long churches, dignified through their sense of proportion and masonry. The three stages and the bay divisions articulate the elevations, while the ornament emphasises the architectural elements through abstract motifs rather than figure carving.

Figure sculpture tends to be confined more to screens and friezes than capitals and portals. Both Canterbury and Chichester cathedrals have fragments of screens with figure sculpture; although neither is in place at least the Chichester figures are intact and very finely carved. Bishop Alexander of Lincoln was known as 'the Magnificent' and embellished the eleventh-century front of his cathedral in the 1140s with a frieze of biblical scenes; the portals he decorated with a series of moulded orders with pillar statues at the sides. In the 1160s Malmesbury abbey added a south porch to their recently built nave. The abbot who had started the work came from Cluniac circles in Burgundy and the nave has Burgundian elements such as the bluntly pointed arches of the arcade. The new south porch has biblical scenes on its side walls in semicircular panels like the tympana of grand French church portals; the Malmesbury carving, although impressive in its own right, never dominates the church in the way the Autun, Moissac or Vézélay portals do.

The technical achievement of erecting high rib vaults over the main parts of Durham was remarkable. Naturally it did not happen without a background of interest in the issue of vaults and their technology; one of the consistent aims of eleventh-century builders, from Germany to Aquitaine, was to develop effective vaulting systems. In England, the mason of the east end of Gloucester abbey (now cathedral, started in 1089) constructed a high, barrel vault over the main choir. He erected half-barrel vaults, reinforced at intervals with quarter-round arches, over the choir aisles and ambulatory; as they worked around the ambulatory he arranged the arches to splay outwards from one point (31). These were not ribs but they appear, whether by accident or design, to support the choir column from forces spreading out from the barrel vault and half dome of the apse above. They seem to show evidence of a man thinking in terms of channelling the forces of a vault, which could combine with the pattern of a groin vault to prompt the idea of a rib vault.

The result of the vaulting at Durham was not that Anglo-Norman masons abandoned the use of all barrel and groin vaults thereafter. Obviously some masons would continue the practices in which they had been trained, at least for some years afterwards, even if all the new men were convinced of the superiority of ribs. It goes beyond this, however. In the south-east of England, notably at Canterbury, there seems to have been a reluctance to change soon; it is in the north and in the south-west, near Durham and Gloucester that the ribs are most popular. Significantly, when barrel or groin vaults were used after the 1130s they were usually in the less prestigious parts of the building; in church crypts, the ground floors of great castle towers or monastic buildings where the floor above was the important one. However, the builders of some major churches, such as

31 Vaults over the ambulatory of Gloucester, showing the quadrant vaults reinforced with arches like ribs

Peterborough or Ely whose resources could certainly have run to a high vault, chose not to erect one; presumably they considered that a timber ceiling, although a fire risk, offered better opportunity for a display of panting.

Durham cathedral owes its prestige in modern scholarship to two things. The first is the high prestige accorded to the earliest example of a feature, in this case the high vault. It is easy to overlook the evidence for a lack of conviction in the new technology at Durham, where the transepts are likely to have been built at first without intending them to have a rib vault which was then added later. The second factor is that it was lucky; uniquely for an English church of its time it has come down to us substantially intact. Parts have been replaced such as the east end and the crossing tower, or removed like the east towers, but we have still a good idea of its appearance inside and out. Added to this is the sheer magnificence of its site above the city and the river Wear, and the glory of its interior. To see Durham as the epitome of the buildings of twelfth-century England is to overlook two other issues. The first is to underplay other influences and intrusions, most notably that of the Cistercian ideals, which aligned with the ideas of Durham. The second is to follow the idea of ordered typology and stress the main stream of development too much. The stream certainly had its eddies in aesthetic design. The most obvious of these is the use of giant columns stretching up from the arcade through the triforium. This device is found at Gloucester and Tewkesbury in the late eleventh century and crops up again in the mid-twelfth century at Romsey, or later at Jedburgh and Oxford. Nor is it likely that Durham was the product of a single mind. We see major stages in the work which lasted at least 40 years. This certainly outlasted three bishops and is likely to have outlasted any one master mason. The work was the product of a continuously changing group of men, not one.

Ireland: a Romanesque microcosm

For some centuries after the conversion of the Irish to Christianity, their tradition was very firmly to build churches in wood; indeed, to Bede in around 700 it was one of the ways in which he contrasted the Irish from the 'Roman' churches. From the ninth century (after the end of the dispute with the Roman church over Easter and other elements of ritual) they started building small churches in stone. It was during the tenth and eleventh centuries that the Irish saw the beginnings of their own version of the First Romanesque ideas. Typically, it concerned the erection of towers, not the towers integrated with the church buildings of Carolingian Europe, but free-standing ones. The tapering round towers became a symbol of Irish monasteries; partly used for storage and display of relics but primarily buildings which proclaimed (they would have been visible from afar) the existence and wealth of the monastery which built them. In form they reflect the stair turrets of a Carolingian or Ottonian church such as St Gall or Gernrode while the occasional use of raised stripwork around openings and triangular heads to doors and windows recalls tenth- or eleventh-century English practice. Their main significance, however, is not in their origin but in the fact that they were constructed at all. They are proof of the existence of an industry which had developed the quarries and lime sources as well as the scaffolding and organisation to construct elaborate stone buildings. To this the masons had probably added, by 1100, the ability to erect a simple barrel vault.

By 1100 the institutional structure of the Irish Church had become seriously anomalous in the eyes of the contemporary reformers in the rest of Europe. Monasteries dominated it with weak bishops who had no territorial mandate or control because dioceses were absent and the monasteries themselves did not conform to the newly established Orders. During the eleventh century in particular the power of a smaller number of kings had also grown, at the expense of the many earlier ones, through greater military power and ruthlessness. These men hoped to establish powers similar to the kings of the new kingdoms of feudal Europe and they allied with Church reformers to achieve their mutual aims. A series of Synods in the twelfth century established dioceses in Ireland, too many for the resources of the land, but they had to placate all the kings who insisted on having a bishopric for their kingdom. The Order of Savigny was the first to establish new monastic houses in Ireland, at Erenagh in 1127; St Mary's abbey, Dublin (also Savignac) was founded in 1139; the first Cistercian abbey, Mellifont followed in 1142. New kings, new bishops and new monks combined to overthrow the old order in Ireland at the expense of the estates of the old monasteries.

All three groups used buildings to reinforce their position and they looked to lands outside Ireland for men, skills and ideas to build them. There are some hints of masons coming from England to Ireland in the quarter century after 1100. The doorway at Killaloe, with attached shafts and a hood mould has (rather controversially) been said to date from before 1125; the church at Dungiven has vertical and horizontal pilaster strips on the east wall and raised stripwork around the window. The Killaloe doorway is a simple design which would be dated to the earlier twelfth century in England; the Dungiven strips recall eleventh-century Anglo-Saxon work. Neither is particularly convincing and Cormac's chapel at Cashel overshadows them both.

Cormac's chapel is like Durham in that it is well dated (probably begun in 1127 and finished in 1134) and in that it is well preserved (32). It is still the key Irish monument of the period, in spite of a number of attempts either to downgrade its position as the occasion of something new or else to minimise its impact. The church is small with a nave and square-ended chancel; within the angle of the junction of the two are two towers. The major elements of the structure derive from English practice of the early twelfth century: the chancel is rib-vaulted while the nave has an arched barrel vault; it was common in England to reserve the rib vault for the east end, while the same combination of ribs and arched barrel vaults occurs at Ewenny abbey. The main decorative elements are blank arcades and chevron ornament, hallmarks of English practice; lesser English elements are the high pediment over the northern door and the rosettes beside the raised strips in it. Cormac McCarthy brought over one or more English masons to construct the church which marked both his own triumph in establishing his kingship in Munster, but also the success of the new archbishopric of Cashel, the site of the former dynasty's stronghold. There are elements in the design which may have come from seeing buildings in western France (the decoration of heads in the chancel arch) or Germany (the siting of the towers, although this is found in England too). These are, however, things which the churchmen involved could have described for the masons to incorporate into the design. The construction of a vault, let alone a rib vault, the drawing out of complex chevrons, these are the masons' business and expertise. At the same time, it is clear that this was not the work only of English or foreign masons. Over the vaults are Irish stone roofs, formed by corbelling in a tradition seen before Cormac's chapel.

The masons working at Cashel trained up a team who went on to train others and to create an Irish Romanesque tradition. Interestingly, they did not continue all the features of Cashel. They dropped the rib vaulting and the twin towers, while the whole range of complex chancel arch, blank arcading, high pediment over the portal and the elaboration of the chevron was never deployed in the one church again. The closest churches in design to Cashel, Roscrea and Ardfert, used the pediment, arcading and chevron. The norm was an elaborate portal and chancel arch. The scale of the churches remained very small. Cashel itself is only some 13m long in total; 20-25m is as long as one of the new Irish Romanesque structures gets, with 15-20m as a norm.

The buildings of the new monasteries contrast with the small, decorated churches of the Cashel tradition. Erenagh is lost completely, with only its site being

32 Cormac's chapel, Cashel

known (its endowments were absorbed into the Cistercian abbey of Inch later in the century), while nothing of twelfth-century St Mary's in Dublin survives. The Cistercian houses have fared better, which has contributed to their overshadowing the earlier Savignac houses. Mellifont has been both excavated and extensively studied. Its church does not conform to the plan of the later 'standard' Cistercian church, for the eastern side of each transept has three chapels, two apsidal with a central one square ended. The earliest of its surviving daughter houses, Baltinglass, founded in 1148, has similarly anomalous transept chapels, but after that the 'standard' plan was followed. The main impression of these monasteries to the Irish eye, especially after their norm of circular sites with scattered buildings, is and would have been of the severe rectangularity of church and cloister along with the wholly new scale of the complex; Mellifont or Baltinglass churches are twice the length of many decorated Romanesque churches, and then there were the claustral buildings. This scale was accompanied by the lack of ornament typical of the Cistercians.

The experience of the Irish was undoubtedly small scale in terms of the general achievement of the Romanesque and contributed no technical or aesthetic development which was imitated outside the island. In terms of modern study, however, it is an interesting example. It allows us to study a relatively straight-forward case of the process of how Romanesque ideas might spread. It required the close co-operation of both masons with their knowledge and the holders of secular and religious power with their patronage; either alone could not have produced the buildings. The foreign masons and craftsmen, however, needed local men who knew the natural resources and who provided the mass of the less skilled workers; the stone roof of Cashel shows that they contributed to the design also. The reform of the Church in Ireland was as important there as the pilgrimage was in France and Spain in stimulating construction. The lay powers, the kings, were also vital for they alone could endow the new church institutions with resource, either new ones or taken from the old monasteries. The influence of the patrons is also clear in the designs; after all, the kings were using the churches as emblems of their power and so were interested in the result.

The largest decision was in the type of institution and building. The resources of Ireland were restricted, but when they were fragmented among warring kingdoms they were smaller still. It would seem that the kings had to choose between small but decorated churches or large but plain Cistercian monasteries; large and decorated was not an option. The same workmen may have been employed in both, if we can explain similarity of ornament as proof of the same workman, so the decision was the patron's. The choice was more than just one of resources, for the needs of a bishop were different from a Cistercian abbey, and so too were their positions in society. Cistercian abbeys demanded solitude and independence. The Irish kings not only founded them away from their own centres of power, where the secular churches or the houses of Augustinian canons might flourish in alliance with them. The examples of Baltinglass and Newry show how the kings appreciated the different place of the Cistercians in society. Diarmait Mac

Murchada founded Baltinglass on lands which divided those of his old rivals for the kingship of Leinster, the O Tuathail. Muirchetach Mac Lochlainn found Newry on lands which he did not own, those of the Mac Guiness kings. They were among the most powerful kings of the resurgent kingdom of Ulster and the monastery estate lay on the direct path which any Ulster army had to take if it was to interfere with the kingdom of Meath to the south. In both cases the kings had placed powerful Church interests in a position to impede their enemies. The original choice of English workmen, and therefore design and technology, for the church at Cashel must be seen in terms of contemporary political relations with Henry I's England and its power in the Irish Sea.

SUMMARY

The church building industry of the eleventh and twelfth centuries saw a massive increase in the scale and numbers of great churches built across Europe. The earlier, First Romanesque, period had created the capacity and desire for the buildings which were now constructed. This was not a matter of the craftsmen alone but also mobilising the resources of society through the patronage of the aristocrats, whether great churchmen or nobles and kings. The church building project ran concurrently with the widespread building of great stone castles; powerful men were using stone buildings to display their influence either in rivalry between each other or over their subordinates. In both cases the masons were working to celebrate and advance the power of their Lord.

The responsibility of the patrons was to organise and direct the work. In part this meant mobilising the resources. A big building project needed money; it employed hundreds of men, trained craftsmen and unskilled labourers taken on seasonally, who had to be supported while they worked. The lords could also facilitate access to the materials needed, principally stone and timber. The lords owned both the forests and the quarries, while it was in their households that the experienced administrators with the contacts across the lordship worked, these people could make things happen. Their main role was to set the agenda for the building. It was the patron who decided the priorities, which would reflect the purpose of the building. The clearest example of this is in the churches of the Cistercian Order, where the religious priorities of the Order, uniformity and simplicity, were overtly expressed in the design of the churches. By contrast Cluniac abbeys were consistent in demanding the highest standard of decoration. In these cases the mechanism of the Order ensured that the message reached across Europe. In the case of the churches built to service (and exploit) the pilgrimage to Santiago there was no institutional link between them. We must imagine that the patrons exchanged ideas about the ways to facilitate the circulation of pilgrims around the relics and how to impress them with displays of building and ceremony.

Individual features may be attributed to the patrons. Bishop Wulfstan of Worcester, the last Anglo-Saxon bishop to survive after the Norman Conquest of England, cannot have been alone in his condemnation of the widespread rebuilding programme initiated under the new regime. His objections were two-fold. He resented the desecration of the old churches hallowed by their past associations with the Old English church. He also anticipated the Cistercian feeling (he was writing a generation before St Bernard) that these new churches were a matter of pride, not religious feeling. The overall length of Durham cathedral was probably within a metre of that of Old St Peter's in Rome while the width of the nave and aisles was also within a metre of the width of Old St Peter's inner aisle. It is much more likely that Bishop William was responsible for transmitting these than that the master mason had visited Rome. Not only did the bishop have the opportunity, but he dictated the scale and the resources. The use of the ambulatory at the east end of St Augustine's at Canterbury not only reflected the deep rivalry of that monastery with the cathedral nearby, but also the personal links of Abbot Scotland who came from the abbey of Mont St Michel which had an apse and ambulatory.

If the patrons dictated the scale and agenda, it was up to the masons to deliver the actual building and ensure that it did not fall down. When it comes to matters of technology we must attribute developments and spread of these to the community of masons. The most obvious example of this is with vaulting. For reasons of fireproofing and acoustics during services, but above all because their rivals had them, the patrons of great churches demanded that they be vaulted in part or as a whole. In the mid-twelfth century it was decided to install vaulting in the old church of St Hilaire in Poitiers; rather than knock it down, the masons inserted columns to carry the vault, which narrowed the space but gave the required prestige effect. A bishop, abbot or king could not design and carry out this aim; that was the mason's work. The solutions they used depended on how they had been trained and on their later contacts; it is among the masons, not the patrons, that a new development such as rib vaulting or some ornamentation must have spread. Laying out a chevron around an arch, cutting the stone of a capital deeply so that the figures stand out proudly or designing the figures in the space of a capital or a tympanum are skills which had to be learned and transmitted among the masons. A patron demanded ornament and said what scheme of decoration he wanted, but it was up to the mason as to which mouldings or carving to use. The Cluniac churches are excellent examples; they were to be highly decorated, but the actual design was in the style of the region. The consistent difference between the figures of Burgundy and of Provence to the south is a clear example of this. The actual laying of stone could vary according to the training of the masons (and the geology of the stone available), as witness the long difference between Saxony and the Rhineland. As the projects grew more ambitious, so the chances of the one master seeing one through from start to end was smaller. The need for continuity reinforced the sense of a team or community, as did the need to bring carpenters, plumbers and other trades into the design process.

The churches are therefore the result of the co-operation of two communities, the patrons and the craftsmen, each with their own agenda and with their own lines of resources, training and development. The communities which were thus formed were not based on political units, but were intensely regional. Solutions to vaulting, from domes to ribs varied according to the region concerned. The emphasis might be on size, as in Imperial Germany or England, rather than the complex carving of Burgundy. The regions are not usually those of political units, as shown in Aquitaine, although it would be impossible to understand the variety of designs and the impulse for the burst of building in England without reference to the Norman Conquest. Against a background of regional identities, the use of imported ideas becomes much more significant. The new scale and ideas of the Imperial basilicas of eleventh-century Germany were as much about the power of the emperor over the Church (to be rejected bitterly by the pope) as it was about the Church itself. When Edward the Confessor chose to build his new show-church at Westminster in Norman plan and design, not the Carolingian style of Canterbury, this was a clear message of the cultural connections he wished to make for England.

4

EXCURSUS: ARCHES, VAULTS AND BUTTRESSES

European builders since the Neolithic had been using timber and learning about its properties. Timber grows naturally with long fibres, so that a length of wood is bound together well; it is hard to break or bend while it is relatively light. As such it is excellent material for horizontal lintels between two vertical supports. It is, however, impermanent. It suffers from rot, especially if it is used in a position where it is prone to get damp and fungus or insects may attack it. It is also vulnerable to fire, a crucial defect when building churches full of hangings, draughts and candles, or which were meant to be high enough to attract lightning strikes. The medieval builders inherited from their Roman predecessors the knowledge of three fundamental building materials: mortar, stone and brick. Brick had never been as prestigious as stone in Rome in spite of its advantages of mass production. Its use was revived in northern Europe in the twelfth century, when it was treated structurally like stone. Stone is composed of mineral grains held together with some form of natural cement. It is bad acting as a lintel: support each end of a length of stone, load the centre of the length and it will break as it bends, because it is only as strong as the cement between the grains. On the other hand it is immensely strong under pressure when the weight simply forces the grains together. It is also much longer lasting in all sorts of positions, at least until the advent of air polluted with industrial chemicals.

Their preference for working in stone presented builders with one fundamental problem of construction: how to span the space between two supports in stone. The Greeks used stone lintels, which is why the columns on their temples are so close together: the Romans used arches to do the same job because they could cross greater spans. An arch is a series of wedge-shaped stones (voussoirs) laid around a curve from one support to the other. It can support great weight at the top, because this simply forces the stone, and the grains which make them up, together. The weight on the top (the crown) of the arch forces the top stones downwards. Then the wedge shape of all the stones, which is essential to keep

Top, above and opposite: 33 The performance of an arch under pressure. A. The arch unloaded and stable. B. The arch deformed at the haunches by weight on the crown. C. Counter-pressure supporting the haunch maintains the arch

them in the shape of the arch, causes the force of the weight to push the stones of the side of the arch (the haunch) outwards. If this is not countered the arch will be broken and fall, so the haunch must be reinforced to prevent any sideways movement (*33*).

This sideways force, however, is also always spreading outwards, not just vertically downwards. The aim of the builder must be to provide a continuous line of support between the haunch and the ground so that the foundations will absorb the forces.

If we put weight on the support, it will also act to deflect the forces more vertically downwards and so contain the spread. An arch with the heavy load of a wall (let alone a tower) on top cannot, therefore, be supported by just two free-standing columns but must be supported by a wall or buttress to the side.

From the tenth century at least, patrons demanded that at least part of the interior spaces of their new churches should be covered by stone vaults between the floor and the roof. They wanted the resistance to fire and better acoustics that vaults could provide, but the main reason seems to have been because they were one of the principle objects of display; a vault was necessary because the other churches had one. This was harder than an arch; it meant spanning a wide space rather than just the narrow strip between two supports. The most straightforward type of vault is the barrel (or tunnel) vault (34). The vault is constructed from stones either cut like the voussoirs of an arch, or else simply flat stones laid at right angles to the line of the curve, with mortar making up the wedge shape to hold them in place. This is essentially a continuous series of arches stretched along the space between the walls, although the stones should interlock along the line of the vault as well as across the span. In either case the vault is very heavy with all these massive stones and needs reinforcement along the whole length of the wall; there is no focus to the forces of the arch design. This is compounded by the fact that these forces spread outwards. If the vault is placed on a high wall, the load must be countered by the wall being built ever thicker towards the ground. A further weakness of the barrel vault is that the greater its length the more prone it is to collapse.

A second technique is in a sense a form of barrel vault, a dome. Here the space over a circle is spanned by what can be thought of as a set of arches crossing the whole series of diameters across the space. If these are made of well-cut stones like a thin barrel vault it is strong and may be relatively light. The problem comes with

34 Walterstown, Co. Meath: a fifteenth-century tower house which has partially collapsed, revealing the form of the barrel vault over the ground floor

the shape of the space it covers, which must be a circle or a semicircle, as when it spans an apse. Stone buildings are, however, usually either square or rectangular; round buildings are very awkward to subdivide. This can be overcome with a square space by building out across the angles of the square to produce a wall on the top of which the mason can draw a circle on which to place the vault. The weight and forces generated by a dome thrust almost vertically, so that the walls have to be strong but do not need to spread so much towards the base. The important points are the corners; if they are strong, the weight between them may be carried on arches and the walls pierced so the sides of the square may be opened out. The result can be spectacular, as shown by St Sophia in Constantinople in the sixth century where the central dome spans an uninterrupted space c.31m across in any direction. The difficulty with a dome is that it is inflexible spatially, confined to circles, semicircles and squares.

A barrel vault is relatively easy to conceive and construct but it places an enormous strain on the design of the walls below and, indeed, the whole building; with walls thick at their base it is difficult to put decent windows in them. The purpose of a groin vault was the focus the weight of the vault on specific points, so the walls in between these would not bear the same load. The means to do it was effectively to place two barrel vaults over a square space intersecting at right angles to each other so that their open ends would form four arches (35). The intersections of the two vaults would produce four lines of intersection along the diagonals of the square; the name derives from the meeting of the vaults along the intersections. If the corners rested on strong columns, properly supported and buttressed, the intervening space could be opened up which worked well. There are, however, important spatial limitations. It is effective over a square space with columns or piers at the four corners. The distance between any two piers is the same, so the profile of the arch is the same as is the profile of the vault they carry. The groins, the line where the sections (the webs) of the vaults meet, run along the diagonals of the square and are easy to predict and define; cutting stones to cross the junctions is therefore relatively straightforward. All this, as with a dome, breaks down if the shape of the space is anything else than a square. The arches, and their vaults, have different profiles, so the groins follow a variety of patterns, difficult to predict, design or cut stones for. If both vaults are semicircular but of different spans, then they will have different heights; to make the narrower one pointed in profile to raise its height results in trying to match a semicircle and two arcs of less than 90°, both difficult and clumsy looking.

The techniques of all these methods of vaulting had been known in Roman times and were probably passed down from then, either directly or through Byzantium, to the masons of the tenth century. In the eleventh century not only were they all practised at least somewhere in Western Europe but it is clear that the masons were thinking about how they worked and might be improved. In Speyer or Cluny, after all, such vaults were being erected at heights not seen in the west for centuries. One of the defects of barrel vaults was that they became weaker the longer they were. Some masons reinforced them at intervals with arches, while

35 St Martin-des-Champs, Paris; groin vaults (foreground) and rib vaults (behind)

the pointed barrel vaults of Burgundy or Provence may have been an attempt to stiffen the crown of the vault longitudinally. The more complex shapes attempted during the eleventh century for groin vaults, especially around ambulatories, must have concentrated minds on the intersections of the different webs. Reinforcing arches and specially carved stones to make the junctions between the webs of a groin vault are not far away from the fourth, and most successful, method of vaulting, the rib vault (35-37).

This depended on building separate arches (or ribs) between the different vault webs of the area to be covered. The webs were then built between the arches and resting on them. This seems to have been the universal medieval practice of construction and it must be based on the idea that the ribs would take the weight of the webs and channel the forces down to the piers and the ground. It may be that the vaults did not always actually function in that way, because in some places, for example at Netley abbey, the ribs have fallen away but the webs are still standing. This can be countered by cases such as Lindisfarne abbey where the reverse has happened; the webs have fallen but the ribs survive. These experiences are probably as much to do with the efficiency and function of the mortar as the design of the vaults themselves, and it seems clear that medieval masons, at least, thought of the ribs as supporting the vault.

There were two great advantages to this system. Firstly the ribs acted to concentrate the forces into one or more points. If the mason reinforced these, the rest of the wall could be free of load. The second advantage was that the ribs

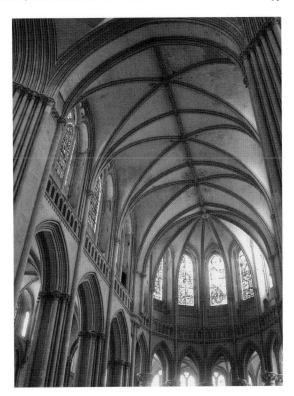

36 Coutances cathedral; a quadripartite
rib vault, but with a further rib added
along the ridge of the vault, as became
common in England

37 Sens cathedral; a sexpartite rib vault

could be constructed to divide up any shape of space: the ribs could be used to overcome the awkward junctions of the groins (*31, 35* and *36*). The oldest surviving major vault of this type is at Durham, where we can also see the master or masters wrestling with problems posed by the technique. The main one was the frequent one of the rectangular space. In the north choir aisle are the earliest surviving vaults and they have to cover such a space. The mason tried to use a semicircular shape for all three arches concerned: the east–west ones over the arcade and facing the choir, the north–south ones crossing the aisle and the ones across the diagonals. Of these, the ones facing the choir were both the most visually prominent and important and near to the average width of the other two. The mason chose to make them a semicircle: to get the narrower ones across the aisle to the same height he started their curve a little higher, while he built the diagonals somewhat less than a semicircle. The raising of one arch (stilting it) is unattractive; the arch less than a semicircle is thrusting outwards more the others. In the nave we see the solution. Here the narrower cross arches are pointed so that they can be carried up to the correct height without using the device of stilting.

As the rib vault became more common, so masons developed variations of the technique. The simplest vault is over a square, and the double bays used at Durham may have been designed to produce that. However, the double bay idea continued and became linked to the idea of the alternating piers seen in German and Norman work of *c.*1100. One variant was to have alternate piers ('strong' piers) support both cross ribs and diagonals in two directions; three ribs leaving the wall there. The other piers (the 'weak' piers) supported only a cross arch. In effect the double bay continued but divided into six vault cells in plan, the so-called sexpartite vault (*37*).

This contrasted with the system where each pier had the diagonals and the cross rib alike; each bay was divided into four cells, the quadripartite system. The reason for the sexpartite system may have been that diagonal ribs cut across the clerestory windows, the main source of light to the main vessel of the building. With only a cross rib on alternate bays, half the clerestory windows were unobstructed on at least one side. A more long-lasting variation was to increase the number of ribs in a bay. There is no real structural need for this, the appeal seems to have been purely for the decorative effect it produced. This could be enhanced by increasing and carving the stones where two ribs met, making them into vault bosses (*38*). The extra ribs have been given different names. A rib running along the crest of the vault is a ridge rib. An extra rib running from the springing on the wall to the ridge is a tierceron rib. A rib running from one rib to another, not reaching the wall is called a lierne rib.

The increasing demands of high vaulting brought with it the need for more support to the walls of the buildings. With barrel vaults there was a problem because they were needed for uniform support along the whole length of the vault. This gave rise to the obvious solution of masses of masonry in the wall; tenth and eleventh century walls were over-engineered anyway, but the desire for vaults increased the tendency to have thick walls. This was not a great help,

38 Lincoln cathedral: the vault over St Hugh's choir of *c.*1200. The best explanation for its pattern is that it is a compromise between a quadripartite and a sexpartite vault

however, if the vault was over the main vessel of an aisled building. In this case the wall would be weakened by arcades and possibly a gallery below the point of the thrust of the barrel vault; the wall was in danger of being bent with the upper parts forced outwards. In spite of this we see the upper walls of Cluny III thickened over the line of the aisles; the extra load had to be countered by later buttresses. This remained a heavy and costly but popular device long into the twelfth century. A more sophisticated way to counter the force of a barrel vault was in effect to prop masonry up against the wall, with half-barrel vaults 'leaning' against the outer wall at the level of the haunch of the vault. We can see these quadrant vaults, as they have been termed, constructed above the aisles at Santiago de Compostella or Gloucester. At the latter, the half barrels are reinforced by arches at intervals: significantly, these reinforcing arches were concentrated on the one pier where the space over the aisles abutted the half dome of the apses.

Rib vaults especially offered the opportunity to make ever more sophisticated support designs. At first, as at Durham, the masons seem to have thought in terms of building counter-arches, complete arches set against the vault to provide thrusts in the opposite direction, a further version of the idea of using masonry props to counter thrust as at Gloucester. This was a poor solution for two reasons. Firstly it added to the weight on the walls, already in the case of Durham thickened above the arcade. Secondly it was misconceived. A buttress is not there to provide extra forces against the thrust but to transmit the pressure from the vault to the ground. It does this by providing a substantial enough line of masonry to face the thrust of a leaning vault (especially when the wind blows against the wall below and the roof above it). The buttress works by meeting the force with a line of stone; stone can take the pressure without crushing and so the force is transmitted to the ground. The buttress must be designed not only to be strong enough to meet the thrust but also to absorb the line of the spreading thrust. The buttress will therefore always take the form of a sloping or arched piece of masonry running from the point of pressure to the ground. This must follow the spreading line of the force but it can be deflected into a more vertical line by placing weight on the buttress but the line of the force will never quite become truly vertical.

These issues became more crucial as the vaults were built ever higher during the twelfth century. The vaults were also placed over the main vessel, the nave or choir, in the churches which had aisles and often chapels on the outside. To build heavy buttresses, either as stub walls cutting across the aisles, or as arches contained within the aisle roof, was impractical. The buttresses had to arch up over the aisle and its roof; they had to become the so-called flying buttresses. When the masons first erected these, in the later twelfth century, they still seem to have thought in terms of a prop against the wall, a counter-arch. The buttresses at St Remi in Reims, for example, meet the wall at the haunch of the vault at a right angle (39). By the end of the century, however, most notably at Bourges, they were redesigned. They met the wall at a steep angle which they continued to the ground. This was much more efficient, containing the spreading forces of the

39 St Remi abbey, Reims: early attempts at a flying buttress. The arches meet the wall at a right angle, as though to prop it up, not at an acute angle to contain the forces of the vault efficiently

vault within a narrow band of masonry and transmitting them to the foundations. The right-angled buttresses worked because, being more massive, they actually did contain these forces within them, but at the cost of an excess of masonry and weight.

It is all very well for a modern non-specialist (like me) to try to understand these principles; there are books by experts with diagrams to explain the lines of force and thrust. These are based on scientific studies through models (literal or figurative) and mathematical ideas. It was very different for a medieval mason. There could be no body of theory, written or verbal, from which to learn; even the words for thrust or force had not been invented, let alone any true definition of them or their study. In spite of this handicap we can see, from the eleventh to the fifteenth centuries a steady advance in the design of vaults and the efficiency of buttressing. This could only have been learned through collective wisdom of successive masons experimenting with new buildings and little by little refining their knowledge and passing it on to the next master, perhaps for further advance. There would have been little role for the lone genius in this process; no possibility either of dramatic new discoveries and no way to communicate them quickly when he made them. Instead knowledge must have been much more a common quality, held and transmitted through numerous building projects across Europe.

The demand for ever more daring schemes of arches and vaulting presented the builders with a further set of problems in their actual construction. They had to be erected on a system of wooden scaffolding and specific supports for each arch; the voussoirs of the arch had to be laid on a wooden framework below, the centring. Designing these, putting them up, at the heights that were achieved, and then dismantling them for reuse in the next bay of the building perhaps, required a massive injection of skill and organisation, from the stone cutters but mainly from the carpenters. The stones to construct them were often large but delicately cut; the prime example would be the great carved bosses at the junctions of ribs. To raise them needed lifting gear but medieval cranes lifted only vertically. They could not swing around like the modern ones so the stones would arrive at a few fixed points at the height required. From there they had to be taken to the point where they were to be laid. This needed a complex, and strong, system of walkways around the site up at the level of the arches and vaults. Designing and constructing it so that it integrated with the scaffolding used for laying the wall stones, and was able to be raised as the walls rose, was no easy task. A great number of men of different skills had to combine together to do the right thing at the right time.

5

THE DEVELOPMENT OF THE GOTHIC STYLE: THE FRENCH KINGDOM 1125-1225

The Gothic style was a clear break from the Romanesque, distinguished in its handling of space, plan and structure, especially of the vault and decorative scheme. Considering the origins of this style raises a number of the issues noted in the Introduction. The first of these is the tension between having a focus on a single line of development and an awareness of the variety of experience and choice in front of contemporary builders. The Gothic style grew out of a number of different lines of development, while each of these lines involved more than one line of experiment existing at any point in time. To ignore this is to compress the story into a straightjacket of typology. The second issue, the selection and definition of a path of development, grows from this. Too often it appears that the style is characterised by a single trait which is asserted to be diagnostic. The source or origin of this single trait is then deemed to be the origin of the whole. In all this the interest is in the prestige of the origin and the earliest example, as opposed to the completion of the process of development. This is marked not by the start of the line but by the point when all the pieces are in place and connected.

The question of origins is intimately connected to the question of definition of the Gothic style. While some stress the aesthetic design, to others Gothic is more a matter of structure. To Harvey 'it is jagged, leaping like a flame', and

it is pure fantasy to attempt to derive the whole towering achievement of the artists of the twelfth to fifteenth centuries from the half-accidental structural evolution of the ribbed vault.

Against this, we have an entry in a recent edition of the *Encyclopaedia Britannica*:

unlike Romanesque architecture, Gothic architecture is systematic. Its principal features – pointed arches, ribbed vaults and flying buttresses – are integrated into a system that distributes the weight of the building to a skeletal structure of vertical shafts.

Neither of these quotations is fully representative of opinion; the writers themselves qualify them later, but they represent a real underlying tension. Recognising or defining Gothic is clearly not an easy thing. How do we define and recognise 'the upward flame' or its first appearance? Where do we stop seeing features as sources of the style and see them as part of the style itself? Should we be looking for the finished achievement or the means by which it was constructed? If we try to weave all these strands into a single line of development, we set up a conflict over the evidence which forces us to take short cuts and to neglect the complexity of the real situation. On the other hand, if we dwell on the individual details too much, we have an account which is incoherent and runs into the sands of complexity.

THE ABBEY OF ST DENIS AND THE CATHEDRALS OF SENS AND LAON

By common consent, the progress, however it was achieved, lay in the area around Paris during the three generations after the 1130s. In this area there were an archbishop (of Sens) and a bishop (of Laon) who were traditionally two of the key supporters of the French king along with the ambitious abbot of a venerable abbey (St Denis near Paris) closely associated with the kings of France. During the 25 years after 1135 these men – and it cannot be a coincidence that all three were involved in competition at the same time – embarked on major rebuilding projects. Between them they introduce us well to the changes, developments and problems of understanding the church building of the period in the region.

The abbot of the monastery of St Denis was Suger (or Sugerius) who rose to great power and wealth both as abbot and as a principal advisor of Louis VI, king of France. Any account of the building of the period is made the more difficult by his existence. It is an excellent example of the distorting effect of the individual attribution and the 'great man' syndrome outlined in the Introduction. He left an account of the rebuilding of the abbey under his direction, which provides us with a rare opportunity of seeing the building of a major church from the patron's view and he also gives us dates. The combination, which we so rarely have, has proved irresistible to later writers and much of the story of early Gothic has been focused on Suger and the building at St Denis. We must remember that Suger was above all a politician and what he wrote was what he wanted us to think about himself and his role in the public life of the times. He wrote a life of the king, Louis VI, with whom he worked most closely, that presents a picture of a strong government suppressing the chaos of the regime of Louis' father when baronial ambitions caused feuds and terror to all. We should take this with more than a pinch of salt. He is as likely to have exaggerated the troubles of the time before his

40 St Martin-des-Champs; exterior from the east, with chevet and south tower

and Louis' efforts brought order to the land as he is to overlook the possibility that the lordship of monks over their tenants may not have been altogether beneficent. Likewise, in his account of the building of his abbey, he fails to mention any other person but himself: it is he who discovers timber in the forest in spite of the denials of the forester; he who organises the supply of stone; he who dictates the message of light for the design. This last we may believe, but we do not have to accept his story wholesale, whether in its omissions or its statements. His story has affected our view of the buildings deeply, however. This is the great man in action as designer and impetus to the work and St Denis is the single origin point of the style.

There are relatively few existing buildings in the Paris area from before the 1130s and they are not as large or impressive as the new St Denis. This absence of evidence has been linked to his picture of baronial chaos before the hand of Suger stilled it, to give us a picture of a region where little building had gone on before. This is inherently unlikely, at time when every other region of France saw a mania of building. In the immediate area of Paris, St Germain-des-Prés has a nave of the eleventh century, while St Martin-des-Champs (*40*) and St Pierre de Montmartre both have surviving east ends from the 1130s or 1140s; St Germer-de-Fly (on the border with Normandy) is of the same date. In plan, Dreux, St Martin-des-Champs and St Germer-de-Fly have the apse at the east end surrounded by an ambulatory with a ring of chapels, which we see at St Denis. To overcome the problems of the diminishing intervals of the columns of the arcade as it goes round the hemicycle of the apse, the builders used pointed arches for the arcade, as the Durham mason had used it in the nave vault there or as it was used visually in Burgundy. At St Germer-de-Fly the pointed arches of the arcade were emphasised by chevron ornament, similar to that used in nearby Normandy, from where the idea of the rib vault came. The ambulatory and apse of St Martin-des-Champs in Paris, built in the late 1130s, are small in scale, but in the eastern chapel and the ambulatory the mason used rib vaults (the symbolism of the cross pattern at the east must have been appealing), although he used awkward groin ones in other chapels. The pointed arch with its varying height was essential both for the structure in the ribs and aesthetically; in these churches we can see that the ideas used at St Denis were already present in the region when Suger set his men to work.

When he started to rebuild his abbey church it was a Carolingian structure but devoutly believed to be much older and miraculously consecrated by Christ himself; this was not a church to be cast aside lightly. It was, however, dark and cramped, neither magnificent enough as one of the key monuments of the new regime nor large enough to cope with the number of pilgrims visiting the shrine of St Denis. At first work went slowly; this may well be in part because, adroit politician that he was, Suger spent much of his earlier effort on new buildings for the monks who might disapprove of his plans. He started about 1130 by building a new west end on to the old church; in 1140 he started the new choir to the east which was substantially complete in time for its consecration in June, 1144. He was impelled to leave the bulk of the old church, from the crossing to the west end of the nave, intact, presumably because of its traditional associations and holiness; it was not replaced until the thirteenth century. It is clear, however, that work continued on the west end until Suger's death in 1151. Both parts have suffered badly in the following centuries: the upper parts of the choir were replaced in the thirteenth century, while the west end was much damaged and restored in its details from the eighteenth to the twentieth centuries.

The overall design of the west end is that of a strong western block, with chapels on a first floor like an earlier German or Norman westwork, and two towers built over the side bays. It is clearly influenced by Christian symbolism: the two towers and the nave between as well as the three stages to the elevation recall the Trinity. There are also three great portals; the central one has a depiction of Christ in Majesty combined with the Last Judgement on the tympanum, with a sculpture of the Wise and Foolish Virgins on the jambs, a suitable frame for the entrance to the House of God, warning to be prepared for the hereafter. In architectural history its main claim to fame is its systematic use of rib vaults over the ground and first-floor bays, following from those of Durham and Caen of the 1120s. The rib vaults are unevenly laid out, especially where they cross the rectangular central bays. The mason found the problems of designing the height of the ribs, which crossed the differing spans between the walls and the diagonals, difficult; as well as failing to get the vault webs to meet smoothly he had to spring them from different heights, marked by capitals at different levels. When it came to the crypt below the apse and ambulatory, however, the vaults are laid out much more truly, with junctions of the webs describing symmetrical patterns of straight lines.

In the choir above, the whole design was aimed at providing a ring of well-lit chapels around the ambulatory which, in turn, surrounded the apsidal terminal of the main vessel (41). Both the bays of the ambulatory and the chapels were to be covered by rib vaults: only these could cover their complicated shapes. This

41 St Denis abbey:
Suger's choir and apse
with pointed arches
of variable width
and rib vaults in the
ambulatory

time, the mason used pointed arches systematically to maintain the arches of the choir arcade at the same height around the apse, and to do the same for the ribs of the ambulatory bays and chapels. The columns between the ambulatory and the chapels were much finer than the heavily over-engineered arches and columns in the west end. This progress in the control of the technology of the arches and vaults has been attributed to a second, and more skilled, master being in charge of the choir after the west end. This is to overlook two points. Firstly, the work on the west end was continuing while that of the choir was proceeding; a second master would mean that Suger had two self-contained work squads in action at the same time, which is hard to credit. Secondly, and more importantly, this is to attribute the progress just to the one mason. In fact, the advance was the result of not only the designer but also the carpenters who devised the centring and the masons who cut the stones growing more expert at the work; it was the team not the single master who were responsible and who were developing their skills.

The complexity of the processes and the composition of the workforce involved is shown by the construction of a new west front at the cathedral of Chartres after a fire in 1134. The overall design of the new front involved two towers at the end of the aisles with a central façade the width of the nave between. The composition of the central portion, below the later rose window, is constructed around a trinity of rectangles enclosing the three windows and portals below. The portals themselves are decorated with figures like those of the portal at St Denis, whose proportions reflect the 'Golden Section' (the ratio of squares whose areas have the proportion of 1:2). Their style is consciously Classical, looking back to Greek and Roman statuary. The themes for the portal are those of the Liberal Arts for which the cathedral school was famous across Europe. The parallels with the design and sculpture of St Denis are clear, but the exact relationship is not. It is usually assumed that the sculptors came from St Denis to work to designs originating among the ideas and of the clergy of Chartres. If this is so, at some point the workforce of St Denis lost a crucial number of its men, again emphasising the place that the team, rather than the single master, had in the achievement, as well as the combination of patron and craftsmen in the design.

The result was certainly remarkable in the way the new work at St Denis achieved its object. The west front was a truly impressive foretaste of the glories of the church and its relics within, while the choir provided a complex of interlocking spaces, choir ambulatory and chapels flooded with light from the chapel windows and the whole was covered with a successfully achieved network of vaults. Given the technological skill displayed in its choir, combined with the documentary record about it, it is easy to see how St Denis and its master mason have been seen by some as the starting point of Gothic style. One assessment of the situations is a good starting point: the choir of St Denis was a 'radically new version of the skeletal structure of the 1130s'. Other buildings followed it: 'The implications of St Denis were explored at a fairly leisurely pace and with surprisingly few consequences.' Here is a classic story: the pace-setting building to give a pattern to be followed, but a sense of surprise that this did not in fact happen in the region. Not only, however, does this underestimate the group dynamics by which the actual building at St Denis was achieved, it also over-simplifies the subsequent story. Its sense of disappointment at the lack of zeal for the new developments betrays a consciousness that the builders did not see it as the pace-setter at all.

It is important to get St Denis into context and not be seduced by our detailed knowledge of its building to construct our story around it. Structurally, the great success of St Denis had been to advertise the possibilities of using the rib vaulting developed in England and Normandy for the awkward spaces of the ambulatory and dependant chapels, but this may not have been entirely new. The two cathedrals, of Sens and Laon, continue the context for St Denis. The seat of the archbishop of the area around Paris was at Sens and there the cathedral was rebuilt from the early 1150s onwards, after a start a decade earlier. The church appears to have been built essentially in the single campaign, to be dedicated in 1163. It survives largely unreconstructed, although the ambulatory chapels have been renewed at different times, so that it gives us a good example of the period. Its plan is interesting for two reasons because it seems to reflect a pattern elsewhere in the region (42).

It has an eastern chevet of ambulatory and chapels, but instead of a transept, just two lateral chapels, which hardly demarcate the choir and nave. This may have been the plan of Dreux church shortly before, and it is also found later in the region. There is also a fundamental difference between the planning of the ambulatories of Sens and St Denis. At Sens, the intervals of the columns around the hemi-cycle of the eastern apse maintain the distance between them of the straight section of the choir: at St Denis, they are closed up. The Sens plan widens the intervals of the bays around the outer wall, inherited form the earlier building scheme, which inhibits the separation of the chapels around the ambulatory. These

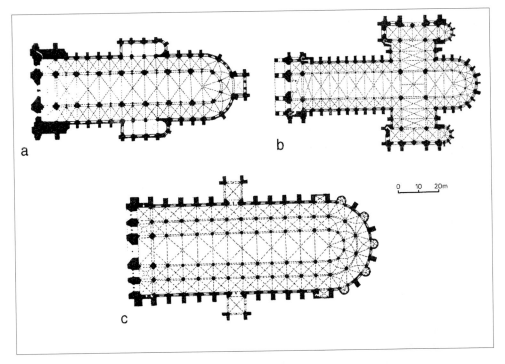

42 Plans of twelfth-century French cathedrals: a. Sens; b. Laon (before the early thirteenth-century extension to the choir); c. Bourges. The complexity of Laon contrasts with the other two

tend to form a continuous space like an outer aisle rather than sharply demarcated spaces, which is a crucial part of the St Denis plan. In plan Sens does not follow the St Denis model, whether at a leisurely pace or otherwise.

The choir and nave were covered with a sexpartite vault. This is a variant of the rib vault, first seen probably in the great churches of Caen in the 1120s, whereby the basic unit of the vaulting was the double bay. A lesser arch divides the two bays within the pair, so that each double bay has six vault webs, hence the name sexpartite: three ribs spring from the major dividing points, with a single rib coming from the minor ones. The logic of the sexpartite system is to have the sort of alternating bay supports seen intermittently in the German and Anglo-Norman Romanesque. This may have indeed been the germ of the idea, taking the logic of the double bays of Durham (which lacks the lesser arch dividing the single bays) to its proper conclusion. Another advantage of the sexpartite system was that the lesser arches, because they crossed directly over the space at right angles to the wall, interfered very little with the light coming from the clerestory windows. One of the main impulses to the Ile de France designs was undoubtedly to increase the amount of light in the churches.

The logic of the sexpartite vault is to carry the double-bay division to the whole design of the internal elevation. At Sens the strong divisions have piers with attached shafts rising from the floor to lead into the ribs of the vault and the 'formeret' arch, a roll which covers the junction between the vault and the wall.

43 Sens cathedral interior from the south-west

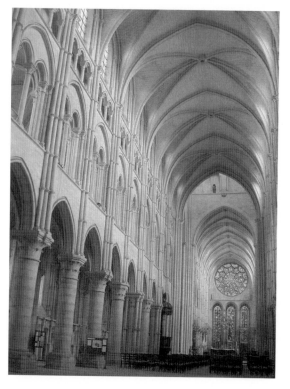

44 Laon cathedral: nave (1180s) and choir, added later but keeping the nave design

The weaker bays have double columns; the shaft for the single cross rib rises from their capital of the inner column. The interior elevation has three storeys (*43*). Above the arcade arches is a passage or gallery of paired, pointed arches opening into the nave. The clerestory above has been widened in the thirteenth century to provide wider windows. Between each stage is a horizontal string course, firmly demarcating the stages, but cut by the rising shafts to the vault. The arcade and the clerestory dominate the proportions of the elevation; the gallery is comparatively reticent, so the whole combines well with the width to give a well-proportioned feel. Outside, the vault is supported by buttresses which arch over the aisles. These meet the wall at right angles below, for the arches describe quarter circles rather than at a steeper angle, and seem designed to prop against the wall rather than transmit the vault forces to the ground. They are additions to the design, but one carried out very soon after the building of the wall and vault within. As such they are part of the early story of the development of the flying buttress.

If Sens is a comfortable building to be in, Laon is much more of an assertive one. Its date is imprecise; the new church was started under Gautier de Mortagne who was bishop from 1155–74; it was started after first year of his bishopric but the builders had completed choir, transepts and crossing by 1178 when they started on the nave. The plan has strongly projecting transepts, which were intended to be emphasised by two towers at the end of either, although only one was built on each (*42*). Along with the central crossing tower and the two towers at the west end, the cathedral was intended to have a display of seven towers reminiscent of Romanesque Tournai. This culminates in the western towers, adorned with statues of the miraculous ox, which helped the carter carry loads of stone up the steep hill to the cathedral site during the construction. The east end had a semicircular apse when it was first built, but when it was extended in 1205, the new choir acquired its existing straight end. The transepts had east chapels and the overall impression of the outside stands in considerable contrast to the simplicity of Sens.

The interior elevation has four storeys, with a wide, vaulted gallery over the arcade; it has twin openings to the nave (*44*). Above the gallery is a triforium of triple openings. Each storey is defined by a horizontal string course. The arcade is mostly carried on rather low, heavy columns, the exception being the two eastern bays of the nave. The vault is a sexpartite one, like Sens, carried on prominent shafts: three for the weak bays, five for the strong. At the eastern end of the nave the strong bay divisions are emphasised by surrounding the column with six detached shafts. All along the nave the weak bay divisions are identified by triple vertical shafts (carrying the cross rib and the two formeret arches); the strong ones are identified by five shafts (the two additional ones take the diagonal ribs). All the shafts rise from the arcade capitals. In the transepts, where the vault is constructed as a quadripartite one over two bays, five shafts to carry the various ribs mark the divisions between the bays. The vault shafts and the shafts outlining the gallery, triforium and clerestory openings combine to produce an interior elevation dominated by shafts. Again it makes a clear contrast with the gentleness of Sens.

The first message of these three churches is variety and contrast. In plan, elevation and possibly vault construction (we do not know how the vault of St Denis was carried out over the main vessel) they stress different elements and provide differing solutions. Two facts emphasise our conclusions from this. Firstly, as already mentioned, St Denis was not the first church to adapt the rib vault to the ambulatory and chapel plan, just as Dreux may have anticipated the lack of transepts found at Sens. The second is that, when the builders of Laon decided to demolish their eastern apse and extend the cathedral choir to the east, not only did they build a square end, but they stuck closely to the interior bay design of the earlier nave. The builders of these three churches were not conforming at all closely to a common programme. Just as the builders of St Denis grew more expert with time, so too the general story is one of experimentation and individual ideas.

STYLE AND DIVERSITY BEFORE THE 1190S

The area of the Ile de France saw much building during the half century after 1150, apart from the three churches discussed above. Overlapping with Laon was the cathedral of Senlis, with building under way by 1153. The choir of St Germain-des-Prés in Paris was dedicated in 1163, while the abbey church of St Remi in Reims was started after 1162. The eastern end of the cathedral of Notre Dame in Paris was also started in the 1160s. These, with the cathedral of Noyon, which is less closely dated, form a good introduction to the great churches of the region during this period. We may consider the question under three major headings. The overall plan expresses the basic organisation of the space in the church; the starting point for a style. The second is the structural system used; in the case of moves towards the early Gothic style this is important because the structural system of vaults and buttresses have been identified as one of the driving motives in the creation of the style. The third is the internal elevation of the walls, which is the first thing to strike the visitor (and the patron) when entering the church.

In the plans there is at least one common element, the chevet: the semicircular apse at the east end surrounded by an ambulatory off which open chapels (*42*). The only major church not to have one is a most interesting exception, the added square east end of Laon. This was erected after all the rest had chevets and, indeed, replaced an apse and ambulatory, even if it had no ring of chapels. By contrast with this common element in plans, is the variety in others. The cathedral at Sens, begun in the 1150s had a minimal pair of transepts; in fact they were later extended. In the 1170s the nave of Notre Dame in Paris was rebuilt beyond the choir, again with a minimally projecting pair of transepts. Others, however, such as Laon, St Germain-des-Prés in Paris, St Remi in Reims or Noyon cathedral have transepts, which are strongly projecting and clearly defined separate spaces. In the case of the south transept of Noyon, it has an apsidal ending like the choir.

The Noyon transept is interesting for two other reasons. It is separated visually from the choir by having the triforium passage below the gallery, when the choir has it above. Secondly the adjoining bays of the choir and transepts are different from the others, with a three-storey elevation without the triforium passage; they appear to have been preserved from the earlier church because they were the part of two towers, set at the outer junctions of the choir and transepts. Towers were a prominent part of the exterior appearance of any church, and they are very much so at Laon. Towers at the junction of choir and transept are found in German Romanesque, but also in the twelfth-century Ile de France, usually in the form of truncated stumps, at St Martin-des-Champs and St Germain-des-Prés above, while at St Remi, the earlier western towers were also retained. As with the idea of the clearly demarcated transepts, they run counter to the idea of a more or less unified interior space seen at Sens and Notre Dame, Paris.

The key question about the structure of these churches is the variant of the rib vault used, and the means of buttressing it. It is usual to think of the sexpartite vault as the typical form for the main vessel of the churches, but at St Remi the builders used the quadripartite form. At Noyon, while the choir appears to have a quadripartite vault, this is in part a result of the survival of the western bay for the tower mentioned above, but in the later nave there was also a quadripartite vault. The story of buttressing is interesting. Here the demands of the chevet with its successive chapels, ambulatory with gallery above and then the choir and its clerestory, made any system of buttressing by means of simple masses of masonry continuous with the wall surfaces impossible to carry out. Instead the buttresses had to arch over the lower and outer levels of the chapels and ambulatory to abut the upper wall of the choir where the vault pushed outwards. Recently it has been shown that the idea of the flying buttress, which has such an arch, runs through the period and does not date from the 1170s and its use at Notre Dame in Paris alone. It is found at Sens from about 1160 and also at St Germain-des-Prés from about the same time. Interestingly they have been adapted during the actual construction at both these churches. The arches of the buttresses describe quarter circles, so that they meet the wall surfaces at right angles. The builders seem to have thought of them as propping up the wall with a counter-arch, rather than the true function of a buttress, to transmit the forces from the vault to the ground through a steeply raked arch. The builders at these churches are working together to explore the solutions to a common problem.

Finally, the structure and the internal elevation are connected. The logic of the sexpartite vault demands a pattern of alternating bay design, with the strong and weak supports. We see this used at Sens, but only at Senlis is it properly followed. In the nave at Noyon, although the vault is a quadripartite one, the arcade arches are supported on alternating pier and columns. Conversely, the sexpartite vault of Notre Dame in Paris is carried on a uniform arcade of columns. The main variation visible in the internal elevations involves the number of storeys. We are accustomed to think of the triple elevation of arcade, gallery or triforium and clerestory as the norm for an aisled church, but this is not always so. The choir and the western bays of the nave at St Remi, and the both choir and transept at Noyon follow Laon in having four storeys, with both a gallery and a triforium passage screened by a small arcade. Notre Dame in Paris originally also had a four-storey design, formed by inserting a row of circular windows between the gallery and the clerestory. We can see a difference in the prominence and treatment of the vault shafts, which define the bays, from the logical but reticent three and one of Sens, to the five and three of Laon, which are also emphasised with horizontal bands: the shafts at Noyon have the Laon treatment. This is complemented at Laon or at St Remi by the horizontal divisions between arcade, gallery and clerestory being emphasised with strong string courses giving an equal horizontal line along the church. The effect is to emphasise the parts of the elevation by lines of shadow cast by the shafts and string courses.

The picture of the Ile de France by around 1190 is therefore a mixed one. The elements of a structural system existed, employing the rib vault to give an articulated skeletal structure which relieved much of the walls from loads. This could then be exploited to give a unified scheme of design, emphasising vertical lines through pointed arches and shafts, and stressing the unified pattern of bays and suppressing the individual plan elements of strongly identified spaces of transepts or chapels. It was not created at St Denis and the ideas were being developed irregularly. The driving force was not the single master of an eminent building but of the group of masters in the region; even the developments at the church of St Denis were the result of dialogue and training of the whole team.

PARIS, CHARTRES AND BOURGES CATHEDRALS

Some time in the early 1160s the canons and bishop of Paris initiated a rebuilding of the church of Notre Dame. The dating of the work is imprecise but we can say that it started with the choir which was complete by about 1179 except for the high vaults which were then added; the nave was started soon after 1180 and completed except for the west end about the end of the century; the west end and the façade were continued into the 1220s. These dates seem to link Notre Dame with Laon at the start and with Chartres or Bourges later and it has been seen as a stylistic connection also. The plan of Notre Dame reflected the double ambulatory and chapels of St Denis and the weak transepts of Sens. In its internal elevation it had rather squat, solid arcade columns which carried a four-storey elevation; between the gallery and the clerestory was a row of round windows opening into the roof space over the gallery vaults. The vaults themselves were sexpartite but the bay system did not alternate to reflect this. In its structure, the mason of Notre Dame pushed the new system of supports further in two ways. The wall of the main vessel was 20 per cent higher than that of Laon, yet the wall was thinner; the pressure of

45 The cathedral of Notre Dame, Paris: interior

the vault was taken up by flying buttresses, renewed in the thirteenth century, more than by the mass of masonry. The nave followed along the same lines, except that the vault achieved a flatter profile with the diagonal ribs not raised up above the side arches. Notre Dame went further than any earlier church, not just in the Ile de France but also Cluny III and Speyer, in its search for height, especially daring because of the thin upper walls. The flying buttresses were not the first as sometimes thought (the ones at Sens pre-date them). The four-storey elevation of the choir provided poor light from the clerestory windows; it was changed to three storeys in the nave and in the 1220s the choir clerestory was lengthened downwards to absorb the round openings above the gallery (45). As elsewhere, the choir of Notre Dame was not a finished and accepted design, but one which was changed when the church was carried into the nave. Rather than seeing it as a link, it takes its place as one more of the range of experiments of the time.

Both Chartres and Bourges lie somewhat beyond the strict limits of the royal domain of France but their bishops had always been closely connected to the French king. By the late twelfth century French power was on the increase and then, in the 1190s, both cathedrals were rebuilt. The work at Chartres was caused by a disastrous fire in 1194 which gave rise to a good illustration of the position of these great churches in contemporary towns. Chartres had a crucial relic of Mary, the tunic which she wore at the birth of Jesus, which attracted pilgrims, prestige and business to the whole town and community of Chartres. The fire, which destroyed

46 Bourges cathedral from the south-east

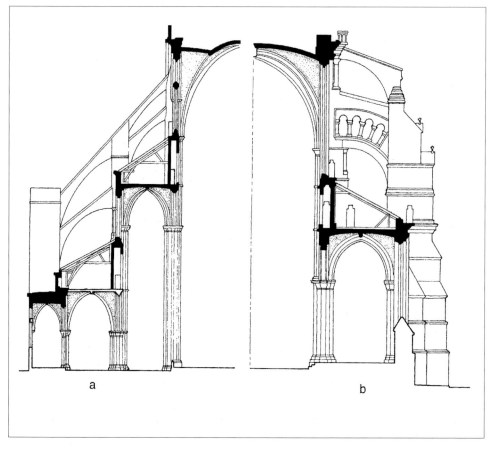

47 Sections through the cathedrals of Bourges (left) and Chartres (right). The buttresses are heavier in Chartres but the clerestory windows take up much more of the height

the whole earlier church except the west end, preserved by its vault, not only physically threatened the relic but might also be a judgement that the Virgin was unhappy about her relationship with Chartres. Fortunately not only was it found that the relic had survived in the vaulted crypt, but Cardinal Melior of Pisa, experienced in canon law and diplomacy, was at hand and able to explain that this was not a sign of the Virgin's displeasure with Chartres as such, but rather that she was unhappy with the old church and that she wanted a more magnificent one in its place. The whole of northern France was then involved in the dramatic reconstruction of the venerated site.

The building of Bourges at the same time, starting in the 1190s, is neither so precisely documented nor dated. The church is a *tour de force* of concentration in unity of purpose (46). The plan suppresses the transepts completely, so there is no interruption between the west end and the apse at the east (42). There are two aisles on either side which sweep around the apse in a double ambulatory. The internal elevation sees all the bays built to basically the same pattern up to the base of the clerestory. In the central vessel, partly because they need to rise to the height of the inner aisle vaults, the arcades are very high, a little over half the height of the whole bay, so that the triforium and the clerestory are correspondingly cramped (47). The bays are not identical because the shafts dividing them are collected in bundles of three or five, related to the ribs of the sexpartite vault above. Each of these elements is explained by major decisions on the design: the height of the arcade resulted from the double aisle; the break in the bay unity from the decision to use sexpartite vaulting. The same clarity of vision applies to the structure. Bourges is very high, some 37m to the crown of the vault (7m more than Notre Dame in Paris) with the roof rising above that again (48). Analysis of the wind load and pressure of weight has shown that its steeply raking buttresses were extremely efficiently designed and distort remarkably little under pressure.

The great new cathedral of Chartres was quite different from the design of Bourges. Because the foundations, the crypt and the west end had survived the fire, its plan could not have the ruthless unity of Bourges; it retained the breadth and the projecting chapels and transepts of the earlier church. The image of separate parts would have been even stronger if the towers planned for the transepts had been built as they were intended; the effect would have resembled the silhouette of Laon rather than Paris or Bourges. The church was a little lower than Bourges, but the master mason embraced the idea of flying buttresses to support the upper walls. However, his design for them involved more stonework meeting the wall at an angle too near a right angle to transmit the forces to the ground effectively. The same analysis, which showed the efficiency of the buttressing of Bourges, exposes the clumsiness of Chartres (47).

The interior is a different matter entirely. With the upper walls now supported more fully by the buttressing, the master took the sills of the clerestory windows well down below the springing of the vault. Where the clerestory of Bourges was a quarter of the height of the arcade, at Chartres the two were of approximately

48 Bourges cathedral; interior of the nave

49 Chartres cathedral; north side of the nave

the same height (49). This flooded the space with light and allowed for a great display of the stained glass directly visible from the ground; the pictures in the clerestory windows of Bourges are much more remote. The internal elevation is also more uniform. The piers and shafts are the same in each bay, and they lead up to quadripartite vaults where each bay is the same, unlike the alternation of the sexpartite system. The triforium stage is a mere passage with an arcade in front of it so that the whole of the wall lies in the one plane with no recessing, a single cliff of stone and glass.

If we consider the reasons why these three churches have been associated, we understand some of the issues involved both for their contemporaries and for us who study them. Although they vary in plan, support systems and in the design and proportions of their internal elevations, there are certain aspirations and accepted principles in common. All three strive for height and for the minimum thickness of walling; in their different ways they accept that support shall come from external buttressing not the internal strength of the upper wall. They aspire to simplicity in the sense of suppressing lesser elements, whether of subsidiary spaces or decorative detail. It comes together in the contrast between the overall looks of their internal elevations and those of Laon and Sens. They reject the alternating bays of Sens but, above all, the prominent shafts and string courses of Laon, which emphasised the parts of the design, either the bays or the storeys; the change from four to three storeys between the choir and nave of Notre Dame is significant. When the canons of Laon wanted a larger choir in 1205, they got a design which followed the one of the 1160s; in part this must have been for harmony with the older part. It can also be seen, along with the designs of Senlis, St Remi or Noyon as an indication that there were those around who still preferred the complexities of their spatial divisions and visual partitions through prominent shafts. Because these principles were not those that the thirteenth-century French builders followed, they tend to be less emphasised by modern academics seeking the linear descent of the later Gothic, but they were very influential elsewhere.

SUMMARY

The ideas of Chartres and Bourges were very quickly followed in the Ile de France at Soissons and Reims cathedrals, so quickly that they were put in place before those two designs were clearly visible. The ideas are likely to have been current among the masons before the work got under way at Chartres. At Soissons cathedral, a new nave and choir appear to have been started within a decade of the fire at Chartres, around 1200, leaving the former transepts to be replaced later. The design took up the pattern of the internal elevation of Chartres, the deep clerestory, the quadripartite vault and the single plane of the wall, but combined these with the raking buttresses of Bourges. In 1210 another of the inevitable fires which punctuate the history of medieval churches damaged the cathedral of Reims. The plan was in part constrained by the site, cramped between the bishop's palace to the south and the canons' cloister to the north but produced a compromise between those of Bourges and Chartres. There was a transept but it only projected one bay north and south, to provide a junction between the single-aisled nave and the double-aisled choir. Like Soissons the internal design is that of Chartres while the buttressing is that of Bourges; in particular the array of flying buttresses over the eastern ambulatory and chapels is a superb design. It is here that we see what was to be the final design element which made up thirteenth-century French Gothic. Many of the windows of the earlier churches were made up of two pointed lights with a circular window above; all three of these units were separated by sections of walling, a system known as plate tracery. At Reims, the mason designed the windows so that the previously distinct three parts were combined and the walling was reduced to simple bars of stone outlining the major lights of glass, bar tracery. In itself, it sounds a small change, but it was both a new basis for design which saw the glass and the stone seen as equal parts of the wall, and the start of a tradition which developed the patterns of stone tracery in the windows.

The first thing to understand from this story is that the Gothic style was, like a complex machine, more than just the sum of its parts. Tracing the structural line over the aesthetic, or vice versa, is no more helpful than tracing the individual elements of either. These trace not the origin of the style but the potential for it to exist. The style only becomes complete when these elements are combined in a particular way. This way was not pre-ordained. There was a constant tension between the demands of one way over another, most obviously in the demands of structural 'progress' as opposed to the aesthetic design. 'Progress' along a particular line of development is irregular, but, above all, proceeds at its own pace. Structurally, the key to Gothic has always been identified as the combination of the rib vault and the flying buttress. However, the idea of the flying buttress may start in the 1160s or 1170s, long after the rib vault. When the flying buttress first appears, it would seem to have been thought of as a prop, meeting the wall at an angle near to 90°, rather than the truly efficient slope transmitting the forces downwards. At which point should we regard it as properly developed: its first appearance, or in its finished, functioning form? When should we see the structural solution of the buttress and the vault as achieved?

Furthermore, the demands of different lines of development might conflict. On the one hand the system of sexpartite vaulting opened up the clerestory windows, gaining the increase in light which was clearly one of the aims of the work. The logic of the sexpartite vault, however, led to the alternation of the bays below, with stronger and weaker shafts leading to the springings of the vault. On the other hand, this ran counter to what was clearly another aim of the aesthetic of Gothic, the unification of the design and the repetition of the bay designs. In the end the solution came at Chartres by expanding the clerestory windows down, breaking the alignment of the sill and vault springing and allowing the vault to be built on the quadripartite system while still giving great amounts of light. The options of design, function and structure must combine in the suppression of the gallery and its replacement by a flat triforium arcade. We do not know whether this is a matter of clerics abandoning the gallery and the use or rituals it served, the replacement of the structural function of its vault propped against the upper wall, or simply a preference for a flat wall without any emphasis on its separate parts. The suppression of the transept, seen from the early twelfth century onwards, must have also set up tensions. Against the aim of spatial unity, most obvious at Bourges, must have been ranged both the need for a division between the nave and the ritual choir and the symbolic effect of a cross at the heart of the church.

What we now know as Gothic style was a long time in gestation. Between the beginning of St Denis and that of Reims was a period of about 80 years during which a lot of different ideas were tried. The builders inherited a Romanesque tradition which delighted in the variety of the parts of the church and their decorative complexity. In some ways the Gothic was a reaction to this, aiming to keep the dominating size (especially height) while still accepting the simplicity of design of a Bernard of Clairvaux. They took up the challenge, and solved it, of the high stone vault which would still allow a maximum of window space. We should not look on this as a period of steady development but as one of great debate about what a great church should look like and how it should be achieved. During it a pool of ideas and experiments existed, out of which other builders could select ones suited to their own taste. This happened as the knowledge of the work done in the royal domain and the Ile de France spread through other parts of France and into the British Isles and Germany. The new Gothic became a common source of style for all Western Europe but not in the same way everywhere.

6

THE EARLY SPREAD OF GOTHIC STYLE

The modern ideas of the spread of Gothic ideas are complex, although not always well articulated, distracted by two issues. The first is the hoary chestnut of the definition of Gothic; tracing the spread of something can be confusing if there is no agreement on what it is or how to recognise it. As we have seen, Gothic architecture is a moveable feast, for it developed over more than one generation and changed along with this development. If we define it only as the finished integrated elements that emerged around 1200, there is a feeling that we have missed the bus; in England in particular, the story is well advanced by then. On the other hand, defining it by one or more element is a trap, as we have seen; to quote England again, the rib vault and the pointed arch were both in use long before the idea of any Gothic style or system. We must recognise that there was a whole range of ideas available in the second half of the twelfth century which could be collected together under the heading of early Gothic, without a single diagnostic feature. Connected to this is the idea of the 'Transitional' as a style or at least as a discrete entity. This assumes that there is a single over-arching Gothic ideal before 1200, made up of a collection of traits and that any time we find one or more of these, used in combination with Romanesque feature, this is transitional to Gothic. The belief seems to be that the ideas which went into the debate in twelfth-century France could be deconstructed and used individually; like flu one could have it severely or less. It leads to two concepts. The first is that the resultant mixtures are somehow the rproduct of men who did not understand the systems or ideals behind the early Gothic experiments but borrowed some elements blindly in ignorance. A variation is that they were somehow unprepared to accept these ideas as a whole, but took some features to look fashionable. Both of these underestimate both the sophistication of the early Gothic debate about what a church should look like and the difficulty of the technological issues at stake. The second concept is well expressed by Bony when he wrote of 'the resistance to Chartres', that there was a single Gothic idea (represented

50 Vézélay abbey; the early thirteenth-century choir

by him as Chartres) and that any deviation from this was a conscious rejection of the ideal.

A second complication is connecting Gothic and political movement. This was the period when the prestige of the French language and literature, especially of the northern French, dominated Northern Europe. The later twelfth and thirteenth centuries saw the kings of France conquer Normandy and the Angevin lands to the south of it and extend their power over lordships to the north and east. In the early thirteenth century the Albigensian Crusade saw the conquest of the south-west of France by the cultural forces of the north. Inevitably the spread of Gothic ideas might be linked to the spread of northern French language and literature but the admitted power of France does not mean that we should not examine the link sceptically. After all, the spread of architectural ideas involved classes of men who may have worked for the dominant levels of society who set the pace in government and literature. Within the British Isles the power of the English and Scottish monarchies expanded at the expense of the 'Celtic' lands to the west: Wales, the Highlands of Scotland and Ireland. Here, too, it was associated with the spread of social structures and language. The discussion of these forces inevitably degenerates into the language of confrontation with concepts of colonisation being used. The movements of the ideas of building are not seen in terms of a potentially neutral network of communication, but in terms of cultural absorption and resistance. This does no credit either to the men of the twelfth century or our own.

51 Auxerre cathedral clerestory and triforium of the nave (1215-34)

BURGUNDY AND NORMANDY

These were two lordships adjoining the royal domain of France, each with a pre-eminent Romanesque tradition of church building by the middle of the twelfth century. While Burgundy was a lordship, friendly but loosely attached to France, the Duchy of Normandy was united to the kingdom of England and had a long history of violent enmity with France. In Burgundy, the abbey of Vézelay was one of the masterpieces of regional Romanesque. In the 20 years before 1215 the monks decided to replace their choir and did so in a contemporary 'Gothic' style. The new choir was two double bays long with an apsidal east end, which appears to have retained the outer chapel walls at least (*50*).

It is has a basically sexpartite vault but the ribs of the eastern double bay are mixed in with those of the hemi-cycle of the apse so that together they make an interlocking pattern. The western double bay has a single arch at arcade level, while the eastern one has two narrow ones like those of the hemi-cycle. As with the vault the spaces are both separated from (the contrast in arcade arches) but interlocked in the similarity of the eastern arches to those of the hemi-cycle. The intermediate cross ribs rise from the base of the triforium in the eastern bay and from the clerestory in the western. Each stage of the elevation is clearly demarcated by a string course which runs across the vertical shafts. The shafts are strongly emphasised with the horizontal bands of Laon (*44*); the triple shafts of the strong piers are set in a row, flat against the wall rather than the traditional projecting triangle, which also makes their impact bigger, especially when it comes to their capitals which give another horizontal line. In the five eastern ambulatory chapels, the vaults and their shafts are carried out in a grey stone which contrasts with the cream limestone of the rest of the walls.

The choir of the cathedral of Auxerre, at the very north of Burgundy, was rebuilt immediately after Vézélay, starting in 1215 when the old choir was demolished and finishing around 1234 when the glass was ready for installation in the windows (51). The main vault is a quadripartite one, carried on triple shafts which, like those of Vézélay, are set in a row with the central one larger. These shafts rise up the inner face of the wall, past both a triforium and a clerestory passage, which separate the inner and outer faces of the wall. At clerestory level this is emphasised by terminating the vault web at the inner face of the wall and having a separate web between it and the outer wall, over the passage. The ambulatory vault ribs and those of the vault of the eastern chapel are interlocked to create a star pattern above the visitor's head. The outer wall of the ambulatory has an upper, 'clerestory' passage of its own behind the vault shafts which are set in groups of three around one thicker one which supports the main arch of the ambulatory vault. The effect of all this, with the spaces of the passages, the shafts and the complexity of the vault ribs is to emphasise the parts of the church, wall faces and vaults, in a way quite different from the unity of plan and elevation of Bourges, Chartres or Reims, but the elements are all derived from the earlier ideas of Laon or others.

The church of Notre Dame at Dijon, in effect the parish church for the palace of the Dukes of Burgundy, was rebuilt in the 1220s, at much the same date as Auxerre choir, but at a much smaller scale. Internally it takes the separation of the vault and shafts from the wall, and the separation of the two faces of the wall, even further. Lacking any transept, the separation of the choir from the nave is achieved by differencing their elevations. The choir, which has no ambulatory around the apse, has a four-storey elevation with a low blank arcade below the first tier of windows. Above these windows is a triforium passage framed by an arcade of narrow arches carried on thin shafts; around the apse, the circular windows behind stress the difference between the inner and outer walls. The main nave vault is a sexpartite one, with alternating triple and single shafts rising from the arcade capitals. The triple shafts are also set in a line, while the triforium and clerestory passages are deeper than at Auxerre; the thin, detached shafts rising in front of, and across, the triforium gallery draw particular attention to the space of the passage behind. The western front is a three-storied screen; it is flanked by small stair turrets but the arcades, which form the stages of the west elevation, wrap around the north and south sides. The two upper arcades have the same thin shafts as the interior elevations. The lower storey has three large arches which open into a porch with vaulting which, like the eastern end of Auxerre, is a display of interlocking rib patterns.

In Normandy we start with the cathedral of Lisieux, begun in the 1160s. It would seem to have concentrated on building the basic church of choir, transepts and nave first, finishing them quite quickly and leaving the central tower and the west front to be completed later, after 1200. The choir has the external proportions

52 Rouen cathedral nave

and plan of the contemporary Ile de France churches with an apse and ambulatory with low chapels. The internal elevations are three-storied, although the triforium passage of the eastern choir changes to an unvaulted gallery in the western choir bays and nave. The main vault is quadripartite, supported on shafts which rise from the capitals of the low arcade columns of French type. The arches of the arcade are bluntly pointed and each bay of the gallery is made up of a similar one enclosing two round ones. This is a church which would be completely at home in the Ile de France of the later twelfth century; there is no sign of resistance or variation in this Norman cathedral.

Two great churches were built in Normandy in the two decades before the French conquest of 1205: the new choir for William the Conqueror's abbey of St Etienne in Caen and the nave of Rouen cathedral, the seat of the archbishop of the Duchy. The choir at St Etienne was as long as its predecessor and it also retained something of its internal proportions but provided the church with a grand apsidal chevet. At Rouen, the work started at the west end of the nave and continued with a number of minor changes to individual bays as far as the crossing. Both have quadripartite vaults and both have designs which are strikingly rich in detail. The elaboration is provided in part by the attached shafting of the arcade piers and the moulding of their arches. Both designs stress the different storeys of the elevation. At Caen there is a strong string course above the arcade which links to the pierced roundels in the arch spandrels. At Rouen there is what appears from the main vessel to be a gallery over the arcade, but in the aisles this can be seen to be fake; the aisle rises through both storeys and what appears to be the gallery vault is in fact the aisle vault (52). Above this 'gallery' is a remarkable triforium passage. At Caen the piers of the outer wall of the ambulatory are composed of a central column surrounded by seven attached shafts. At Rouen in the aisle the 'gallery' level is supported by brackets carried on clustered shafts, some with rings and all with their own capitals.

In the next generation, the cathedral of Coutances and the additions to Lisieux show the same trends. At Coutances there is a chevet with the raking flying buttresses of early thirteenth-century Gothic style. The whole is dominated by the central tower, turrets at the ends of the transepts and slim towers flanking the choir. The central tower, in particular, is decorated by a multiplicity of shafts; internally it is embellished by a complex of arcades and the ribs of the central vault. Internally the high arcade of slender pairs of columns and the high lancets of the clerestory dominate the choir; the triforium passage is shrunk down to a very low blank arcade. The ambulatory vault is carried, on the outer side, on detached shafts with a passage behind, like those in Burgundy. Similarly, the central tower and the west front of Lisieux cathedral are decorated with lancets and arcades; with strong horizontal lines of string courses and spandrel rosettes balancing the high shafts.

To the south of Normandy, the cathedral of Le Mans added a new choir at the same time, after 1217, which provides a contrast both with the earlier nave and the Norman buildings to the north. The nave of the 1160s looks to the south, to the lands of Anjou or Poitou, with its wide bays covered by domed rib vaults. The choir plan has strongly projecting chapels around the ambulatory (reflecting the east chapel at Coutances) but otherwise is firmly based on Bourges with its double ambulatory and thin, steeply raked flying buttresses. The main vessel of the choir is high and lacks a triforium or gallery stage, so that the arcades, particularly in the hemi-cycle of the apse are very steep.

In Burgundy and Normandy we can see the masons bringing in ideas from the Ile de France over the generations after 1160. They do so from the rich mixture on offer and they integrate them into the traditions of their own region. Perhaps this is more easily seen in Normandy where the practice of building the rib vaults was well established, but here we should note their readiness to take up the ideas of the raking flying buttresses, as at Coutances and at Bayeux, after rather tentative efforts at St Etienne, Caen. In both areas the element which they found most popular was the detached shafting. This they used, as it had been in Laon, as a prominent feature to divide up the elevations along with the string courses and other horizontal elements. The Burgundian masons carried out most thoroughly the aim of separating the parts in terms of the wall and the internal spaces, but the Norman love of towers and their decoration reflects the same spirit. It is most important to understand the history of these ideas. The process clearly starts before 1200 in both cases. It has its beginning in the period when the ideas that were to become a coherent Gothic style were still very much a matter of debate. This means that they were not a matter of rejecting the Gothic ideal, as it later developed, so much as picking up some ideas and then, after assimilating them with their own traditions, carrying on with them. Nor were they connected with any process of political developments; in Normandy the French conquest after 1205 was not a significant milestone and Burgundy had a different political history but a similar process of borrowing and assimilation, at least until the 1220s or 1230s. These are points which are important when we come to consider the case of England, linked politically, of course, to Normandy.

ENGLAND 1160–1200

We can understand the course of events more easily in England if we bear these patterns in mind. England presents us with three opposing scenarios for the spread of the Gothic ideas: introduction gradually, suddenly or regionally. Firstly we have what might be termed the 'gradual' model. Major elements of Gothic style were present in England before 1150 such as the rib vault and the pointed arch; the latter was used structurally at Durham to overcome the problem of having arches of differing spans coming to the same height. Among the Cistercian churches, with their Burgundian connections, Kirkstall is the best preserved of those from the 1150s and 1160s. The arcades have bluntly pointed arches with a clerestory of round windows above. The piers are moulded and the aisles are rib-vaulted, giving a more spacious feel to the church than some of its contemporaries. Roche abbey dates to the 1170s and is more elaborate, with a triforium stage. It combines pointed arches at arcade and triforium level with round ones in the clerestory. The church had rib vaults throughout, rising from shafts which linked to the clustered shafts of the arcade piers. The prominence in history and the extensive preservation of their northern abbeys of the twelfth century may have exaggerated the role of the Cistercians in the story of English Gothic. The ideas we see in their churches, such as the clustered pier, were also found at other churches, for example Ripon cathedral in the north. Malmesbury abbey also has an arcade of pointed arches carried on columns, but surmounted by a triforium gallery of round openings decorated with chevron ornament in the Romanesque style. It was probably built in the 1160s and is attributed to a Burgundian abbot; significantly the work also included a splendidly decorated entry portal. Clearly ideas which are found later as elements of Gothic style were to be found spasmodically in England before 1175.

The second scenario, the sudden introduction, is tied to Canterbury. In 1170 knights of King Henry II's household murdered Thomas Becket, Archbishop of Canterbury, in his cathedral after a long and bitter dispute with the king. In 1174 the eastern end of the cathedral was almost totally destroyed by fire. The combination of the martyrdom of its archbishop and the funds which flowed from the pilgrims to his tomb, along with the need to rebuild, resulted in an unprecedented effort of construction. The eastern half of the cathedral, as big as many a complete church, was rebuilt essentially in a decade. A monk of the cathedral community, Gervase, has left us a detailed account, year by year, of the work. This is as good a source as Suger's account of the work at St Denis but the

53 Canterbury north side of the choir built by William of Sens

difference in tone and emphasis is striking. Suger tells us of his energy, motivation and organisation; he omits all mention of the men who actually did the work. Gervase never explains his own role but concentrates on the unfolding work and the masters who designed it. His language and the story he has to tell are vivid. He tells us that after the fire the monks summoned masters from France and England to advise them and how the first master, William of Sens, got the contract by concealing from the monks the amount of rebuilding necessary. At the beginning of his fifth year at the work, William fell from the scaffolding and was paralysed, but tried to carry on the supervision from his bed through the medium of a young monk, who is not named but may have been Gervase himself. He had to retire, to be succeeded by a second William, 'by nation English, small of body but large in skill'. With such immediacy of incident and the details of the annual progress which he gives, inevitably Gervase's account has dominated our view of church building in England during the later twelfth century.

Two further things compound this. Firstly, just where Gervase says the change in master occurred, we can see a change in the design. This confirms one of the basic tenets of modern scholarship, that we can detect the identity of a master from the building style. Secondly, the work carried out by the two Williams, but the first, William of Sens, is undoubtedly very close to contemporary work in the Ile de France (5 and 53). Here, therefore, we have unequivocal contemporary testimony that a building of 1174-84, of early French Gothic style, was built by a French master. The conclusion seems inescapable; this must be either the point of introduction of the new style to England or at least a very significant turning point in the story.

The third scenario splits the story up into regional ones, which allows us to have gradual introduction in some areas, particularly the north and the south-west, and to allow Canterbury to dominate the south-east with the sudden introduction. This has the 'advantage' that it places the most clear-cut story of introduction near the capital, at the chief cathedral of the country. It then allows the more 'peripheral' or 'remote' areas to catch up with a gradual introduction. These also make up the core of the 'Transitional' story; places away from the mainstream of development which may be expected to be a little slow to take up the new fashions.

The new work at Canterbury is, indeed, a good starting point, undoubtedly a work entirely in the style of the early Gothic of the Ile de France of the 1170s. As with Chartres, early on the plan was inherited from the foundations and lower walls of the earlier building in so far as they survived the fire. William the Englishman added an apse and ambulatory to the eastern end, followed by the Corona, a projecting, nearly circular chapel for Becket's relics. The vault under both masters was sexpartite in the French manner; William the Englishman introduced tentative versions of the sort of flying buttresses being used in 1180s France. The main support came from the thick upper walls, with clerestory passages suitable for the relatively low building which the height of the surviving church demanded; again this is the sort of thing found at Laon or elsewhere at the time. The internal elevation of William of Sens especially has the columns with capitals very similar to examples from northern France; from these rise triple shafts to the main ribs for the vaults, single shafts to the minor ribs.

There are variations, as one would expect. The system used by William of Sens, alternating the columns between round and octagonal and the use of the clerestory passage were both probably inherited from the older church (53). The triforium gallery, with two paired arches in each bay may have been the same; one of the changes which William the Englishman made was to convert this into a triforium arcade of four equal arches per bay. One new idea, which was to prove very popular, was to use dark Purbeck marble for many of the shafts, giving a contrast between it and the white stone of the rest of the walls. One of the interests of the building is in the variations between the work of the two masters. William the Englishman's introduction of the simple fliers and the remodelled triforium has been mentioned already. In the new part, east of the old end of the church, he raised the floor of the choir over a heightened crypt. To keep the roof line and the heights of the three storeys of the elevation in keeping with William of Sens' work, he had to lower the arcade columns; to avoid them seeming stumpy he doubled two slender ones up, like the Laon design. Like other masters, he clearly felt no compunction to follow his predecessor's design to the letter. Nor is there any hint that, despite Gervase's description of him as 'the Englishman', the second William built in any less a 'French' style than his predecessor.

The problem for the 'sudden introduction' scenario is that there are no really clear or immediate close imitators of Canterbury as there should be if it was the origin of English Gothic. The cathedral of Chichester suffered from a fire in 1186, when the work at Canterbury was just finished. It was refurbished but the work did not involve a major reconstruction. The clerestory was rebuilt and Purbeck marble shafts were added to the openings of the lower storeys. Rochester cathedral was closely linked to Canterbury and when its eastern parts were rebuilt around 1200 (finishing in c.1227), we might expect it to follow the Canterbury example. Instead, it has a unique design with an aisle-less presbytery projecting beyond the choir. It is covered with a sexpartite vault but massive external buttresses support the whole, the antithesis of the French moves towards the flying buttress. The interior elevations of the north and south walls are dominated by four large blank recesses at ground level with a clerestory and passage above; Purbeck shafts divide the bays. The Purbeck shafts and the vault may derive from Canterbury and France but neither the supporting system nor the internal design has anything to do with it.

The churches in the north of England are related to the famous and large Cistercian houses in the region, from Yorkshire well into the Lowlands of Scotland. The earliest are typified by Byland (Cistercian) and Ripon (Augustinian Canons), of the 1170s or 1180s, which have a full three-storied elevation, relatively new to the Cistercian Order. The triforium passages especially were stressed by means of arcades (with a mix of round and pointed arches) carried on shafts, with the clerestory windows also decorated with shafts; the arcade piers were formed of clustered shafts. Neither of these was vaulted, so the shafts from arcade to the top of the wall functioned purely to divide the bays, giving an equal balance to the vertical and horizontal lines. Later churches in the north added high, plain lancets to the formula, in some places as the terminals of transepts.

The most often cited example of the regional story comes from the west of England; sometimes, indeed, referred to as the Western School. As a 'School', which should mean a group of craftsmen sharing a coherent training as evidenced by repeated use of the same devices, the Western School fails to convince. The list of common features is not long nor does it cover fundamental elements either of design or structure. Nor is it clear that all the churches said to belong to it possess all these elements; we are back again on the problem of definitions; what number or proportion of features must be present to join the club? The hallmarks of the School may be the continuous arch order, whereby a shaft goes right round an arch without a break for a capital, and the application of carved roundels or plaques to a blank ashlar surface, often in the spandrel of an arch. These are not fundamental elements and they occur at Malmesbury. The best-dated example of the School is the Lady Chapel at Glastonbury, built in 1184-6 after a major fire in 1184. It is a masterpiece of elaborate surface decoration, involving complex chevron ornament and interlocking arches in arcades, but is not a particularly Gothic building. The design of the main church at Glastonbury, rebuilt after the Lady Chapel in response to the same destruction, uses the pointed arch much more. The most prominent feature of the choir design was the way in which the major arches of the arcade embraced the triforium as well as the arcade, and the use of chevron ornament to stress the lines of the arches. Perhaps the most elaborate scheme is to be found at the cathedral of St David's in west Wales, rebuilt on a scale consonant with the dreams of Welsh churchmen that it be elevated to the status of an archbishopric independent of Canterbury. It also combines two storeys, the triforium and the clerestory, and uses a full panoply of chevron ornament. It seems to have been at least planned, and quite possibly constructed, to take a compressed sexpartite vault (with each bay divided into two half-bays for the vault) which domed up above the walls. If it was built, this would account for the severe lean that developed at the top of the walls, for the support system is clearly inadequate to contain the thrust of a vault.

The re-dating of the rebuilding of the cathedral at Wells to a start in the 1180s, that is contemporary with the second part of the Canterbury work, has shown up the great variety of ideas current at the time; it was finished with the west end of around 1240. There are two crucial points about the Wells design. The first is that we can see a continuous development of ideas through the choir, the transepts and the nave. This involves a steady reduction in the emphasis on the bay divisions: in the transepts the shafts start from the arcades and divide the triforium, but in the nave the latter is a continuous arcade and the vault shafts only spring from its top (54 and 55).

The second is that whole design is built around the idea of clustered shafts in the three stages. The arcade piers are composed of a whole array of shafts, each

54 Wells cathedral north transept; the triforium stage is divided by the vault shafts

55 Wells cathedral nave: clustered piers and capitals in the arcade with the undivided triforium stage
above. The X-shaped arches were added to support the new tower of the 1330s

emphasised by having an individual capital. The triforium is the same and then come the shafts and the ribs of the vaults. On the nave arcade piers, the capitals are carved as leaves (the so-called stiff-leaf foliage) which are interlocked together to give the effect of a band of carving rather than individual capitals. The arches are carved with a multiplicity of mouldings, so that each is an array of lines of light and shade. In the nave also, the band of the triforium, with roundels carved in each spandrel, runs right across any sense of bays and stresses the length of the whole wall. In one sense this is quite counter to the spirit of the developing ideas of unity and height to be found around 1200 in France. On the other, the arches and openings are much more sharply and systematically pointed than the French practice. It is not surprising that Wells was treated as something of a problem of date and interpretation until recently. So it was also in the early thirteenth century; as with Canterbury, there are no close imitators of the Wells design, although individual elements were copied.

In 1185, it is recorded, there was an earthquake which destroyed the cathedral of Lincoln. More recent scholarship has pointed out that it was a remarkable earthquake, which did little, if any, damage elsewhere, and that it was probably a failure in the structure which caused the collapse. If so, this might explain why it was not until 1192 that anything was done to repair the building, which makes it an almost exact contemporary of Chartres. Lincoln had another problem; it lacked a saint whose relics would add renown to the cathedral and bring in pilgrims and alms. The canons were at the time trying to get their founder, Remigius, beatified and so, when they came to rebuild the east end they included an eastern chapel for relics; in the event it was not Remigius but their bishop at the time, Hugh, who was made the saint.

The new choir, whose east end we know only from nineteenth-century excavations, was built to a unique plan and apparently had a five-sided apse with an ambulatory and chapels (64). The rest is preserved and it, too, is a remarkable structure. It was covered by a vault of unique pattern, a compromise between a sexpartite and a quadripartite design (38). It has been termed a 'crazy' vault, but a good case has recently been made that it was a serious and logical attempt to combine the wider clerestory windows of the sexpartite with the uniform bays of a quadripartite one. In the event, the result was a vault which made an interesting visual pattern above the choir, emphasised by a structurally useless rib along the ridge. The plan and internal elevation of the choir takes a number of the features of Canterbury: the two pairs of transepts, the eastern chapel like the corona, the three-storey elevation of similar proportions, the bluntly pointed arches of the arcade, the Purbeck marble shafting and the thick wall system of buttressing (56 and 64). The arches of the arcade were much closer to the complex shafted piers of Wells than the plain columns from Canterbury, and both the triforium and clerestory had more elaborate shafts and capitals, like the northern bands. What with the Purbeck shafts alternating with limestone and the elaborate crockets attached between them, the whole surface was much more richly decorated than even Wells. The shafts which mark the bay divisions, although they are picked out

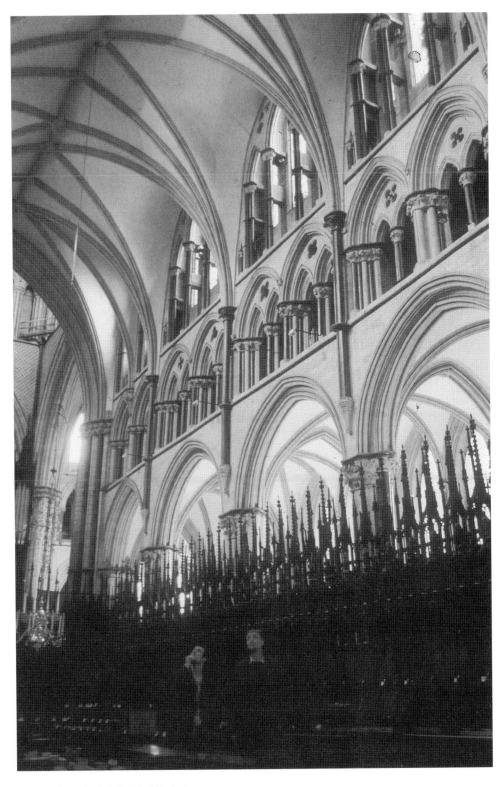

56 Lincoln cathedral; St Hugh's choir

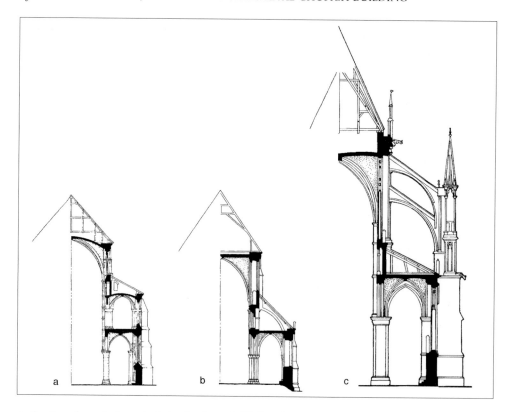

57 Sections through the cathedrals of: a. Laon; b. Wells; c. Reims. Wells relates to the lower, and earlier
Laon rather than to Reimss

in Purbeck, rise only from the spandrels of the arcade and do not do much to
stress the vertical. The design of Lincoln is as much longitudinal as vertical.

It stands in sharp contrast to its contemporaries in France, Chartres and
Bourges. What all these English buildings show is the same propensity for eclectic
choice as in northern France. Interestingly, as with Normandy and Burgundy,
what the English masons picked up most from France was the love of shafts.
Unlike Burgundy, however, where they were used to stand free of the wall and
separate it from the vault, in England the shafts were very much integrated into
the wall, giving an overall system of decoration to its surfaces. Again, we are led
back more to Laon than to Paris, with the balance between the horizontal and
vertical divisions. This aligns also with the English structural system. The English
rejected the French push for height and preferred to keep the proportions of their
Romanesque tradition. Equally, they failed to appreciate or follow the French in
their desire to unify the space of their churches. Canterbury had two transepts as
did Lincoln and all kept the strong transepts and crossings of the Romanesque
ideal. Their long, low churches did not need the elaborate flying buttresses which
French height demanded (57).

Certainly they showed little interest as a whole in the sexpartite variant of the rib
vault. They took many of the features of French Gothic and used them in a different

way. The vault and buttresses they toned down in height but used for decoration. They seized on the idea of multiple shafts, applied it to their piers as well as the vault supports and linked them to string course, to balance the bay division. They took to the pointed arch and used it to make strong lines for their windows and arcades. In doing all this, they used some of the principles of the early Gothic but took them down a different path, noticeably less divorced from their Romanesque traditions. This of course means that to those areas of the British Isles looking to England for their knowledge of Gothic, the rules of France would not apply.

BEYOND ENGLAND: SCOTLAND, WALES AND IRELAND

While northern France contained political boundaries, generating more or less tension but a common social structure and language, the British Isles present us with both political and cultural boundaries. The boundary between the twelfth-century kingdoms of England and Scotland, which controlled essentially the Lowlands alone, was almost entirely a political one. It generated the occasional war but no great permanent tension, as shown by the absence of the proliferation of castles along the borders. The kings of the two countries were related by marriage and culture by the middle of the twelfth century and the kings of Scotland encouraged the inward migration of English aristocrats as well as Flemings and others. They encouraged the building of great churches either through their patronage of abbeys belonging to Continental Orders or cathedrals. The later twelfth and early thirteenth centuries saw a great burst of church building in Scotland, with some very large projects such as the cathedral of St Andrew's (longer than Winchester cathedral). The design of the churches at the end of the twelfth century tracked that of England, particularly the north, closely. At Arbroath the surviving south transept shows the use of the long, bluntly pointed lancet like Tynemouth Priory. At Jedburgh abbey, the clustered shafts of the piers and the arches at triforium and clerestory levels reflect those of the Cistercian abbeys to the south; the strong horizontal stress of the three storeys is also typical of the English trend. As with England, the Gothic influence is very much a matter of decoration – pointed arches, shafts and capitals – rather than a large-scale redesigning of the idea or arrangement of the whole church.

England's other political land border, with the lordships of Wales, was far more confused. Instead of two reasonably homogenous political kingdoms, as in England and Scotland, the land was divided between rival English (or Anglo-Norman) and Welsh lordships; war was much more a feature of the life of the region. Between the English and Welsh lay cultural differences of language, law and tradition, although there was also much personal mingling and borrowing, notably of the idea and practice of building castles by the Welsh. St David's cathedral, English in its staffing and estates, but preserving ancient Welsh ambitions of independence, was a notable example of English church building at the end of the twelfth century (58). Within the Welsh lordships, the emphasis was on monastic rather

58 St David's cathedral; north side of the nave

than on cathedral building, partly because the bishops' sees lay in the hands of English, but also because of the ancient order of the Welsh church.

The main monastic influence was that of the Cistercians, with the abbey of Whitland adopting a prominent role. Its first daughter abbey was Strata Florida, founded by an Anglo-Norman but quickly taken over by the Welsh Lord Rhys in 1165, a year after its foundation, after which it became a repository of Welsh literary culture. In its buildings, however, it was a Cistercian abbey, subject to the international, French-biased, rules of the Order. Strata Florida is poorly preserved, but we can see it as essentially a Romanesque church built to a Cistercian plan; the most prominent survival is its west door, round-headed with jambs of clustered shafts and horizontal bands without capitals. In 1201, the Welsh king of Powys founded the abbey of Valle Crucis, which was built in the succeeding decades. The architecture is not particularly ambitious, with vaulting confined to eastern chapels of the transepts, and intended for the nave aisles. The east wall saw a composition of three pointed lancet windows in one storey below two above; the piers had clustered shafts. There is nothing here which would be out of place in a similar abbey in England; any differences are due to resources not culture.

In Ireland we find all these divisions and assimilations together. The incursion of English lords was later than in Wales or Scotland, starting in 1168-9, and rather more structured; the king of England tried to control events more than in Wales. Although the relationship has usually in modern times – thanks in part to nineteenth-century nationalism but also to the sixteenth- and seventeenth-century religious wars – been presented as particularly antagonistic, the lack of Irish castle building may imply the contrary.

Something of the cross-currents between cultures and contemporary political and ecclesiastical worlds can be gained from the connections of Cistercian abbeys. Mellifont abbey was founded before the English came and the nexus of abbeys founded from it were always different from the English-founded ones. The affiliation of the Gaelic Scottish world, or at least its southern part, to Ireland is shown by the fact that Reginald, son of Somerled, Lord of the southern Isles, chose Mellifont as the mother house of his foundation of Saddell abbey in Kintyre in the later twelfth century. Likewise the Romanesque architecture of Iona nunnery is Irish in character. John de Courcy, English conqueror of the kingdom of Ulster in 1177, with his wife founded two Cistercian abbeys. One was Inch, which seems to have been the inheritor or even re-foundation of Erenagh abbey which we have seen as the first of the new Order abbeys in Ireland; certainly he chose Erenagh's mother abbey of Furness as the mother for Inch. His wife found Grey abbey, choosing Holm Cultram as mother; this was an abbey founded in Cumbria in 1150 by King David of Scotland as part of his attempts to expand his kingdom into England. As we saw with its impact on Romanesque building, the twelfth-century reform of the Irish Church was a major upheaval and was still proceeding when the English incursion started. All in all, we should not expect simple patterns in church building here.

The reform movement had brought bishops to Ireland, but the cost of getting the support of the various kings was that each kingdom tried to have its own bishop; the result was too many poor dioceses. The story of the church building of the late twelfth century is dominated by the monasteries, particularly the Cistercian monks and the Augustinian canons, who tended to inherit the old Irish monasteries. The result is that Gothic style came very cautiously to Ireland. Like England there were Burgundian contacts, visible in the eastern end of Boyle abbey, for example, with its pointed arch and barrel vault, in the far west of the island. As with Wales it is a matter of these pointed arches and vaults confined to the lower parts of churches. I would identify Inch, in the 1180s, as the earliest example of Gothic style in Ireland, benefiting from its closeness to its mother church of Furness which completed its nave in the 1170s, and from its inheriting the organised lands of Erenagh giving it a head start. It resembles Valle Crucis in its display of pointed lancets in the east wall and its use of rib vaults, with clustered shaft piers, for the transept chapels. Others would identify Grey or others as the first; the difficulty is one of precise chronology, but also one of deciding precisely what constitutes a Gothic church.

This is well illustrated by one story: perhaps in imitation of English scholarship, Ireland has also seen the identification of a 'Western School' of Transitional architecture, first proposed in 1960 but repeated in 2001. It is an interesting study in methodology. Its supporters list the features which they believe serve to identify a building belonging to the 'School'. Although they tend not to be explicit on the exact number of instances where these features occur, one can still make up a reasonable list of eight of them. The results of a survey of the occurrence of these features candidate in the candidate churches is rather variable, with some churches having 6, or 75 per cent, while others have only 2, or 25 per cent. Identification is often subjective, especially when analysing the alleged affinities of the designs of capitals, for example; it is not clear why one trait should be significant and another not. There is also the issue of the uniqueness of the feature being compared; in this case Leask identifies finely wrought and jointed masonry as one of his identifying traits, but this is hardly unique. As Mannion pointed out, all his traits can be found in St Magnus' cathedral on Orkney. Some of the traits are found either outside the area concerned or earlier than his defined period; should we view these as sources of the ideas or as a problem? The mechanism problem is really a question of asking what this assemblage means; how did it come into being, if it did, and how was it maintained. The implication is the old one that a similarity between two pieces means that the same workman made both, or that the two workmen learned their trade in the same workshop, hence the name School. This is a real problem when it comes to having a number of buildings going up at the same time. Then there is the obvious difficulty that it assumes that craftsmen ere uniformly unimaginative through their careers. This is easier to believe when we are dealing with technological practice such as the erection of a vault or the overall proportions of a church. Here the workman may well not understand the theoretical issues well, as with the forces of a vault, so that he has not the basis

59 Boyle abbey; west end of the nave with a different design on the north side from the south (most notably with pointed arches in the north arcade and rounded ones in the south)

on which to experiment with new ideas, and is driven to repeat what he knows because he dare not change.

Both in this context and in a more general one, it is important to note that in the case of this 'Western Transitional' School, it is defined entirely in terms of decorative traits, not major structural or design ones. This also tells us much of what Gothic meant in the British Isles. One lesson is that it was a fund of individual features, such as the shape of arches or the decorative effect of shafts, much more than the overall scheme of the church. That would come during the thirteenth century but not until then; just as it had not been a uniform line of development in France. The other lesson is that these ideas could cross not only political but also quite profound cultural boundaries. Admittedly, the Gothic of Boyle (59) or Inch abbeys is as long a way conceptually from Canterbury, Sens or Bourges as it is physically, but this is as much to do with resources as it is with the ideas themselves. The vision is greatly attenuated; there is little of the Harvey's 'upward flame', or indeed of the elaboration of vault and buttress, and the elements are as much derived from Cistercian practice as they are the main principles of the Gothic of the Ile de France. The Cistercian connection is notable because by the 1220s some of the Irish Cistercian abbeys were rebelling against the international discipline of the Order. In building, however, the fashion of the pointed arch and the rib vault proved stronger than the divisions of politics, society and language.

GERMANY

A lack of resources was not a problem for the German church. The cathedrals and abbeys were wealthy and their prelates powerful; the craftsmen could look back on as long a tradition of training and expertise as any area beyond the Mediterranean. It is not until the second quarter of the thirteenth century, however, that we can point to systematic use of Gothic ideas in Germany. This has always been a problem to academics, because it challenges directly the story of the inevitability of the adoption of the Gothic style across Europe, and the further we trace back our definitions or origins of the style, the more acute the problem becomes.

There can be no question of believing that the German patrons and masons were ignorant of the developments of the later twelfth century in France. The church of St George at Limburg-an-der-Lahn of the 1190s has sexpartite rib vaults and pointed arches in the arcades, gallery and crossing, but these are applied to a traditional plan with towers, external gallery to the eastern apse and other Romanesque features. The great cathedral of Magdeburg was burned out in 1207 and the rebuilding started in 1209, reaching the crossing by 1232. This was a most significant church, founded by Otto I as one of the main centres for the German military and evangelising expansion into the pagan Slav lands east of the Elbe. It was closely associated with the Premonstratensian Order, one of whose centres was in Picardy, and the archbishop in 1209 had studied in Paris. The work started

60 Magdeburg cathedral; east end chevet

with the eastern end, with a five-sided apse surrounded by an ambulatory and chapels; a French chevet (*60*).

The choir, ambulatory and chapels all have rib vaults; the choir has strong and weak piers, as though to lead to a sexpartite vault. The vaults are carried on bundles of shafts which formally rise through the horizontal string courses; the arches of the three storeys are all at least bluntly pointed. All these elements may be traced back to the generation before in the Ile de France but the overall effect is not early Gothic of *c.*1200. The predominant stress is horizontal. In part this is because the builders or, more likely, the patrons, wished to reuse four stout porphyry columns and their capital in the apse. They sit on compound shafts but reach only to the string course at the base of the gallery. Here they support life-sized statues and link up visually with the plaques and smaller statues placed along the other bays of the choir just below the string course. The gallery itself has arches which are framed with strong shafts, so the whole cuts right across the vertical lines of the vault shafts. The component elements of Gothic are outweighed by the powerful Romanesque tradition of the place; the builders were aware of the French developments and chose to use some, but not to follow the system behind them.

The greatest number of early thirteenth-century churches in Germany is found along the middle or lower Rhine. Again there is clear evidence of the builders' knowledge of French Gothic elements. The church of the Holy Apostles, Köln, has a sexpartite vault accommodated to a system of double bays. In the same city, the remarkable octagon, inherited from late Roman times, of the church of St Gereon was rebuilt between 1219 and 1227, with arcades of pointed arches set between shafts leading up to the rib vault. The Minster at Bonn, of the 1220s, has a quadripartite vault supported by simple flying buttresses on the outside, along with a Gothic south portal. However, the church of the Holy Apostles at Köln also has a common, even diagnostic, feature of these lower Rhineland churches of the early thirteenth century: the east end is short, with an apsidal ending, which is reflected in apses at the ends of the transepts. The apsidal transept is a feature of Soissons and Noyon and thus can be part of the early Gothic design. However, the internal design of the Rhenish apses is very different from that of early Gothic Noyon. They have banded barrel vaults and clearly separated horizontal arcades of round arches, in contrast to the rib vaults and elevation held together vertically by the shafts at Noyon. The sexpartite vault fitted into a pattern of plans in Germany whereby the nave is composed of two squares, each of two double-bays, a tradition going back to the eleventh-century. Behind the arcades of each of these bays is a pair of square aisle bays, emphasising the separate parts of the plan. The plan type, the proportions of the heavy piers and arcades, the thick walls and the round openings, along with the clear separation of other elements of the church plan, choir, transept or nave and towers, are all essentially part of a Romanesque idea of a church. The Gothic elements, vault or arch, are assimilated into this, rather than changing the basic principles of design behind it. To the south the transepts of Strasbourg follow the same pattern, with Gothic elements but a plan of a four squares around a central pier derived from the Rhenish bays.

61 St Elisabeth's church, Marburg; the nave from the south-west. The two rows of windows light the high aisles of the hall church

This pattern of Gothic elements in a traditional frame continues well into the thirteenth century in Germany. The church of Our Lady in Trier, poorly dated but from the first half of the century, has a remarkable plan: a cross of equal-length nave and transepts with a choir prolonged by an eastern chapel, the whole surrounded by a circle of eight chapels. The windows have the bar tracery of Reims cathedral; the vaults are complex ribs supported by high shafts rising from the ground. The exterior is less convincingly Gothic, particularly the west front with a Romanesque portal and the upper windows enclosed in round arches; on either side it is flanked by two stair turrets. The church of St Elisabeth in Marburg is, by contrast, precisely dated because it was a church of great political importance within Germany. It commemorated Elisabeth, Countess of Thuringia, who died in 1231 and was beatified in 1234. The impetus for the cult and the building came from an alliance of the Count and the Master of the Teutonic Order of Knights; it was started in 1235 and consecrated only three years later. Its interior with its high columns, shafts and vault, along with the window tracery are Gothic in spirit as well as elements. However, the church is not constructed like a conventional French Gothic one; it is a hall-church (*61*).

This has no triforium or clerestory to the nave; the arcades rise to the roof because the aisles are the same height as the central vessel so that all the light comes from them. The design is like those churches of the later twelfth and earlier thirteenth century from the west of France but had been found in Westphalia before the building of Marburg. In the west of the region, after 1228, the church of Herford was built as a hall-church with three aisles, each of three bays long. Paderborn cathedral was probably of the 1230s, essentially contemporary with Marburg, while Munster cathedral followed in the 1250s. It has been much debated whether or not they derived the hall idea from Anjou. On the one hand the distance and lack of known connections seem to militate against it; on the other, independent invention at the same time is difficult to believe. It must be significant that both Paderborn and Munster in the same region use domical Angevin vaults.

The story of Germany, even more than the British Isles, is of the gradual use of Gothic elements within a strong regional and Romanesque tradition. In one sense this is the true Transitional, with the number of the Gothic elements gradually rising until they had made something different from the whole. In another, it is the exact opposite, for there is no sense that there was any appreciation of a movement towards the ultimate achievement of Gothic building; no sense of working to a pre-ordained agenda. Instead the agenda continued to be a traditional German and Romanesque one. The Gothic elements show that the builders were aware of the Gothic but were indifferent to its system when it conflicted with either their ideal or, as at Magdeburg, traditional associations were more important.

ANJOU AND THE SOUTH AND WEST OF FRANCE

When the lords of Anjou and Poitou deserted King John after 1204 and transferred their allegiance to Philip Augustus of France, that was all there was to it: as they showed on a number of occasions later, they could transfer it back again. The idea of a conquest of the land, in the modern terms of a State-sponsored occupation of the land and its government, is an anachronism in the Middle Ages. At best, the process is better described as one of replacing one set of lords with another. In France during the thirteenth century, the developing bureaucracy did expand into new lands, such as the south-west, but this was a slow process, really only getting under way after 1242 when the lordship of Poitou and much of the south was transferred to Alfonse, brother of King Louis IX.

This is important to clarify because the French kings' expansion of power is often described as conquest, just as the similar expansion of new lords into lands in Scotland, Wales or Ireland is so described. It is also one area where the ideas of Gothic had no impact during the earlier thirteenth century. Before 1150, various groups of masons in the south-west of France had developed their own idea of a church. It was based on breadth rather than height and on the unity of the interior space. In plan, one expression of this was the 'hall-churches' of Poitou, where the aisles were the same height as the central nave and the arcade, giving the effect of three equal spaces. It was linked to the idea of 'vaulting' the interior by means of a line of domes, first seen in the Périgord at the start of the twelfth century. The idea of the domes was picked up by the masons further north, as far as the Loire in Anjou, as seen at

Fontevrault abbey church or the extraordinary pyramids of Loches. In the 1150s, the cathedral nave at Angers, the see of Anjou, was rebuilt. It was divided into three bays, some 16m square, by strong piers inside and out. On these piers the masons built rib vaults, crossing this wide space. Perhaps because of the wide span, perhaps because of the ideas of domes, the diagonal ribs of the vault were considerably higher than the arches cross the nave or along the wall. This domical effect was not unique to Angers or the region, for it occurs occasionally wherever rib vaults were used in the earlier twelfth century. What was different was that the patrons and the masons clearly appreciated the effect and both continued with it and exaggerated it.

The cathedral of Poitiers, the rival to Angers to the south, started to be rebuilt in the 1160s. The space is a straightforward rectangle with square ends to east and west and no projecting transepts. It is a hall-church with three spaces of equal height; the aisles are somewhat narrower, although there is not as much difference as the usual aisled church. The bays of all three spaces are covered in the domical rib vaults ('Angevin vaults') of Angers. The first bays to the east had four ribs to the bay, the quadripartite system, but this was changed to eight ribs as the work moved to the west, perhaps by the 1190s. In the succeeding decades masons developed these ideas (62). They adopted the eight-rib design; it had no structural advantage but it was decorative, especially in churches which were wide and open with few opportunities for embellishment. They made ribs and the shafts steadily thinner and elaborated patterns of the ribs with subsidiary ones. In part this may reflect the love of complicated shafting which was so much a part of the late twelfth-century early Gothic, whether at Laon or Wells, but this is to stress the source too much. The overall idea of the churches of the region was based on different principles from those to the north and east. The builders continued their Romanesque tradition of breadth and unity, simply adopting the rib form to articulate the coverage of more complex spaces than they could with domes and then to embellish them.

In the south, Toulouse was one of the centres of the enormous County of that name. From the late twelfth century it was riven by the existence of the Cathar heresy, with a Crusade launched from the north in 1208 against the lands of the Languedoc and the lords who protected the heretics. During this a start was made on rebuilding the cathedral, with the nave of three bays being constructed. They are wide and covered by vast, but relatively low, quadripartite rib vaults; one of the bosses is decorated with the arms of the Count (63). East of Toulouse, in Narbonne, the builders of St Paul's church, after 1224, adapted some of the northern ideas to the local tradition. There is a chevet of sorts, with bluntly pointed windows (but also round arches between them), but the proportions and the overall impression is of a low, wide building. The interior is similar, with the width (emphasised by the later strainer arches across it) and the two-storey elevation more dominant than the simple rib vault.

Because these churches use rib vaults and have occasional pointed arches, particularly on the arches at the sides of the vault bays, they are sometimes linked to the early Gothic ideas. Conversely, because they do not share the principle of

62 Candes St Martin; nave with an Angevin domed and ribbed vault

63 Toulouse cathedral; the low, wide nave of the early thirteenth century contrasts with the later choir beyond

verticality and the three-stage design of the main bays, to others they are a 'dead-end', because they do no fit into the advancing stream of Gothic development. Both these descriptions are mistaken. The structural device of the domical vault over square bays arises from the ideas practised by masons in the area since the early twelfth century; this cannot be part of the spread of Gothic. The criticism that it was static and did not contribute to the wider style of Gothic is equally wide of the mark. The builders had their own ideas of how a church should look; it was indeed different from those elsewhere, but that does not make them wrong. To label this as resistance to the Gothic, to identify it as a conscious rejection of northern French ideas, in the wake of the 'conquest' after 1204, is probably equally wide of the mark. The ideas were developed long before 1204, so they pre-existed any conquest, let alone the gradual suppression of the powers of the local magnates. Nor is it clear that those involved in the political life or the wider cultural differences between the Languedoc and the Languedoil identified the church building style with their literature or society. It might be labelled conservatism, except that in Anjou and Poitou in particular the experiments with developing the design of Angevin vaults and churches based on width, not height, went on apace.

SUMMARY

The differing ways towards the development of Gothic building style and its spread across Northern Europe are not a simple story. The two strands of the rib vault and the structure dependent on it, and the visual design of the pointed arch, shafts and vertical emphasis were brought together by the masons in the area north and east of Paris. It is crucial to realise, however, that there were a whole variety of features, some stressed more than others in any individual church, as those who picked up the ideas were aware. To some it was the shafts which were the most striking feature, to others the pointed arch, to others the structure. They combined them in different ways, from the stress on the separation of wall surface from structure of Burgundy to the variety and colour of the shafts in England, at Wells or Lincoln. Resources played a part, also, as we see in the poorer parts of the British Isles, where the ideas of Gothic became so attenuated as to be only recognisable as Gothic by the locals. There was no Gothic building style, in the sense of an agreed pattern for designing the plan, structure or interior elevation of a Gothic church, before 1200.

This was the work of the masons, not of the patrons. The features which were used, whether the structural ideas or the decorative details, were not such as could have been transmitted by patrons. It is most unlikely that a churchman, even one so involved as Suger of St Denis could have understood and explained the way to construct a rib vault: indeed we see the gradual progress there of the whole team. The provision of shafts may be done by putting separate pieces of stone against the side of the wall, detached from it, or by building up lines of carved stones with the wall or pier. How this is done, and how to explore the different effects created by the two techniques is the realm of the mason. The proportions of the storeys of the elevation, the arcade, triforium and clerestory have to be decided before the work starts, and by the mason not the patron. It is the same with the design of the major openings, arches and windows; this requires the organisation of the masons, the scaffolders and the glaziers. The result was to reinforce what we might term the community of masons, along with their fellow craftsmen. Unlike the earlier Romanesque, when we can envisage the patrons, orders of monks or bishops, deciding on major elements of the design, such as the demand for towers or vaults, and taking ideas from region to region, the Gothic was a matter for the professionals.

This connects in to the difficulty of aligning this with political currents, in the narrower sense of politics. In neither of the two main regions where there was little enthusiasm for the Gothic style before the 1240s, Germany and the south-west of France, can we really align this with political trends; neither the chronology nor the political positions support this. Conversely, in Ireland, where there was real tension between the local Cistercians and the international Order, there was no suggestion of the tension being reflected in the building style. What we are seeing are the links and cultural connections of the builders in the narrower sense, the men who were actually doing the work. These would be bounded or expanded, of course, by wider cultural connections of the society in which they worked and lived. This story, in fact, provides us with a line into the connections, not of the aristocracy, but of the craftsmen of the various regions. In Ireland or Wales it acts as a counter-balance to the story of insular hostility of the native communities; in Germany or Poitou it shows us their self-confidence in their own traditions.

There is a second side to be emphasised in this story. The period of debate in the Ile de France, and the other areas we have been considering here, only lasted until the beginning of the thirteenth century. The reaction of the various regions to the questions and solutions raised in France show how radical these ideas were about the whole nature of church design and construction. While it is correct and reasonable to draw attention to the lack of clarity among the proponents of change and the lack of a concerted response elsewhere, we must not lose sight of one crucial fact. Everywhere we can see the builders reacting to the challenge to their Romanesque traditions, even if they did not accept the new French agenda. They were both aware of the debate in the Ile de France and they took it seriously. After 1200 the debate in France was resolved, with the reconciliation of the ideas found in Chartres and Bourges, as we have seen in chapter 5. This would give a fresh impetus both to the prestige of France and the full Gothic system developed by the builders there; after 1200 the conditions for building churches would be different.

7

CLASSIC GOTHIC: 1200-1330

THE NORTH OF FRANCE 1200-1330

This was the time of the maximum population rise of medieval Europe. It was a time of boom for those who controlled land and of poverty for those who did not; the latter provided a pool of labour for the building industry in particular. Little wonder, therefore, that the great ecclesiastical institutions, cathedrals and abbeys, found themselves with the resources in this period to undertake much building. France was the most powerful land in Europe, both economically and politically, thanks to the foundations laid in the later twelfth century. Church building in France boomed on the basis of the wealth and power of the great landed institutions, especially the cathedrals.

When we conjure up a picture of Gothic buildings, it is often, or usually, one based on the buildings of the thirteenth century; this is the time of the most spectacular churches in Europe. In part this is because after 1300 we have fewer completed large churches of the one style; they exist, of course, but not in the same numbers as those of the thirteenth century. This is probably the period of both the greatest number of major church projects, but also the greatest expenditure, so they inevitably loom large in our consciousness. Added to this is the legacy of the nineteenth-century studies, when medieval church architecture was first analysed. At this time, in France and in England, the thirteenth-century style was held up as the purest of the medieval church styles, between the rougher Romanesque and the degenerate late Gothic. This is one justification for using the word classic. The other is the nature of the building, particularly in France. On the basis of the experiments of the later twelfth century the builders of the thirteenth century in France developed, and adhered to, a clear style. They subscribed to a series of principle, rules even, which applied to the plans, structure and elevations of their churches. Within these constraints they pushed

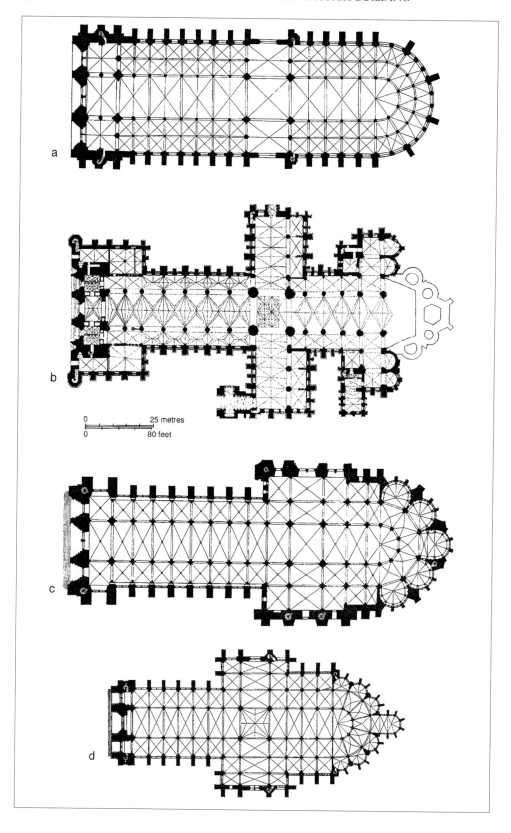

0   25 metres

0   80 feet

their ideas to the limits like Racine containing great human emotions within the three classical unities. This is the time of the maximum tension between Harvey's 'upward flame' and the structural system; the two defining features of Gothic building.

The style, as we saw in chapter 5, is a consensus or compromise between the ideas seen at Chartres or at Bourges and is to be found at Soissons or at Reims. Soissons must have been around 1200 or earlier because it was dedicated in 1212; Reims cathedral was started in 1210. The works at Chartres only started after 1194 and those at Bourges can only have been a little, if at all, earlier. At the time when it came to planning Soissons or Reims, Chartres and Bourges were far from complete, although a fair amount of their ideas may have been visible. The ideas of Reims were quickly followed. Amiens was started in 1220 after a fire of 1218, Rouen was started in 1214 and Le Mans 1217-54; the west end and upper parts of the choir of Notre Dame in Paris dated 1200-45. The chronology is too compressed for the ideas to be spreading through the conventionally supposed mechanism of developing ideas seen in one church before starting the next. The builders must have been drawing on a body of agreed ideas developed around 1200 or very shortly afterwards, which were ready to be put into place when each contract came up.

The churches are built around two principles, both derived from the earlier work. The first is that they should stress unity of the church, both in plan (64) (suppressing the Romanesque separation of spaces) and also in their elevations, with uniform bays and decoration. The second is that they stressed height over either the length or breadth of the church. In plan they use the chevet design for the east end, a short choir, an apse and an ambulatory with a ring of outer chapels. The transepts are neither suppressed, as in Sens or Bourges, nor as strongly projecting as in the Romanesque tradition, but project at least one bay beyond the nave and have clear façades to north or south but tend to blend into the choir aisles. The naves are fairly short; chapels are accommodated in the chevet or along the aisles. The result is to strike a balance between the extremes of unified space at Bourges and the demands for a defined choir, nave and chapels, as well as retaining the overall plan of a cross. Towers are confined to the western façades. The structure is designed around a high quadripartite vault, supported by raking flying buttresses. The sexpartite vault is abandoned, presumably because of the tension it set up between the logic of the differing bays and the desire for unity. The flying buttresses had now been perfected to deliver the height which could exceed that of late twelfth-century Notre Dame in Paris.

The plan and the structure feed into elevations which stress both unity and the vertical. The main elevations are those of the transept façades and the west fronts. On the outside, the transepts follow Chartres in their design of a large portal surmounted by a rose window and then the gable. The western façades

Opposite: 64 Plans of three French cathedrals with one English: a. Bourges; b. Lincoln (before the addition of the Angel Choir after 1255); c. Reims; d. Amiens. The simplicity of the French plans contrast with that of Lincoln

65 Reims cathedral; the east end with
the chevet chapels and flying buttresses,
completing the earlier experiments,
with the new window tracery

66 The south choir wall of Beauvais
cathedral; its height and the lines of the
inserted bays crossing the earlier arcade
are visible

are based on the traditional twin towers and a central unit, again dominated by a rose window. The towers front the aisles, they centre the nave and each provides, logically, a grand portal to reflect the three vessels of the nave. The exterior is a clear reflection of the interior and vice versa. Bays defined by prominent vertical shafts dominate the interior. Wall surfaces are kept to a single plane as far as possible. The older galleries are abandoned and replaced with shallow triforium passages, interrupted visually by the bay divisions, so that the strength of their horizontal is diminished. The bays culminate in high clerestory windows whose sills were well below the vault springing, the Chartres solution; often approximately the height of the arcade.

The one new feature, not found before 1200, is the appearance at Reims of the bar tracery in the windows, with a common formula of two lancets surmounted by a circle (65). Until then, if a window was to have two lights beneath a circular opening, the three elements were kept separate. They appear as individual openings with sections of walling between, the so-called 'plate tracery'. At Reims the master made the decision to bring them together and separate the units purely by narrow bars of stone, hence the term 'bar tracery'. This invention was to have a massive impact on the design of the windows as they grew ever more prominent over the succeeding centuries. In the context of the principles of design of the church as a whole, it is interesting to note how this led to the standardisation of the pieces of stone which made up the window tracery, with repeating stones of the same shape assembled to give the whole design.

The result of this work is a series of stunning churches, still, rightly, seen as major works of Western European culture. Reims and Amiens continue to dominate and decorate the centres of the cities around them. Obviously these churches are not identical; an important part of the whole appeal of medieval buildings is that each was individual, unlike the canons of taste imposed by eighteenth-century classicism. In the choir at Le Mans, for example, the whole triforium stage was suppressed entirely and the elevation consisted of a high arcade and clerestory alone.

They were also always pushing for ever more spectacular effects. One of these was in height and the result was to achieve what was probably the technological limit of the stone vault. In 1225 fire destroyed the choir of Beauvais cathedral; there was a short period of money-raising before work began to replace it in the 1230s. The greatest effort here went into the stunning effect of the internal height of the church. The apex of the vault of the main vessel is 48m above the floor, the highest cathedral vault in Europe, higher, by 2m, than its nearest rival, Köln. The roof rises above this vault; the whole is the height of a 15-20 storey building. This is achieved in part through having a very high arcade, with stilted arches, especially in the apse (66). During a storm in 1284, the vault partially collapsed and the choir was rebuilt with eight narrow bays rather than the original four; research has also shown how the buttresses were reinforced at precisely their vulnerable points of stress. We can only admire whoever it was who stood near the collapsing masonry to identify these weaknesses.

67 St Denis; the thirteenth-century nave which linked the two parts of Suger's church

They also, inevitably, explored new possibilities of decoration, which have sometimes been detached from the main body of the style and been labelled the Rayonnant style. The 'style' amounts to the increased emphasis on tracery in the windows, accompanied by larger windows and more tracery in general; it is better seen simply as one end of a spectrum of elaboration in decoration. It starts with the completion of the church of St Denis, which involved building transepts and a nave to join the two separate parts left by Suger in 1151, and rebuilding the upper parts of his choir to match. Along with this is stress on the mullions of the tracery by embellishing them with mouldings and making the ribs narrower and with similar mouldings to align with them. The feature of the nave at St Denis with the most immediate impact is the piercing of the outer walls of the triforium and glazing both inner and outer faces. The clerestory window tracery is continued down to include the triforium, so that everything above the level of the arcade is traceried and glazed (*67*).

The impact of this is seen at the cathedral of Troyes, where the choir chevet had been laid out and taken to triforium level by 1228, when the work was damaged in a great storm. The triforium was renewed in the 1230s, with an exterior glazed face and an open arcade on the inner side. The work continued through the rest of the century to add the transepts and nave; they reproduce the St Denis internal elevation almost exactly. The cathedral choir of Tours of the 1240s also follows the same design.

King Louis IX received the relic of Christ's Crown of Thorns (a miracle of survival and salesmanship) in 1239; shortly after 1243 he started a new chapel in his palace in Paris, which we know as the Sainte Chapelle, finished in 1248. It is not large, as befits a palace chapel (*c.*40m long) although it is much bigger than any purely personal, private chapel. It is constructed on two floors: the lower one for servants; the first floor at the level of the principal lodgings of the palace. The upper chapel is simply a frame of narrow stone piers giving four straight bays and an apse, with vaults above; between are windows which make up the majority of the walls. One of the great fortunes has been the survival of a great quantity of the original glass, even if the internal paintwork dates from the nineteenth-century restorations. It is a simple and unified glass and stone box on two levels. The same spirit and agenda was carried on at the church of St Urbain at Troyes. It was founded in 1262 by the son of a shoemaker of the town who became Pope Urban IV and built the church on the site of his father's shop. The whole is like a jewel box, with the stone work reduced to the absolute minimum that would stand up; the walls are as much a screen of glass as the simpler Ste Chapelle. The buttresses are reduced to a beam of stone supported on a slender arch. As well as this, in many places there is one layer of tracery placed in front of another. Outside, the traceried gables set over the windows rise in front of pierced parapets, which themselves stand in front of a roof or a blank piece of walling. Inside, some windows have an inner layer of tracery of one design in front of the tracery which holds the glass, so that the one design seems to contradict the other. The whole is like the castle imagined by the fourteenth-century English author of *Gawain and the Green Knight*: 'just as though it was cut out of paper'.

One feature which really did cause trouble was the relationship between the column or piers of the arcade and the shafts which led up to the vaults. Two principles were in conflict here: one was that the vaults should be seen to be 'supported' by shafts rising from the ground; the other was the integrity, observed since the temples of Classical Greece, of the column and its capital (*68*). One had to cut the other, but, whichever that one was, the result was always clumsy and each of the churches had a different solution.

Above left: 68 Troyes, the church of St Urbain; the elaboration of later thirteenth-century French Gothic
Above right: 69 Reims cathedral: the integration of the capital of a single arcade column and the shafts rising to the vault gave a real problem to thirteenth-century French builders

A further problem was that, if the shafts were to rise from the capital of the column, which was the most usual solution, then the capital must project beyond the line of the wall face. This contradicted the aim of a flat wall face and stressed the arcade too much. Interestingly at Rouen nave, before 1200, one solution, found commonly in England, was used: to support the arcade on piers with multiple shafts, some of which could continue up to the vault. This was then rejected in the choir of the same cathedral, when it was built after 1214 and not used elsewhere. At Bourges and Le Mans, the columns were wider than the wall above with eight thin attached shafts; the thin vault shafts rising from the capitals were less noticeable against the height of the columns. At Chartres, by contrast, there were four large attached shafts, one for each compass point on the column; the main vault shaft then rose through the capital of the column; this was the system more or less followed at Soissons, Reims and Amiens. At Amiens, however, the main vault shaft lacked a capital, and the arcade column capital was interrupted on the side of the nave; only the abacus above continued round to interrupt the shaft. However, the lesser vault shafts there, which rose from the column abacus, were given bases of their own although this made their origins more prominent.

The ideas, of plan, structure and elevation, worked out in the early thirteenth century continued to be used into the next century and were used across northern France in areas where there had been some independence of tradition before. The choir of Séez cathedral was started in the 1270s, in contrast to the great churches in the Norman manner, like Coutances or Bayeux, of the earlier thirteenth century. The nave of La Trinité, Vendome, was started in 1306, while the choir of the great abbey of St Ouen in Rouen was begun in 1318; all in classic French Gothic style. The nave of the cathedral of St Benigne in Dijon of the 1280s and that of Auxerre cathedral in 1309, mark the same transition for Burgundy. The choir of the cathedral of the County of Flanders, Tournai, another of the semi-independent lordships surrounding the kingdom of France, was rebuilt from 1243-55, dwarfing the twelfth-century nave. It was laid out with a chevet and aisles, steep flying buttresses to support the quadripartite rib vault, and an internal elevation based on a high clerestory. All of these follow the same formula; although in the case of the nave of St Bénigne in Dijon in a rather impoverished or stripped down way.

One of the variations that we can see is the continuing debate about the relationship between the arcade columns and the vault shafts or the mouldings for the arches. The choir at Séez is the latest of this list to have simple columns with attached shafts in the arcade. The others, from Tours onwards, tend towards having piers with the shafts, if not actually suppressing the capitals, at least running so strongly through them as to make them secondary in importance. At Auxerre and St Ouen, the capitals are minor excrescences on some of the shafts; at Vendome, they are missing both from the shafts and the mouldings of the arches.

Some of the variations can be linked into a series to give us examples of typological 'progression'. The design of piers and shafts is one; another is the series of western facades. Around 1200, there were two formulae to be found as models.

The façade at Noyon, constructed after 1205, survives with scars of shells from the First World War still visible; some of them aimed in 1918 by Maurice Bowra, later an eminent Greek scholar and Warden of Wadham College, Oxford. This façade and the one of Notre Dame, Paris, are built with a strong, square central element, the width of the nave and two aisles and a similar height, and this is stressed with lines of horizontal arcading. The portals are either set in a continuous porch, as at Noyon, or are cut into the façade as at Notre Dame; in neither do they have gables of their own. The façade at Laon (from c.1190) lacks the square centre, as does that at Bourges (perhaps because it fronts double aisles), and both are dominated by the great gables of the portals. Reims and Amiens follow the latter formula, abandoning the regularity of the square for the emphasis of the portals. The elaborate detail of the decoration at Amiens certainly contrasts with the overall design, but whatever our view of its aesthetics, we must acknowledge the ingenuity of the master there at contriving to build the towers over the portals and so shrinking the space that the whole façade occupied. This became the standard western façade in France and continued as such down into the sixteenth century.

All deployed rose windows in the design, which later generations used extensively in France as the traceried centrepieces of façades of the transepts as well as the west ends. Here again we can detect 'development'. The round window at Laon and the one in the façade of the south transept at Chartres (themselves preceded by the one in the western façade of St Denis) have tracery based on an inner circle. At Notre Dame in Paris this is replaced by something more like the spokes of a wheel which is the design followed at the west fronts of Reims and the south transept at Notre Dame itself. Historians have detected a conflict between the rose window and the ideas of verticality for the whole façade. They see the inclusion of the rose within the tracery of the main nave window at Reims as part of a design to mask this conflict, and the same with framing it within a square at Paris. Perhaps the best example of this is in the south transept rose at Tours cathedral where the whole shape is distorted to a diamond with curved sides to fit it into the window, while still keeping the idea of a dominant traceried rose. The rose's shape is reflected in the common use of curved triangle in the tracery (a motif popularised by the Ste Chapelle) but apart from this, the tracery is very much based on the idea going back to Reims, of two lancets and a circle above.

SOUTHERN FRANCE

This is the region of Northern Europe, south of the river Loire, where different ideas from those which produced the Gothic style were strongest; not until the middle of the thirteenth century did buildings come here. The cathedral of Clermont-Ferrand was started in 1248 in the northern style. The clerestory tracery is in the style of Reims and the triforium is an unglazed arcade. The arcade piers reflect the move from column to pier, with only the mouldings relating to the arcade arches receiving capitals; the vault shafts run straight up. The choir at

70 Narbonne cathedral, seen from the south, marked the spread of classic north French Gothic style into the south but only the choir was finished (1272-33)

Bayonne, of the 1260s, has a northern French chevet with the flying buttresses and tracery of the style. The choir of Narbonne cathedral owes its existence to a pope, like St Urbain in Troyes. In 1259 Guy Foulquoi, one of Louis IX's councillors, was appointed archbishop; in 1265 he was elected pope as Clement IV. In 1272 he started the rebuilding of his cathedral, where the choir alone was completed, by 1333 (*70*). It has the full plan and structure of a French Gothic chevet with steeply raking flying buttresses. Inside the bay design has a minimal triforium, unglazed but linked to the tracery of the clerestory windows above. The arcade is based on columns with thin attached shafts. There are no real capitals, however, rather a line of an abacus and the mouldings of the arches spring directly, at different levels from the sides of the columns, while the thin vault shafts rise unbroken through the line of the abacus.

In the same year as the choir at Narbonne was started, the choir of Toulouse cathedral was replaced. It was on a different alignment from the old nave of the cathedral, of the early thirteenth century. However, it was only finished in the seventeenth century; only the work up to the top of the triforium is of the thirteenth century; as with Narbonne the arcades lack much in the way of capitals and these are followed by others, such as Limoges or Rodez. Perhaps the cathedral of Béziers is representative; it has a new apsidal choir and vault added to the Romanesque part; the apse in particular has a design with high single windows between the vault shafts, like that of the Ste Chapelle in Paris, but the actual amount of work done was not large nor was it done quickly.

There were churches in the region which were built much more according to the traditions of the area. The cathedral of St Nazaire in the great fortress town of Carcassonne, received a new choir. The apse of the choir, like that of Béziers, is reminiscent of St Chapelle, with its high, narrow windows; the occurrence of spherical triangles in the tracery, popularised there, reinforces the feeling. Its details and structure with a fine rib vault are all in the northern style, but the plan is not. It consists of two large transepts with a short apsidal choir; the transepts have an eastern aisle in front of a line of three chapels each to the east again. The transept chapels and aisles are of the same height as the apse and the transepts themselves, and are only separated by thin piers, so that the whole interior feels far more like a hall-church, with the traditional southern breadth, than a northern one; it is also not high, perhaps to align with the old nave which was retained. The Dominicans in Toulouse, the nerve centre of the Inquisition against the southern Cathar heretics, built an enormous new church in the second half of the thirteenth century. It is large but its plan is straightforward: a rectangle with an eastern apse, the whole being divided longitudinally into two parallel naves. It is of undecorated brick and presents formidable façades to the outside. The Dominicans were preachers and this may explain the design of the church. The two parallel naves were of the same height, separated by slender columns which support the vaults; nowhere in the church has its view of the altar obscured (*71*). Equally, although it is high, there is more than a suggestion of the local tradition of unified space, seen in the hall-churches of twelfth-century Poitou or the lines of domes of the Périgord.

The cathedral of Albi belongs very much in the same context; it was started in 1282 by a Dominican bishop, a fierce pursuer of heretics. It, too, is of brick with an even simpler plan. It is a single rectangular space with an eastern apse and a line of chapels along the sides. These were originally open to the nave, although later screened off at ground level; in effect the walls between them acted as buttresses supporting the vault above. Like Toulouse, it is high and austere and its Dominican associations also must be considered, but it is still very markedly different from the northern model and must prompt the thought that the builders were affected by the local tradition. This is not because of hostility on the part of the bishop; even if he was cool towards the royal officials and policy, he was quite unlikely to be sympathetic to traditions associated with the older regime which had been so closely associated with protection of the Cathars. As with Carcassonne, the builders could adapt their technology, the use of brick, and the idea of the spatial organisation of the church to the new technologies, the high vaults, and the forms of design, from the north.

ENGLAND 1200-45

In England, as in France, the first half of the thirteenth century saw a massive amount of construction, especially of the great cathedrals. If the French builders

71 The north aisle of the Dominican church in Toulouse

set a pattern of building based on Chartres and Bourges combined, in England Canterbury, Wells and St Hugh's choir at Lincoln occupy the same position; all were finished or well under way by 1200. From Canterbury came the basic ideas of the first French Gothic but also the use of Purbeck marble to pick out shafts in contrasting colour. From Wells came the sharply pointed arches and multiple shafting for the piers with grouped foliage capitals. At St Hugh's choir the bay design and Purbeck marble of Canterbury were combined with the shafts and capitals of Wells. The Lincoln vault, although probably developed as a device for improving light, showed the possibilities of multiple ribs for creating patterns.

At Lincoln the work of rebuilding continued after the completion of St Hugh's choir probably before 1210. It was followed by, first, the western transepts and then the nave which was under way in about 1225, after the great, western transepts had been finished. Work, and therefore employment of the teams building there, was essentially continuous until the 1240s. The project was an epitome of the Early English Gothic style as it coalesced over the first half of the thirteenth century (72). It differs from the French in a number of ways. The plans continue the Romanesque idea of separate parts and they continue to stress length over height. Structurally, as a result, there is less elaboration of flying buttresses; vaults are as much part of the decoration as virtuoso structural feats. The elevations are elaborate compositions of shafts and string courses giving a rich pattern of lines, horizontal, vertical and arcades, and like the plans emphasising the parts of the composition more than the unity.

We confront the differences immediately at the west transepts at Lincoln; they not only replicated St Hugh's eastern ones but are large and prominent spaces. They were covered with rare (for England) sexpartite vaults which arose from a double-bay elevation; the strong bay divisions are marked by single shafts rising from the ground, the weak ones by shafts from the triforium sill. The arcade piers on the east sides have clustered shafts and even the lesser supports for the triforium arches have three shafts, one of them Purbeck marble. The north façade of the north transept has a version of a rose window but composed of individual elements piercing the stone, without even the rudimentary ribs of the wheel at Laon. The nave is a magnificent piece of work. The wide arcades are carried on piers with eight shafts; the problem of how to provide a series of close-set capitals and still have individual ones visible was solved by a fully worked-out row of the 'stiff-leaf' capitals pioneered at Wells and used hesitantly in the transepts. It was made up of stylised, curling foliage of which the individual fronds of adjacent shafts could be made to interlock. It was an ingenious solution which, at its best with the deeply undercut swirling leaves, could both create capitals which were a delight in themselves and gave a layer of deep shadow at the top of the pier. They were also abstract and did not demand the individual attention of a capital with figures telling a story, like the ones of Romanesque Burgundy; they acted to link the piers visually rather than to separate them. The triforium has paired round arches over three lesser ones; here are multiple shafts and capitals with the blank tympana pierced. The clerestory is shorter than in the vault springing (contrast

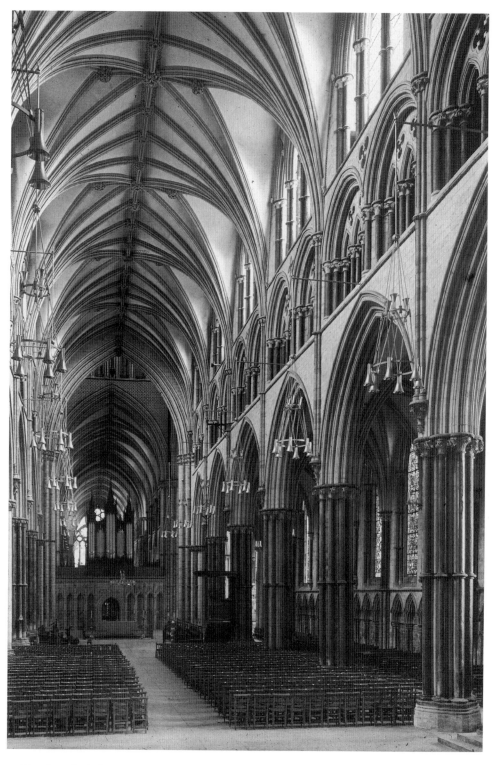

72 Lincoln cathedral nave

73 Salisbury cathedral from the north-east; the square east end, two transepts and low proportions of the thirteenth-century building are rescued by the spire added in the early fourteenth century

the deep French clerestories) and is made up of three separate lancets per bay. The vault is the most original composition, with extra ribs springing from the walls (tierceron ribs) and meeting at a ridge rib which has no real structural function but, by running down the length of the nave, completes the visual closure and emphasises the length of the nave.

The cathedral at Old Sarum had been established there in the eleventh-century reforms of the English cathedral sees. It was in a former Iron Age fort and Anglo-Saxon burh on top of a windswept hill, cramped in its relationship with the royal castle there and located in a place that trade was deserting. By 1218 the bishop resolved to move down to the river valley below the hill, and in 1220 the start was made on the new cathedral of Salisbury. This was the only English cathedral to be built in the thirteenth century on a totally new site and one of the few to be built in accordance with a single design in one campaign, which lasted until about 1260 (73). Other dated examples of major works in the period are a series of eastern extensions: at Winchester, started in 1202; at Worcester, from 1224 to 1232; Ely, started in 1235; Durham, started in 1242. These, along with others, give a clear basis for an appreciation of the buildings of the period.

The great majority of east ends in England rejected the chevet of the French design in favour of square fronts. With the main altar normally placed one or two bays at least west of the termination, there was a clear demarcation of the choir space as opposed to the retro-choir and chapels behind it to the east; this contrasts with the blurring of French space in the apse, aisles and ambulatory chapels. At Durham and at Fountains abbey the eastern space was extended into T-shaped crossings, transepts without the eastern projection. The Durham 'transept' was called the chapel of the nine altars, which tells us one of the main purposes of these east ends, to provide a range of chapels facing east, another advantage of the square end. English builders continued to like a gallery, at Ely choir of the 1230s, for example, instead of the flat blank arcade of a triforium which the French used from the beginning of the thirteenth century. Why these were still built is a question. In common with the others, the Ely gallery is wide and open to the main vessel, but there is no clear access to it; certainly nothing of the sort of width and dignity seen in castle stairs. It can hardly have been for dignitaries, either senior churchmen or visiting laymen. If it was for ritual, when the French did not need it, it is difficult to explain, not least because the difference would surely have attracted some contemporary comment.

None of the arches, of the arcade, triforium or clerestory, was allowed to be single if possible; they must be given an array of hollows and rolls so that they provided a series of highlights and shadows around their individual curves. Further effects were created by using jagged nail-head or dogtooth mouldings (themselves descended from the Romanesque chevrons) to pick out a dominant line. Likewise the verticals were, as far as possible, a collection of shafts, just as the arcade piers were not single columns. The light and shade effects of the shafts were stressed by the popularity of Purbeck marble, dark against the limestone or plaster. The love of pattern can lead to creating effects by doubling up an arcade, as in the superimposed arches seen at Lincoln or at Beverley. Curiously, perhaps, the one set of decorative patterns which the English ignored was the idea of window tracery, for years after it had been used at Reims. In particular they did not often use the rose window which would appear to have been ideal for the great square façades which they contrived.

Within this tidal stream of the development and course of the Early English style there were eddies and counter-tides, groups or even individual churches which showed different designs. Some of these were simply because of cost. The full display that we see at Lincoln nave or at Beverley, with Purbeck shafting, stiff-leaf capitals and complex arcading was very expensive; indeed it may have been costlier than a bay of a contemporary great French church. These costs could clearly be cut if need be. Salisbury has plain ring-capitals which required considerably less time to cut than the equivalent foliage ones. Even more drastically, instead of a stone vault, a timber ceiling with the shape and details of a vault could be erected instead, again a considerable saving on craftsmen's time. An excellent example of this can be seen in three Irish churches. Christ Church cathedral in Dublin was built by an English master with a vault and complex carved capitals; the triforium is subsumed into the clerestory. The cathedral of Kilkenny also had similar capitals (with a combination of foliage and human heads) and the master may have used the north door of Wells as a model for his west door. Inside, however, there is no triforium at all and the nave was always open to the wooden roof; the arcade is composed of moulded arches resting on piers of four attached columns while the clerestory is made up of quatrefoil windows placed over the apex of the arcade arches. Near Kilkenny is the smaller collegiate church of Gowran. Here the builder has taken the example of Kilkenny, with the quatrefoil windows and the four-column piers for the arcade; there are a few carved capitals with foliage and human heads. However, the arcade arches are unmoulded and the clerestory windows are placed, not over the apex of the arcade arches, but over the piers, so that they, and the nave walls, may be lower.

There were also individual groups of masons with independent ideas. The work at Pershore abbey illustrates both this and the way the Early English style could be adapted to circumstances. The choir was erected in two campaigns, separated by a fire which diverted resources to the repair of the rest of the building. The first phase, before 1223, saw the monks commission a new choir to replace the Romanesque one, elaborately decorated with marble shafts and complex carving in the mouldings. The 1230s saw the work renewed again on the choir, but this omitted some of the expense, with simpler mouldings and no marble; crucially it also omitted a stone vault. The fire and the repairs it required, had significantly trimmed the budget for the new design. This design, however, also reflected a local, west Midland, idea (perhaps derived from Worcester cathedral) of producing a two-storey elevation by carrying down the shafts of the clerestory to become the shafts in front of the triforium passage. In effect the two storeys were united into one, so that the design gives us an arcade with a deepened clerestory above it. This was not unlike the aims of the later builders of churches in France when, as at St Denis, they glazed the triforium and linked its tracery to that of the clerestory, but in neither case did the idea become popular and lead to two-storied elevations.

Obviously, the elaborate expenditure of the sort of full double-transepted east end was beyond most of the churches of the time. Even the rich diocese of Winchester decided to make its eastern extension a one-storey affair, wrapping around and beyond the older apse, but this may have been as much because the ground was less firm to the east. There was a similar choice at the west ends. At Peterborough, Wells and Salisbury the west end was given a screen front of masonry; something of the same was done at Lincoln. These fronts projected north and south of the width of the nave and did not clearly reflect the nave and aisles as the three-part French façades did. They also lacked the massive French gabled portals – the doors at Wells have been described as like mouse holes – but they provided space for a grand display of statuary. In the case of Wells an internal passage also probably accommodated a choir to sing to crowds assembled in front of the cathedral. Undoubtedly they are less successful than the clear logic and proportions of the French façades, but again they emphasise the willingness of the English to separate out elements of the church for special treatment. Perhaps the most remarkable example of the variability possible in the Early English style is provided at Selby abbey nave. Not only are the two sides of the nave quite different, but each is a design unlike any other. It is said that they were built at two different times, by two different designers, but there are problems with this. Firstly it requires that the same abbey employed two different men of remarkable originality. Secondly, there is the question of how the church was roofed during the process; was it walled up at the crossing with the first wall left exposed until the second was built, or was a temporary wall built and then replaced?

ENGLAND 1245–1300: THE EARLY DECORATED MANNER

In 1245 the pope authorised King Henry III to take over the building works of the new Westminster abbey which the monks had started but which they were finding beyond their resources; the costs and Henry's motives are discussed in the Introduction. The new church, whether because of the rivalry between the kings or not, was as French in its overall design as had been the rebuilt Canterbury cathedral of the 1170s. Its plan was French, with one of the handful of thirteenth-century chevets built in England at the east end of a typically short French choir. It was higher than any English church and had the full set of high flying buttresses. Internally the elevation is dominated by the clerestory, with its sills in French fashion dropping well below the level of the springing of the vault. Perhaps the most dramatic of the French innovations, however, comes with the windows. Here, best seen in the chapter house which was finished by 1253, they are filled by the sort of tracery, based on the twin lights surmounted by a circle, first used at Reims some 30 years before.

Westminster is not, however, a purely French church, any more than Canterbury had been. It used the English Purbeck marble widely. The vault has a ridge rib, emphasised by the use of a number of prominent bosses at the junctions with the other ribs. The mass of masonry at the vault springing conforms to an English, not French, structural tradition, as does the coursing of the stones in the vault webs. Instead of a French triforium, there is a gallery. There has been much debate as to how we think of these English elements, against the background of the overall French principles of the design. Is it a question of compromise in the mind of the master mason or is it a question of delegation by a French master to gangs of English workmen who then carried out his wishes in their own way? The use of Purbeck, at the least, cannot be as simple as that because this was a decision with obvious consequences; Henry III as the patron may well have been involved here.

Few of the French features of Westminster were copied in England, just as the French design of York at the end of the century was also little imitated. The one element which was popular was the bar tracery of the windows, picking up from Reims. There is a small by-issue here. The churches of Netley and Binham abbeys, both apparently constructed in the 1230s or 1240s, before the work at Westminster had reached the windows, also have bar tracery of this French design. Should we therefore see them as the point of introduction of this idea to England, or should we follow the assumption usually made that only the more important church would have set the fashion? Leaving this aside, for some reason a feature which the English had ignored for 30 years was now eagerly copied and provided a stimulus for a new phase in English church building. It was at first concerned almost entirely with the window tracery, hardly a qualification for identifying it as a style, although in the second phase of this, the Decorated manner, it went much further.

One of the first major examples of this was at Lincoln, where the chapter wished to respond to the expansion of nearby Ely cathedral with a new choir of their own. They wanted to build even further to the east, which involved cutting through the city wall; they sought royal permission to do this in 1255 which dates the start of the work to about five years from the Westminster windows going up. The new east front was dominated by a grand composition of ascending pairs of lancets and circles up to the final circle, which is too large for the regular cusping of the lesser ones, and is filled a set of six circles around the central one. The composition of windows above it, which light only the roof, inserts a fifth lancet into the series, between the two pairs on either side, a move towards variation which had a great future. Within the new choir, only the window tracery is French; all the rest is a gorgeous display of English shafts, capitals and statuary, including the angels in the triforium spandrels that give it its name (74).

The same façade display, based on the twin lancets and circle design, is seen at the west end of the Cistercian abbey of Tintern as well as many others. The builders of Salisbury, having finished the west façade of the cathedral, turned their attention to providing a cloister and chapter house in the 1260s. They adopted

74 Lincoln cathedral: the Angel choir

the new tracery with enthusiasm, especially in the window display of the chapter house. The eastern transepts of Durham were slow in building; by the 1270s, when they were being finished, the two façades also incorporated great windows of this tracery. The rose windows of the Westminster transepts were imitated at St Paul's cathedral in London, again for the east end; from there the design seems to have been copied on tiles and even clothing but there are (perhaps surprisingly) few other clear examples of direct imitation from the Westminster rose.

The Angel choir at Lincoln has a gallery behind the elaborate screen of shafts and tracery, a strong element of English continuity. Perhaps the latest of these galleries, before their replacement by triforia, was at St Mary's abbey in York of the 1270s. Given the difficulty of finding a practical use for these galleries, in the face of their abandonment outside England and their replacement, they are a powerful element of tradition in England of the thirteenth century. The answer may be structural; although they created difficulties for the vaulting, they did contribute to the English practice of loading the wall at the point of springing of the vault.

The cathedral of York was a curious sight at the end of the thirteenth century, with a grand transept of the 1230s and 1240s reached through the narrow eleventh-century nave and leading to the twelfth-century choir. Archbishop Le Romayn is credited with starting the work on the nave in 1291, half way through his term of office. He was rich (the son of a former treasurer of the cathedral), with a conscience about his birth; pushing on with the building would be a good thing. This feeling was not shared by his successors, for the west window would not be completed until 1338 and the wooden vault not put in place until the 1350s. Whether or not it was related to his foreign ancestry and training in Paris, or rivalry with Westminster, the design was a second example of French work in later thirteenth-century England and sits at the end of this phase of design. The failure to complete the vaulting means that it is difficult to assess the structural system and the plan was inherited from the earlier nave. The total height, of c.31m, would have been the same as Westminster abbey and St Paul's cathedral in London; England's second archbishopric was making a statement here. It is the bay design which shows its French character. The bays were defined by the vaulting shafts running through the arcade capitals. Within this the arcade and the clerestory dominate the proportions. The latter has wide windows with the geometrical tracery of lancets surmounted by circles. The sills run well below the springings of the vaults and the vertical mullions link through to the shafts of the triforium, which is a flat arcade of sharply pointed arches. The whole is a design very close to that of Clermont-Ferrand, for example.

THE LATER ENGLISH DECORATED MANNER 1300–1340

During the 1290s and the years after 1300, there were a number of elements introduced into the range of motifs used in England. Individually they were small and appear to be concerned entirely with surface decoration, but the builders went on to add spatial re-organisation so that the effect was considerable. Within tracery, designers began to make use of the double or ogee curve, which seems to have started a whole fashion for inventive designs. Together with the ogee curves went an increased and more elaborate use of cusping, the triangular projection on the inner side of arches, not new but certainly more prominent. The English had been from the beginning of the century using extra ribs from the springing of their vaults, the tierceron ribs. From about 1290 (the first example may be that of the choir at Pershore begun after 1288) they introduced other extra ribs, running between individual ones above the springing; the lierne ribs. These began a second fashion, for composing more elaborate patterns for the vaults. A third feature was the increasing emphasis on niches, used not just on the outside or for occasional statues on major elements of the interior design but as a large and prominent body. They are best seen at first in such things as shrines or tombs, where they can take up a large part of the structure, and where they act to dissolve the face of the structure into a series of openings. An example of these things used to give a new composition would be the tomb in Westminster of Edmund, Earl of Lancaster, who died in 1296. A wise man builds his tomb in his lifetime, for his heirs can often fail to see the necessity for spending much on it; this may therefore date to the 1290s and is a riot of niches, tracery and cusping. The principle which lay behind these became one of surprise and pattern, of producing designs, for example, of tracery which played with the old concept of a pair of lancets and a circle to lead off into new patterns. This went on from patterns in elements such as windows into the spatial arrangements as well. Where the English had stressed the separation of their spaces, in contrast to the French elimination of them, a new idea was developed. This was to bring surprise and novelty to space as well by interlocking what would be expected to be separate or playing with vistas and perspective.

Throughout the thirteenth century the English had been building centrally planned chapter houses, either circular or polygonal, since the one at Worcester of the late twelfth century. They became much more spectacular through the century with the elaboration of the tierceron vaults, especially with a central pier, which appeared to burst into a forest of ribs at its top. In secular architecture, polygonal towers had become more prominent, as with the great Eagle tower of Caernarfon castle built by Edward I in the later 1280s. The whole castle of Caerlaverock of the later thirteenth century is in the formal plan of a triangle, an unprecedented (and distinctly impractical) conceit. The ideas of variety in plan and spatial organisation were, therefore, around at the end of the thirteenth century in England, but not used in any consistent way. Indeed the whole spirit of the later Decorated was to be original not consistent.

Exeter cathedral is one of those rare cathedrals whose surviving fabric was essentially built in one campaign from the 1280s to about 1240; like Salisbury, it straddled changes in design. The changes mostly concern the window tracery. In the choir they are based on the two lancets and a circle pattern, but are variations on this rather than repetitions. In the east window of the Lady Chapel, which projects out to the east, there are two major lancets but the circle connected to them is both much larger than the classic model and also drops well below the normal position; below it the two major lancets are separated by a lesser one. The major lancets themselves are divided, not into two lights and a circle but three and a circle; the central light being made out the intersection of the other two. The windows of the aisles and clerestory show the same sort of variations on the pattern, with over-large circles and intersecting lancets, all elaborated with cusping. The nave, built after 1320, shows the effect of the new fashion adopting the ogee curve. The designs are a riot of invention, each design different, abandoning any formality of the basic pattern.

The plan of the east end of Exeter also shows change. Fundamentally it is a repeat of Salisbury; for example, a square-ended choir and presbytery with an ambulatory around it from which a Lady Chapel opened out to the east. Ending the presbytery with a central pier and two arches makes the difference; east of these is a screen between the presbytery and the ambulatory proper. Looking east down the choir the first, central pier stands in front of the central opening to the ambulatory, and behind that is the light of the Lady Chapel, a sequence which distorts the classic symmetry and perspective. Throughout, the interior is marked by a wealth of detail of carving: the mouldings of the piers and arches of the arcade, the foliage ornamenting the corbels supporting the vault shafts, the triforium arcade and its parapet. The vault is an elaborate composition of tierceron ribs, stretching down the whole length of the choir and nave and embracing the clerestory windows. The wealth of decoration culminates in the screen dividing the choir from the crossing, which has two storeys: the lower is an arcade with an elaborate 'vault' (the space it covers is so narrow that it cannot be called a true vault) supporting an arcade of blunt ogee arches. Every fragment of the whole is carved with deep foliage and cusping; it took years to accomplish.

The later Decorated manner came together in the two decades after 1300, seen on a grand scale at the great churches of Bristol abbey (now cathedral) and Wells and Ely cathedrals. Bristol has two remarkable features. It is a hall-church, unique as such in England, giving a broad space rather than a high one. It also needed large aisle windows, which gave an opportunity for a display of tracery. This was different from the usual patterns of the period for, although it used the ogee curve, it is characterised by angularity rather then the flowing and intersecting curves found elsewhere. The hall-church also gave prominence to the vaults of the spaces, the main vessel and the aisles (75).

The main vessel has a vault with what appear to start as four tierceron ribs in each bay. Of them, alternate ones do not rise to a ridge rib, however, but split into two to create a number of diamonds, ornamented with cusps along the line of the ridge. The aisles have a unique design of vault with arches across the space which carry a 'beam' of stone across the aisle. A fan of ribs arising from the centre of the beams over the arches support an upper vault; it is an extraordinary mixture of complexity and exposure of the structure. This structure is marked, however, by a perverse over-strengthening of the arches and beams as opposed to the actual vault.

75 Bristol abbey, now cathedral, the nave; it is the only hall-church in England but both the main vessel and the aisle have remarkable patterned vaults

76 Wells cathedral: the east end. The ambulatory behind the high altar and the Lady Chapel interlock in a maze of columns

The canons of the cathedral at Wells renewed the whole east end of the cathedral in the 1320s. The work involved a new choir with an ambulatory and a Lady Chapel to the east, in the general pattern of Salisbury or Exeter, reflecting the use of the Salisbury rites at Wells, with their arrangement of chapels and altars. The result was a totally different organisation of the space. The Lady Chapel is egg-shaped in plan, blunter to the west than the east; the west end is formed by an arch carried on two piers, with arches opening to the north and south of this. The choir terminates in a three-bay screen, with two smaller piers supporting the central arch. Between the choir and the Lady Chapel the ambulatory is divided up by four piers. They are not placed in a line from north to south, but reflect the curve of the west end of the chapel. Because arches, not walls or screens, mark all the divisions, there is no clear distinction between the spaces. Viewed from within the Lady Chapel, it seems clearly to end at the two western piers, but from the aisles this is not at all clear, and the west of the chapel appears to belong to the ambulatory (76). The dissolving of perspective in the view up the choir, which is visible at Exeter, is much more extreme at Wells, because the two inner piers of the ambulatory are further apart than those of the choir termination; where you expect the piers to narrow with perspective, they widen out. The chapels at the ends of the aisles have no clear boundaries at all, except two outer walls. The vault of the choir is also notable as a magnificent exercise in its elaboration with lierne ribs to create an overall pattern, while that of the Lady Chapel creates the pattern of an elaborate star over the space, appropriate to its dedication.

The work at Ely cathedral was caused by the collapse of the central tower of the cathedral in 1322 which brought down the western bays of the choir as well. The work began promptly, partly because the bishop and monks had already started to collect funds and material for a new Lady Chapel. It involved both the features of the Decorated manner: a dramatically unexpected organisation of the cathedral space and elaborate decoration. Ever since builders had put towers at the crossing of churches, the pillars needed to support them had resulted in a narrowing of the space from the choir, nave and transepts; the tower roof or vault usually resulted in this space also being darker than the rest of the church. The bishop, sacristan and designer at Ely set about turning these facts on their head. The crossing was to be both wider than the spaces leading to it and it was to give light to the whole. The idea proceeded briskly at first, with the construction of a broad octagon of eight stone piers and arches in the space of the crossing, absorbing the first bays of the choir, transepts and nave. This presented them with the enormous problem of roofing this area, more than 20m across, too wide to span with either a vault or beams of wood. After some delay, the master carpenter designed a technological *tour de force*, a system of cantilevering a ring beam of wood out from the stone walls of the octagon. The ring beam carried eight great vertical masts of wood, which formed the frame for a tower over the crossing. Between the masts were eight windows which flooded the area with light, so that on good days, the crossing appears as a pool of light against the relative darkness of the rest of the church. Perhaps the most remarkable aspect of the scheme is that the monks carried their choir and its screens across the new space, placing their ritual needs above the whole basic point of the new work.

The three new bays of the choir were good examples of the new elaborate style of ornament, but they were over-shadowed by the display in the new Lady Chapel which followed after the rebuilding of the church. Its interior is now bare, but three features dominate it. The east window is a showy piece of tracery, again a variation on the lancet and circle pattern; the circle has become a curious lozenge, while the lancets are divided into four lights whose tracery interlocks at their head; it is impossible to admire it as a composition. The lower part of the walls are faced with rows of conjoined niches, each crowned by an arch which is a so-called 'nodding ogee', i.e. where the double curve acts in three dimensions, pushing the point out from the wall. Every inch of the arches is carved with a whole variety of detailed carving, foliage and figures. The vault is a web of ribs and bosses at the intersections.

These major projects are simply the highlights of a very fertile period of production in England. There were other individual examples of individual features. The elaboration of vaulting seems to have been particularly appreciated in western England with examples such as the new choir vault at Tewkesbury (*77*). The chance to create special designs of window tracery result in the elaborate variation of a rose in the west front at Exeter or the conceit of a heart at the centre of the west window of York Minster. Not all are so elaborate. As in the earlier thirteenth century, there were smaller churches, often parish churches where the

77 Tewkesbury abbey choir vault; such elaborate vaults were a hallmark of the west of England in the early fourteenth century

work was confined to an arcade perhaps, or new windows. Here the elaboration might be cut down further by having the same design for all the windows rather than requiring a different one for each.

From the beginning of the century, English builders made provision for towers in many churches, particularly at the main crossing. There may have been something of a coolness for them around the middle of the century because towers at a number of major churches were either not completed or left distinctly low: the west front of Wells an example of the first, the crossings at Lincoln and Salisbury of the second. This coolness, if it was such, and not just a pause to gather resources, was remedied at the end of the century. There were a number of parish churches, notably in the Oolite belt of Oxfordshire and Northamptonshire, which added spires as the century proceeded. It is fitting that the abbey church of St Frideswide in Oxford (now the cathedral) added one in the last quarter of the century, bringing the fashion into the great churches. The crossing at Lincoln was completed with a tower in the first decade of the fourteenth century. More spectacular was the spire added a little after 1300, probably before 1330, to the short tower over the crossing at Salisbury, which now makes the famous composition of the exterior (73). At Wells the eastern end was completed by the addition of a tower over the crossing.

Both of these projects placed an enormous strain on the earlier foundations; the spire at Salisbury is estimated to weigh some 6300 tons. The result is visible in the distorted piers of the crossing there, which can give serious concern to an innocent visitor who catches sight of them, and which had started before the spire was finished. The spire itself was built with as thin stonework as possible, and braced internally by an elaborate framework of wood. This was the scaffold for its construction but it ended by being suspended from the pinnacle and may have been designed to act as a pendulum to counteract the swaying of the spire in a wind; it may even act like this in fact. The pressure seems to have partially relieved by two X-shaped strainer arches across the entrances to the eastern transepts; these were effective, but a pair of arches across the north and south arches of the main crossing, added in the early fifteenth century, appears to have contributed little. From very early on the builders at Wells faced up to the same problem, by inserting the four spectacular X-shaped strainer arches into the crossing arches. An alternative was to build the spires of timber, which could achieve great heights such as the one said to be 500ft high over the crossing of Old St Paul's cathedral in London. The use of timber, but above all the sheer technological expertise displayed, unites all these with Ely.

SCOTLAND

During the twelfth century Scotland's builders had been driven by the need to accommodate the church to the new organisation, and, like the Irish, the monasteries had played a leading role in this. By the end of the century, the Scots

78 Glasgow cathedral; the north wall of the choir

participated fully in the ideas which resulted in the development of Early English Gothic, particularly those ones associated with the Cistercians. The thirteenth century saw a great expansion of wealth in the country and the buildings followed; the community of masons and builders continued to be closely associated with the English ideas. The abbey of Holyrood was rebuilt in the first quarter of the thirteenth century. Its internal three-storied elevation has the clustered piers with foliage capitals of the Early English style. The western end had two towers (one is now buried beneath the seventeenth-century palace buildings) projecting out beyond both the line of the west of the church and the side aisles, like the front of Lincoln or the later screen fronts of Salisbury and Wells. The feature which does not follow a fully English agenda is the division of the bays and the vault. The latter is a sexpartite structure that requires subsidiary shafts which rise from the sills of the gallery and divide the main bays in two; the main shafts are rather awkward; like the arcade arches, they sit uncomfortably on the massive piers.

In about 1240 the cathedral of the west of Scotland at Glasgow, perhaps in rivalry with St Andrew's in the east, embarked on a total rebuilding, starting with the choir raised up over a crypt. The choir elevation is a purely Early English composition dominated by the tall east lancets. The vaulting arrangements of the crypt are interesting. It seems obvious that they were built early in the work, because inserting them later would cause havoc to the choir above. However, they display a stellar pattern of ribs which we associate with a later fashion and they contrast with the main choir. This was left unvaulted and covered with a wooden ceiling (78). Triple shafts divide the bays and it may be that a complex vault along the lines of the crypt was planned but never achieved. The nave followed later in a slightly different design, caused by the bay intervals having been already decided when the aisle walls were laid out. The mason used this to give an elevation which stressed the vertical elements and which also divided the clerestory arcade into two arches so that the single bay was clearer. He also brought the clerestory shafts down into the triforium to link the two storeys; the result is a much more tightly defined bay.

In 1273 Devorgilla, Lady of Galloway, founded a Cistercian abbey called Sweetheart in memory of her husband John de Balliol whose heart she preserved and carried around (after his death in 1268) until her own death in 1290. The east window and those of the choir show the geometric tracery, the two lancets and a circle, of the period. The nave elevation, perhaps in line with Cistercian tradition, was of two storeys rather than three; so, too, were the cathedrals of Dunblane and Elgin, smaller dioceses than Glasgow. The wars of independence at the end of the thirteenth and beginning of the fourteenth century undoubtedly caused great economic damage to Scotland, and the building suffered. Flowing Decorated tracery of the early fourteenth century English type can be found, however, at Dunfermline abbey refectory around 1330 and in the south nave aisle of Glasgow cathedral.

IRELAND

Among the institutional problems of the medieval Church in Ireland, was the fact that the Archbishop of Dublin had two cathedrals in the city, with the resources at best for one. The older of the two, Christ Church, was given a new nave between 1215 and about 1234 with a remarkable design. It was one of those where the shafts which divide the three lights of the clerestory were joined to those which divide the three arches of the triforium passage. Its similarity of ideas with churches in the West Midlands, such as Worcester cathedral or Pershore abbey, is so close that we must conclude that the canons of Christ Church recruited a master from the region. This conclusion is reinforced by the fact that Christ Church is earlier than the other two, so it cannot have been copied from them. In this it contrasts with the west door of Kilkenny cathedral, probably of the 1240s or 1250s, which appears to have a design based on the north porch door of Wells cathedral. It is only based on Wells, for the proportions are different, but both have the general design of a double door in the archway with a quatrefoil flanked by angels in the tympanum. While this shows a clear knowledge of the Wells door, it need not have been transmitted by a mason who worked there, unlike the Christ Church design which is far too complex in its working out to have been anyone else's idea but a master's. William Marshal founded the new town of Ross at the end of the twelfth century; the parish church is presumed to date from the early thirteenth century. It has broad transepts west of the choir, which is dominated by the three high lancets in the east wall, outlined by banded shafts and mouldings; the nave has been destroyed. New Ross, along with Christ Church and St Patrick's cathedrals in Dublin and Kilkenny, show that the builders in Ireland were directly aware of the principles and designs of Early English Gothic.

These ideas were not only introduced directly into Ireland but local builders adopted them. At Christ Church cathedral, in line with other churches of the West Midlands, a common design for capitals, particularly on the arcade piers, is to have human heads peering out of the normal Early English foliage. The capitals of the cathedral at Cashel, whose choir perhaps dates from the 1230s and crossing from the 1250s, and a smaller number at Kilkenny, follow the pattern. The church of Gowran, which we have noted as being a cheaper version of the bay elevation of Kilkenny, also has the same patter of capitals. The knowledge could be fairly precise, as in the mouldings of the door to the choir at the large Augustinian abbey at Athassel, but it could be very simplified as well. The abbey of Hore, close to Cashel, is the last Cistercian abbey to be founded in Ireland, in 1272, yet its architectural details and general style, with eastern lancets and a plain arcade, could have been put up 50 years earlier.

A wider example of the spread of ideas within the community of masons in Ireland is seen in the choirs at Cashel and Kilkenny cathedrals. In both of these there is a line of high lancets, in the south and north walls; they are surmounted by little quatrefoil windows at both, although the ones at Cashel are set within niches on the inner side. The lancets are a good idea, for in Ireland a reader needs all the light he can get, but the quatrefoil windows serve no purpose except embellishment of the plain wall; they clearly link the designs of the two churches. The more general idea of the row of lancets in the choir was carried out also in the cathedral at Ardfert in Kerry and in a number of the friaries of the later thirteenth century. The similarity of ideas, and the sharing of the masons implied is interesting from the wider cultural point of view. Kilkenny was a cathedral with English bishops sited in the centre of a part of the island densely settled and controlled by English lords. Cashel also was in English Ireland, but the archbishops of the see throughout the thirteenth century were Irishmen; Ardfert was in an Irish lordship. The ideas and the men, as we saw with Boyle and the Cistercians of the early years of the century, did not observe the political or linguistic boundaries of the lordships in thirteenth-century Ireland.

From the start of the fourteenth century, we can see a similar awareness of the new Decorated manner from England. There are details such as the ballflower moulding (characteristic of western England in the first decades of the fourteenth century) at Jerpoint abbey or the pier mouldings of Mellifont in the 1320s. Obviously it is in window tracery that we would expect to see the influence shown. It is there in the east window of Tuam cathedral from before 1312; it has the typical Decorated conceit of the enlarged circle over two lancets (each with two lights) which are separated by a central light. The church of the Dominican Friars at Athenry was enlarged after 1324 with a choir extension and a new north transept; the windows in the choir are lancets with restrained Decorated tracery, but the north transept window is a large display of the style. The Franciscan friary at Kilkenny founded a fraternity in 1347 for the building of a tower between the nave and the choir, in a position characteristic of friaries elsewhere in Europe. It served to restrict access and views from the nave, which was dedicated to preaching to the public and the private choir, but the design at Kilkenny was one which was to become typical of later Irish Gothic style.

THE GERMAN EMPIRE

The Empire may have been declining as a political unity and force during the thirteenth century but it was still a reality, stretching from west of the Rhine into the lands east of the Elbe where German settlement and power was steadily advancing. This expansion was given the title of a crusade, against the pagan Slav lordships, with all the conflict that the name implies. From the eleventh century there had been signs of difference in the church building between the lands along the Rhine and west of it on the one hand, and the lands to the east on the other. The great expansion east of the Elbe had tended to distance these two regions further.

79 Strasbourg cathedral: the French style
of the Gothic nave contrasts with the late
twelfth-century German choir beyond

The Rhineland and the west

In the upper Rhine city of Strasbourg the bishop had started to rebuild the
cathedral from the east at the end of the twelfth century; in the 1230s they came
to the nave, which was finished by 1275 (79). The internal design is purely French,
with a high clerestory, each window marked by tracery of two lights and a circle
like Reims, reaching down below the springing of the vault. The triforium is
glazed and the arcade piers have shafts rising through the capitals like those of
Tours.

Outside the vault is supported by the system of flying buttresses. The west
front, started immediately after the nave was finished, and taken over from the
church authorities by the city, was even more spectacular. It adapted the delicate
and complex tracery of St Urbain at Troyes to the basic two-towered façade
with rose window of the classic French pattern. The designer, whose sketches
explaining the design to his patrons have survived, had a German name, Erwin,
but he produced a masterpiece inspired from France. The cathedral of Köln was
one of the key centres along the Rhine, in the richest city of the Empire and
with a rich and aristocratic chapter. In 1247 they resolved to reconstruct their
cathedral after a fire on such a scale that construction finally finished only in the
later nineteenth century. The choir was completed by 1322 in a purely French
style. It had a chevet, chapels and aisles; the vault was built only 2m lower than
that of Beauvais (and it did not collapse later), supported by an array of flying
buttresses.

Strasbourg and Köln were simply the two most spectacular examples of French style along the Rhine. The work on the nave of the cathedral of Metz proceeded more slowly after the start in 1239 (it was not finished until the building campaign of 1328-48) but the structure and the internal design are French. So, too, was the new Cistercian church of Altenberg near Köln, started in 1259 and dedicated in 1276. Its plan is very close to the French abbey church of Royaumont while it dominates the area through its height. Although the triforium is unglazed, it in every other respect reflects contemporary northern French style, in proportions and window tracery. Towards the mouth of the Rhine, the lordships of the present Low Countries also built according to the same style. The cathedral of Brussels, in Brabant, was laid out according to French ideas, with a chevet and unemphasised transepts, in 1220, although much of the present building is later. The French plan for great churches remained the norm in the Low Countries, as at Maastricht or Utrecht to the north.

The Eastern lands

East of the Rhine, between it and the Elbe and north of the mountains of the Rothaar and the Harz was the old core of the Empire of the Ottonians, Old Saxony. Here we can find a different view of a church. French Gothic elements are first seen here at Magdeburg, but more extensively in the church of St Elisabeth in Marburg, discussed in chapter 6. The Gothic elements are here grafted on to a hall-church, where the basic form of the church has three parallel naves (rather than a nave and two aisles) all of the same height; there is no triforium or clerestory in the central nave, the light coming entirely from the aisles through the high arcades. This is a very different idea of space from the classic northern French one. Instead of height and an organisation of the internal elevation around the three storeys of the bays, we have breadth and just the single storey for the central vessel. Hall-churches are not as high as the French Classic Gothic, and because they have no lower aisles, they cannot use the whole system of the rib vault to carry thrust out over the outer walls.

Hall-churches proved very popular in the region. Paderborn cathedral was constructed after 1231, with Minden cathedral from 1267, although rebuilt after 1945. They used the tracery windows and the capitals of the Gothic style but heavier piers and walling to compensate for the lack of flying buttresses. The builder at Minden stressed the separation of the side naves by roofing each bay at right angles to the line of the church, resulting in a series of gables. Among the later versions of the plan, the builder of the church of St Severus in Erfurt, in Thuringia, the eastern part of the region, took it further. He made the church with five parallel naves and then emphasised the whole with his piers (80). These are slim with minimal capitals so that the interior appears as a forest of them; the ribs of the vaults rising in four directions from each of them are equally prominent. This is a centralised and unified space quite unlike the directed verticality of French Gothic. The exterior is also unified, so that the mason added an elaborate, and rather bizarre, eastern front to give it a focus.

80 Erfurt; the five-aisled hall-church of St Severus

East of the Elbe, the north German plain stretches out across to Poland and the Baltic, the lands of the Teutonic Knights' crusade against the pagan Slavs. It lacks any decent building stone or quarries, so that since the twelfth century major buildings here, and in Denmark, had been made of brick. The demands, or possibilities, of brick affected the design of the churches in German Backsteingotik. It lent itself to the construction of decorated façades, using moulded bricks to create elaborate compositions. In the late twelfth century, the west front of the church of the Premonstratensian abbey of Jerichow had been built with decorated portal and arcading of brick. By the end of the thirteenth century at the Cistercian abbey of Chorin in Brandenburg, there was an elaborate western façade of brick, using French Gothic tracery motifs. Further east, in east Prussia, the Teutonic Order developed a distinctive plan for their centres, building the example of Mewe by the end of the thirteenth century (81). These were half monastery and half castle. They were built in a formal square around a cloister in the interior, but contained within a strong perimeter wall and a single defended gate. At one corner is a strong tower, reflecting their knightly, fighting role; opposite it is a principal range accommodating the chapel and chapter house for their life as monks.

By around 1300 three further features are to be found in German churches which diverge clearly from the classic French model. The first innovation is that of traceried stone spires whose designs go back to the tracery of Strasbourg, with the west tower at Freiburg started before 1280. It has a square base section which supports an octagonal one, composed of eight piers with open windows between. Above this, and a ring of pinnacles, soars a spire of open traceried stone, decorated with crockets so that the whole is an exercise in fretwork. In the second quarter of the fourteenth century work started on the massive western façade of Köln cathedral; the choir had been finished in 1322 but there was no nave. Only the lower two sections of the south tower of the twin-towered block were completed when work stopped in the early fifteenth century. It was not resumed until the later nineteenth when the whole façade was finished according to the early fourteenth-century drawing preserved in the cathedral archive. The design of the tower is articulated into sections by string courses, while the buttresses are decorated with shafts, niches and pediments. A second innovation is the use of window tracery which elaborates on the classic French lancet and circle design or the geometric patterns which followed. At Minden (1267-90) the design of the hall-church gave a series of large, gabled windows along the aisle. These were treated like small transept façades with elaborate tracery of roses cut by lancets. At Oppenheim the window tracery is developed away from the French lancet and circle type using circles and curved triangles as well as curious (to British eyes) Y-shaped elements. Stellar vaults are a third introduction, found in the eastern lands and designed with a proliferation of ribs especially liernes. They are found at Peplin before 1300 and at Kulmsee cathedral we find the use of vaults, to give stellar patterns.

Both the elaborate window tracery and the idea of creating patterns with the vault ribs were found in England in the later thirteenth century. It is therefore

81 Mewe the castle/abbey of the Teutonic Knights

very tempting to derive the German style, in two of its essential features, from the English Decorated style of the end of the thirteenth century. The problem is that there are really very few close parallels between the two countries. The tracery at, for example, Oppenheim is not particularly close to English examples; the motifs derive rather from Köln, and the flowing ogee curves of English work of *c.*1300 are missing. English vault patterns arise from a multiplication of tierceron ribs, combined with a strong ridge rib; they relate well to the long English churches. In Germany the development is much more of the stellar type of centralised patterns, based more on liernes and more suitable for use in their short, broad hall-churches. It is quite possible that the idea or stimulus to build such patterns came to Germany from England, but, if so, it was quickly transformed.

SUMMARY

The strongest impression of the period is that of the cohesion of the community of the professional builders. The twelfth century had seen the steady increase of the craftsmen's influence over that of the patrons and this continued through the thirteenth. There were individual churchmen who had a strong influence on the buildings, either as organisers or as designers. Elias de Dereham was recognised as an expert at the organisation of building, at Salisbury cathedral especially. The Ely tradition credited the cathedral sacrist (the monk in charge of the cathedral buildings) with at least the inspiration behind its great octagon. It is, however, unclear if he actually designed the solution to the problem, or just posed it; a compromise may be that he was the man who decided to hand it over to a carpenter not a mason.

The cohesion displayed by the builders poses a real problem for later interpreters of the programmes. We can see how a building such as Reims in France or Lincoln in England foreshadows later work; the ideas used in it are those which follow after it. This is unlike the impression of debate and variety displayed in the twelfth century, either in the regionality of the Romanesque or the complexity of the evolution of the Gothic style of Reims or Lincoln. What we see is an agreement about how a church should be planned and organised and coherent principles of its internal elevation and decoration. One solution to this problem is the idea of the pace-setting church, project or master. This creates a problem of communication; without the equivalent of an architectural journal being widely and regularly distributed to masons across Europe, how did they know what the latest style was? In part, of course, they did not; there are cases of 'advanced' and 'retarded' work (to use the language beloved of modern historians) to show that. This may beg the question of what is 'advanced' for it depends on the idea of typology, of placing each work along a line of development. More seriously, because the judgement is often based on details, it often obscures the overwhelming general similarity of the works in the thirteenth-century Gothic style. An alternative is to stress the probability of debate and agreement before Reims or Lincoln; to see them as the outcome of consensus not the creators of it. This explains the subsequent history but provides no account of how the debate took place or was settled in so widespread a manner.

On the other hand, the weight of the consensus and the prestige (then and now) of the French masons has led to descriptions of the period as a single style. In part this arises from the emphasis on the origins of Gothic style; tracing its roots back to a common origin in France inevitably stresses the common features of the style. However, it is surely an over-simplification to ignore the differences between the Early English or Decorated styles and those of France. Likewise, the existence of such strongly French models as Köln or Strasbourg cathedrals has obscured the independence of the builders east of the Rhine from French ideas. This independence requires a further explanation when we note the common features between England and German churches especially in the early fourteenth century: the decorative use of vaulting and free tracery; the popularity of spires. The close parallels of details, which art historians would use to trace individual masters travelling from one country to the other, are missing. The chronology is also very close, so it is difficult to say whether one was the progenitor of the other. Again we are confronted with the vagueness, so unsatisfactory to those who wish to explain these things, of a consensus and a community, rather than one or more individual masters.

However the consensus occurred, there can be little dispute about the size of the achievement of the thirteenth-century builders. On the grand scale, there is the achievement of the height of the French churches, not to be excelled until the later nineteenth century. Parallel to their height was the formidable logic of their unity in plan and elevation. In England there was the same clarity of vision, adapting the Gothic style to the Romanesque proportions they inherited, rather than replacing them; it led on to the spatial ingenuity at the beginning of the fourteenth century. In both cases we see great practical engineering skill, not least in coping with collapse and disaster, ever present in medieval buildings. The device of the strainer arches at Salisbury and (more successfully) at Wells to counter the weight of the new towers is impressive. So, too, was the response to the collapse of the high vault at Beauvais in a storm in 1282. The mason doubled the number of bays and their supports, but also, as Mark has shown, reinforced the flying buttresses at just those points which his research with photo-elastic modelling predicted were weaknesses. How he was able to detect these points, short of sending a man up to the roof to watch the buttresses sway about him and note them, we do not know.

The skill levels were extraordinary on the smaller scale as well. Perhaps more in England than in France the effects depended on the ability of masons to carve an endless series of variations of foliage capitals. Everywhere the elevations depended on repeated mouldings up shafts and piers or around the arches. These required a whole series of stones placed on top of each other, cut to precisely the same profile, because our eye will detect easily any variation in their vertical lines. The process is relatively straightforward in principle: the stone is cut to a horizontal level and a profile, cut in a template, allows the cutter to mark it out on the level stone. A plumb bob can then keep the lines of the cutting vertical and at right angles to the level surface. What is impressive is how considerable numbers of men were trained to cut to the precision required as a matter of course. It is no surprise that we can see a new emphasis on systematisation of the stone cutting during the period. It became more common to have the courses of the same height and the new bar tracery lent itself to being designed with a number of similar stones to be assembled together.

8

LATE GOTHIC

The later stages of movements generally receive less attention than the more glamorous innovations and this has applied to the church buildings of 1340-1540. Building historians have taken their cue from documentary historians who, until the 1960s, tended to dismiss the fourteenth and fifteenth centuries as a period of gloom and decline and have been slow to pick up on the change of mood after then. The fourteenth century has inevitably been seen by later generations in terms of disaster for it is the century of the Black Death and the Hundred Years' War when the population of Europe shrank to a little over half its earlier numbers, with consequent massive economic dislocation. In this, historians sometimes missed the key point: that, in spite of the problems and disasters, which would have caused a lesser civilisation to collapse, Europe not only survived but emerged the stronger. The fifteenth century saw Europeans on the verge of world domination. More attractively, the fourteenth century was one of great innovation and achievement in the world of church building.

The economic power in society shifted away from the great land owners, whether lay lords or the great ecclesiastical corporations. Merchants, the lesser lords and skilled craftsmen in turn were the gainers as real wages rose and agricultural prices dropped in the face of the population fall. Just as renting out their land to more flexible and entrepreneurial tenants became the solution to the management of great estates, so the structure of the great building works changed. In place of direct control, it became more common to employ a general contractor, who managed the design, the supplies and the wages as a single enterprise. As well as these new contractors, we find a greater emphasis on the status and control of the masons and builders. This is the period when we begin to find written descriptions and definitions of master masons, carpenters, etc., as opposed to lesser grades and to the lodges as permanent upholders of standards and restrictive employment practices. The period was also one of political and social tensions; the Hundred Years' War was only one of the many conflicts of the time. War was if anything more destructive in the fourteenth and fifteenth centuries than earlier and to it were added a series of peasants' revolts. Literacy increased in Europe and there was a rise of vernacular literatures to replace the universal Latin and French of the thirteenth century. Inevitably these linguistic shifts have been seen in terms of a rise in general cultural division and this has been aligned with the rise of conflict to create a view of the period as one of growing nationalism.

GERMANY

The late Middle Ages saw the Germans adopt a new style of church building, differing from the work of earlier builders in plan, structure and elevation. As we have come to expect with a new style, the individual, diagnostic features by which we recognise it are to be found independently before they come together to make the style. The hall-church is found in the earlier thirteenth century; traceried stone spires from the 1280s; stellar or patterned vaults and elaborate window tracery from just before 1300. It is not until about a generation after 1300, however, that we can see these combined. Traditionally this was explained by attributing the creation of the new style to the genius of a father and son, Heinrich and Peter Parler.

A sculpture in Prague cathedral bears an inscription identifying it as the portrait head of Peter Parler, son of Heinrich Parler. It further states that he was summoned to the cathedral from Gmund by the Emperor Charles IV in 1356 and that he worked on it and other named projects until his death in 1399. This is linked to a statement that the master of work at Gmund in Swabia was called Heinrich. The identification of the masters of two major works in the new style, at Gmund and Prague, has proved irresistible. The work at Gmund did not start until 1315, with the western façade; the nave does not seem to have been begun until about 1330 and the choir not until 1351. The west front is unremarkable, the nave a full exercise in a hall-church, which is the first in the region, marking a significant spread of the form (*82*).

The columns of the nave are slim with thin ring-capitals separating them from the later vault. The windows in the aisles have alternate tracery patterns based on the use of curved triangles and diamonds with cusping. The plan of the choir breaks with the classic French Gothic plan where the outer bays of the ambulatory reflect the pattern of the bays around the apse. At Gmund an ambulatory of seven bays surrounds an apse of only three; the chapels are flattened in plan, fitting between the buttresses around the outer wall. When seen from the outside (*83*) the flat roof over the ambulatory is hidden so that it appears as two tiers of windows, the ambulatory and the clerestory, separated by a pierced stone balustrade. The choir vault is also later, but the windows of the ambulatory are good examples of the same cusped tracery as the nave. The plan of hall nave and apsidal choir of the Gmund type proved very popular in Germany in the next 150 years.

82 Schwabisch Gmund interior of Holy Cross church from the west; the nave and choir are of the
fourteenth century but the vaults are later

83 Schwabisch Gmund: the outside of the east end

84 Prague cathedral: the choir interior

The cathedral of Prague is interesting in its own right (and not just as a type-site) because of the extent of our information on the masters and the process of its construction. It was started because the Emperor Charles IV had made Prague his centre and had secured its promotion to the seat of an archbishopric in 1344. The emperor supported the construction, and negotiated for a French master, Mathew of Arras, to start the work. He laid out the plan of the choir on the classic French plan, with a semicircle of discrete chapels around the ambulatory. From the details of the masonry we can see that he had proceeded to erect the arcade piers and arches in the apse and the first two straight bays of the choir, but he died in 1352. There was then a gap before the young Peter Parler was summoned from Gmund and his father's tutelage in 1356, which gives us the exercise of detecting the change from the masonry. Parler was bound to continue the basic scheme of an aisled basilican church with flying buttresses on the French model he inherited, but seems to have made a number of drastic alterations to the design.

He completed the last three straight bays of the choir, changing the design of the bases, shafts and capitals, simplifying and strengthening them; he separated the shaft mouldings from those of the arches. His aim was to stress the individuality of the parts of the design more than Mathew. He created a glazed triforium which consisted of a low balcony and arcade, topped by a string course between it and the clerestory windows (84). The windows match the arcade in effect. Not only are the windows a grand display of tracery but their side lights are angled in to the face of the piers on either side; the whole window resembles an open triptych.

The angle is emphasised by the strong string course at the top of the triforium arcade which breaks out in a point to cross the piers, stressing the horizontal divisions of the zones; a similar string course exists in the choir at Gmund. The main vessel has a vault with a pattern of parallel pairs of Y-shaped (triradial in the jargon) ribs springing from the piers. They do not meet at the ridge of the vault which is unmarked, either by an English-type ridge rib or even by the apex of cross arches; as if to stress this there is a line of bosses in the centre of the webs along the ridge line. The different internal spaces, the Wenceslas chapel, the Sacristy and the south porch are all distinguished by various forms of stellar, centralised vaults. The sacristy has a pendant in the western bay; the south porch a skeleton vault, where the web between the ribs is omitted. The porch is a complex space in itself, with a wide triple arcade to the outside narrowing down to a pair of doors to the inside.

There are two problems with the traditional story. The first is that it is not quite the classic of the equation of document and architectural attribution that it might be. The inscription at Prague tells us the Peter Parler was the son of Heinrich Parler of Köln and came from Gmund; it seems likely that his father was the Heinrich recorded as master there. On the one hand, at Prague we can see links with Gmund in the tracery and the string course. On the other, academics have tried to find physical evidence of links between the work of Heinrich at Gmund and work at Köln, but without success. The inscription also names Peter as the master at Kolin-an-der-Oder where a choir was added to the nave. Here, however, the plan and structure are much more straightforward and traditional. The vault is a plain quadripartite one over a two-storey elevation; the choir has the Gmund plan of ambulatory chapels. At Prague we can see the master's known background in the masonry but not at Gmund: at Kolin the same man produces a very different design from his work at Prague. Tracing the individual through parallels in the design is not a simple matter. The second issue is that of chronology and the invention and spread of the German late Gothic style. All the elements were present by 1300, yet the work of Heinrich Parler at Gmund, the nave which is supposed to mark the beginning, does not start until 1330. The new style spreads very quickly; the nave of St Mary's church at Soest (1331–76) has slender, elegant piers whose shafts blend into the vault ribs without the interruption of any capitals at the springing of the arcade arches and Soest is in Westphalia, home of the hall-church. As with the combining of ideas which went up to make the classic Gothic of France about 1200, it looks much more likely that the ideas for German late Gothic were generally current before the work of the Parlers. Their work may be better seen as excellent examples of these ideas in practice than as the start of them. The overwhelming impression of the work of early and mid-fourteenth century Germany is that it breaks with the classic French pattern as seen in Germany at Köln and Strasbourg. Instead the inspiration comes from the work done further east in the years before 1300. The Francophile Emperor Charles IV may have brought Mathew of Arras to lay out his new cathedral in Prague in the French manner, but it was completed in a German style. This was the style which we find in the lands of the Empire for the next 200 years.

The immediate sign of this is the popularity of the hall-church, which is the plan of the great majority of German late Gothic churches. Combined with the choir and ambulatory with its ring of narrow chapels like Schwabisch Gmund it provided a good balance between the need for a wide open space for the congregation and the desire for private chapels for individual or group patrons. The hall was normally three vessels wide, but it could be of five vessels, as at St Severus in Erfurt, built on either side of 1300. The space of a hall-church is centralised rather than divided and longitudinal as in a basilican design. The lack of a storey above the arcade diminishes the stress on the bay and tends also to unify the space. As a result, we find the German vaults doing two things. They are the focus of decoration, for the bay elevations cannot provide many possibilities but do not lend themselves to longitudinal patterns (as in England) but to centralised ones. Instead they are usually stellar and net vaults, reflecting the space below them. In a hall-church the thrusts of the vaults and roof are carried directly to the outer walls; there is no need for the elaboration of flying buttresses to support them. The German buttresses are therefore found either against the outer walls or else, as with the Gmund-type choir plan, absorbed into a line of chapels built between them.

Counteracting the unified shape of the church were the towers, which were a further prominent feature of German style. The hall-church plan did not lend itself to crossings and central towers, so the towers are placed to flank the naves,

85 Strasbourg:
the cathedral still
dominates the city

most often to the west but also to the north or south. The spire of Freiburg and
the elaborate stages and buttresses of its tower and that of Köln were the basis for
many similar structures (*85*).

Late in the fourteenth century work started on a south tower at Prague. It was
followed by the south tower of St Stephen's cathedral in Vienna, where work had
started on the nave in 1359; the tower was completed in 1450; both are marked
by the open tracery work. The culmination, perhaps of these towers, is that of
the Minster at Ulm whose west tower occupies the western bay of the nave.
It was started about 1390, like Köln before the nave was finished; the city may
have wished for a grand symbol of their opposition to the power of the Dukes
of Wurttemberg who had defeated their militia in 1388. The first three stages are
square with tracery like Strasbourg in front of the wall faces and windows. Above
this, the next stage is an open octagon, flanked by open staircases at the angles like
those of Prague's south tower. It was meant to be surmounted by an openwork
spire but work stopped without it being finished. This was finally done in the
nineteenth century; as at Köln the design drawing survived and was followed, to
create the highest spire in Europe.

The trend for hall-churches dictated the form of internal elevations, for they
really only permitted piers and arcades. The need to stress the feeling of a wide
open space meant that the piers were kept as thin as possible and the arches of
the arcade also relatively plain. The capitals of the piers were often omitted, which
again avoided drawing attention to the piers; the arches seem simply to grow out
of the piers in a single, uninterrupted line. On the other hand, the hall-church
provided great opportunities for elaboration in the tracery of the wide aisle
windows. Another way to give decoration was in the provision of lesser features.
Porches were a favourite example of this: not only were they elaborate, as at Prague
or at Ulm, but they could take different forms, such as the triangular one at Erfurt

86 Kutna Hora; the elaborate vault of *c.*1500

cathedral, decorated with figure sculpture. Similarly, in the cloister at Magdeburg at some time in the late Middle Ages was added a small projection, now called the Tonsur; it has a display of skeletal vaulting as well as traceried windows.

During the century after 1350 there were no systematic changes to the German late Gothic style; the individual churches were variations on the same themes. At the end of the fifteenth century there is a phase of what we might call Baroque Gothic, an intense interest in fantastic elaboration of the earlier decorative motifs. This is confined purely to decoration of individual features without any change in the overall plan or elevation design. The main concentration is on the principal area of the vault, the focus of earlier elaboration. In the so-called folded vaults, the cells are set at sharply pitched angles and the ribs hidden so that the effect is of folded paper in stone. The main effort concentrates on elaboration of the rib patterns. There are remarkable looping ribs criss-crossing over the vault surface, so that it is impossible to see the actual structural scheme (86). The looping rib patterns seem based on making the lines flow naturally and this can be carried further when ribs are given knobs and spurs to make them look like branches of trees.

In contrast there is a renewed interest in the idea of skeletal ribs. Some vaults break the canonical rule which had dominated vault construction and rib patterns for centuries and have the springing of the ribs from the same pier set at different heights. They employ what is the reverse of the twelfth-century device of stilting the narrow arches upwards; they have the wider ones springing from below with all having a similar profile, but the effect is remarkable to someone used to the Gothic norm. The capitals may not only be omitted but the ribs may be prolonged so that they seem either to cross each other or to pass through the pier only to be cut off on the other side. The whole effect of these developments is both restless and disturbing.

ENGLAND

The story of late Gothic in England is concerned with the practice of what has been known since the earlier nineteenth century as Perpendicular Gothic. By the 1320s and 1330s, the Decorated manner in England had reached remarkable level of elaboration. The insistence on the individuality of each project and the complexity of detail had combined to produce a style which was extremely expensive in terms of skilled labour and which could be tedious in its excesses. The result was a reaction. At Canterbury there are works which show tracery in which the curves of the Decorated manner are no longer flowing but are defined with angular cusps and lines. This was carried to London, probably by Michael and Thomas of Canterbury, working above all at Westminster palace in the 1320s, where they continued with their spiky, angular tracery. At the front of St Stephen's chapel Thomas placed the large west window in a rectangular frame with turrets up the side and a horizontal arcade over the apex. William Ramsey from Norwich rebuilt the chapter house of St Paul's cathedral in London, starting in 1332. Here, as well as a door placed in a rectangular frame, the vertical mullions of the window tracery above are carried down to link with the verticals of panelling below the sill. These are all features which would be part of the Perpendicular style, but they are not a full exercise of it. What they show is that by 1330, there were people who both rejected the flowing patterns of the Decorated and thought that a rectilinear design was better.

The church where these ideas were transformed into the basis for the total design of a church was at the abbey of Gloucester. Because the achievements of successive abbots of Gloucester have been recorded, we have a clear idea of the chronology of the fourteenth-century building at the church. Under Abbot Thokay who died in 1329 the south aisle was rebuilt (starting c.1318): crucially, in 1327 he accepted the body of Edward II, after his murder, for burial. In 1330 Edward III carried out a coup against his mother and her lover; a proper tomb was built over Edward's grave and pilgrims came to it. Abbot Wigmore rebuilt the south transept; the local chronicle records that money came from the royal tomb and that the work took six years of his abbacy before he died in early 1337; it can thus be dated to the building seasons of 1331-36 inclusive. His successor, Adam de Staunton, ruled from 1337-51; in his time the choir was built; it is recorded that the work included both its vaults and stalls which shows that it was finished by 1351 because internal woodwork like stalls would be the last parts to be put in place. The high altar and the presbytery (again its stalls are mentioned) were built under Abbot De Horton between 1351 and 1365. The design of the choir runs unbroken through to the presbytery; it would have been clear what it was to look like before the choir was finished in 1351. It was followed by a new north transept that is precisely dated; it was started in 1368 and finished in 1373.

The first two works are the south aisle and the tomb of Edward II. The south aisle was carried out in the Decorated manner; its windows in particular are festooned with the typical motif of the Decorated churches of western England, the ballflower. The vaults to the east are also decorated with this motif but, in a clear indication that cost was important in the project, this was abandoned in the western bays. The tomb of a king, and Edward III's father, was almost certainly made by a court craftsman, possibly away from Gloucester because it did not fit into its position well when it was installed. Cost cutting, seen in the south aisle but not in the tomb, remained a crucial part of the next building project, which was to rebuild the south transept, thus making it a more difficult engineering problem than it might have been (87). Instead of sweeping the old masonry away and starting anew, the south-east and south-west turrets were retained, which meant supporting them when the south wall was taken down. The new south wall reused many of the stones of the old one; some, such as the voussoirs of the arch of the old windows were reset in something like their old position but re-cut to fit the new great south window. At the same time raking buttresses had to be incorporated into the design of the east and west walls to support the crossing tower. The vault was one with a pattern of tierceron and lierne ribs

87 Gloucester cathedral; the south transept from the south west. The raking strut in masonry visible in the west wall is part of the engineering required to support the tower during construction; the great south window is the earliest full Perpendicular design

88 Gloucester cathedral choir; the first fully developed Perpendicular composition

but no expensive bosses at their intersections. At one point in the east wall, a miscalculation of the vault's curve meant that, had the ribs been carried down as originally designed, they would have met the wall in a window. They had to be built horizontally to come into the wall above the window. These problems and the range of day-to-day decisions required make it very unlikely that the master could have been absent for much of the time of the work.

The master of the south transept produced a design in which the windows had tracery patterns composed largely of straight lines, dominated by vertical mullions. This pattern was expanded to encompass the whole interior elevations of the walls. The mullions were carried down through the sills of the windows to form blank arcades. The inner face of the walls was refaced or rebuilt to give an overall pattern of blank arcading. The story continues with the choir and presbytery (*88*). The rebuilding of these followed straight on from the completion of the transept and was carried on until the north transept was built in 1368-73. If the south transept was practice, the choir had shown by 1351 what the new manner was all about. It retained the three-storied elevation of its Romanesque predecessor; the arcade and triforium were cut out from the old masonry. The triforium was a screen in front of the old gallery with a newly built, high clerestory above it. All three storeys are connected not just by the shafts on the piers but by the vertical mullions in the openings and the blank arcaded panelling. There is no carving; all the detail so beloved of the Decorated manner, is omitted in favour of the abstract lines of the panels. The only stone decoration comes in the vault. It is a flat tunnel covered by a maze of ribs and bosses but with two dominant lines. The flatness gives a stress across the space; the triple ridge ribs counter this with a strong axis along the church. The result is a very straightforward composition of vertical lines, with minor horizontal ones, framing up, across and along a simple, open, rectangular space. The whole culminates in the great east window of the presbytery, composed of tiers of high rectangular panels filled with figures, which occupies the whole of the east wall. The background colours, blue and red, are the costliest to produce in glass – the economy of the transept has been truly thrown off – and the panels are ideally suited to rows of figures painted on the glass. These are a representation of the tiers in the hierarchy of the universe, from the lords temporal at the base (shown by their coats of arms) through the lords spiritual to the saints and heaven above. A final invention in the church is provided in the eastern cloister of the 1370s. Here there is a new kind of vault, the fan vault, composed of half cones of stone which support flat lozenge-shaped areas of vault between them. Again, the cones and the flat lozenges are covered by a regular pattern of tracery. The change from the economy of the south transept to the choir and presbytery is to be explained by increased money, either because Abbots De Staunton and De Horton were far greater spendthrifts than Abbot Wigmore, or (more likely) because the abbey had more to spend. A major reason for the new choir was to provide a splendid backdrop for Edward II's tomb. Edward III visited it several times and he was a man who rewarded loyalty such as that shown by Gloucester in risking the wrath of Isabella and her lover Mortimer, when they took his body in for burial. The continuity of ideas shown between the transept and the choir and then the completion of the presbytery exactly to the choir design argues for the continuity of the same master.

All this is relevant to the identification of the mason in charge. It has become the accepted view that he was mason from the royal works in London, either William Ramsey or Thomas of Canterbury. Both of these men were involved in other projects during the time, 1331-36, when the transept was being constructed, but it is said that he acted like a modern architect – in overall charge, but not present at the works more than occasionally. This runs counter to the evidence of the *ad hoc* solutions to problems such as the re-working of stone or the rib design. The new work shows a series of on-the-spot solutions; it is difficult to see how an occasional visiting mason could have controlled the new transept work in particular and this is where the key design innovations were made; the choir follows on from it. Finally, the elaborate vault pattern argues for a west of England man not a royal mason (77). The actual tomb of Edward II is likely to be London work; it is in the spikiest Decorated manner and this is the style that a royal mason from London would have been likely to have used for the transept.

The new Perpendicular work at Gloucester, and as practised later, rests very largely on the designs of the elevations of the buildings which were organised so that all the elements stressed the vertical and horizontal lines and framework of the design. There is a general trend towards simple rectangular open spaces as opposed to the occasionally complex plans of the Decorated manner, but there is no such drastic re-organisation as the adoption of the hall-church in Germany. Structurally, while there are developments in the realm of vaulting, they are neither universally applied nor are they associated with the start of the 'style' and cannot be regarded as part of its definition. If we are to try and make a rule that a style needs to be definable through structure, plan and elevation, then the Perpendicular of England must be termed, in the terms of the introduction to this book, as a manner, not a style. This makes it different from the story of German late Gothic, and also explains why it is easier to define its origin. Because it is a coherent aesthetic idea, primarily applied to the elevations and decoration it is easier to define than a style, composed of a combination of lines of thought which come together to give a new idea of the whole church: plan, spatial organisation and structure, as well as decoration. Interestingly, however, the pattern of development and chronology of England and Germany show parallels.

In England during the 1350s the new Perpendicular manner was used in a number of new church projects, two of them linked to Bishop Edington of Winchester. Before his death in 1366 he had started to rebuild the nave of his cathedral from the west, pulling down the two Romanesque towers and substituting a relatively plain front. Under his patronage the lower parts of the west front, including the west porch, and the first bays at the west were rebuilt. The west porch has canted walls to increase the sense of depth (like the use of space at Prague or in a Decorated church) but the panelled tracery is Perpendicular like Gloucester. The nave bays were not fully rebuilt, but cut from the Romanesque fabric, like Gloucester but

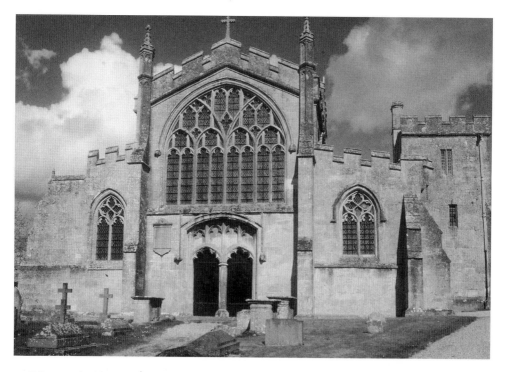

89 Edington church, west front; the central window is Perpendicular in design, the side ones Decorated, yet they were built together

more drastically. The walls were taken down to the level of the springing of the gallery arches, which became the level of the top of the horizontal framing of the main arcade and the sill of the clerestory windows. Edington church was very different in conception, a small church for a community of canons set in the village of his birth, later changed to the (for England) exotic Order of Bonshommes. It is a cruciform church with an aisled nave but unaisled choir and transepts. The exterior is of plain, but excellent, smooth masonry, the walls unrelieved except for slight buttresses and ornamental battlements at the top. The interior is unvaulted and the nave has a simple internal elevation of two storeys: decoration is confined to the window tracery. The whole took only nine years to build, from 1352-61 (an almost exact contemporary of the Gloucester presbytery) and the occurrence of the same masons' marks around Edington church argues that the same group of masons was employed throughout the project. The windows have a mixture of tracery designs. The main east and west ones have Perpendicular tracery, while the choir side windows have the uniform reticulated tracery originating earlier but used because of its uniformity in the Perpendicular; only the aisle windows of the west front really look Decorated (*89*). Also of the 1350s is the Perpendicular work found in the Deanery and chapter house at Windsor castle and the south cloister of Westminster abbey; the royal works picked it up quickly. Outside the major centres we can find Perpendicular work at Donington in Lincolnshire, where Henry, Lord Percy gave money towards the cost of the work in 1351, and at Sandon in Hertfordshire (a manor of St Paul's cathedral) where the contract for the work was issued in 1348 but modified, perhaps after a pause during the onset of the plague.

Not all the new projects of the 1350s, even major works which might be expected to be up to date, were carried out in the Perpendicular manner. In the case of the west front of Exeter, it was started in 1346 when the Gloucester choir was half built so its fame may not have spread. The design also consists of rectangular blocks with tiers of sculpted figures; the central window is placed in a rectangular frame, but the tracery is a typical piece of Decorated work. It is as much evidence of the spirit of reaction to the decorated as of its continuity. The central tower of Worcester cathedral is later, started in 1357 and completed in 1374, yet it is not Perpendicular. The Gloucester invention of the fan vault was not taken up with great enthusiasm; it was not used over the main vessel of a church until the choir of Sherborne abbey in the middle of the fifteenth century. There is little sign of any 'transitional' work, other than some small windows where the tracery is not thoroughly dominated by vertical lines. This is because the Perpendicular was based on the one idea, of a simplified vertical design, not a number of different ideas; it is difficult to imagine a partly Perpendicular church.

Through the later part of the fourteenth century, after the crisis of the Black Death, the Perpendicular manner became accepted as the normal one; it was used in all major projects. The nave of Winchester was nearly completed by Edington's successor as bishop from 1366–99, William of Wykeham (90). The work was essentially a continuation of the scheme of his predecessor's; a re-cutting of the older building with the same rather heavy mouldings and proportions.

He accompanied the work at the cathedral with his two academic foundations: New College, Oxford, and Winchester College, both examples of the same style. The archbishops and canons of York replaced the eastern end of the Minster in the 40 years after 1361. The eastern bays (built first) have the notable feature of an outer and an inner skin of tracery in the clerestory: the outer vertical mullions in a square frame alone, the inner with full Perpendicular tracery. The great east window was the only one larger than that of Gloucester. The nave of Canterbury cathedral was fully rebuilt, starting about 1370; money was being gathered for the project in 1369–70. The result was a magnificent example of the new manner. The arcade is high in proportion to the rest and appears thin so that the aisles are very visible from the main vessel: the triforium and clerestory are connected by the mullions of the former running into the panelling of the latter. The vault gives a strong closure to the design, with the prominent springings and tierceron ribs.

It is interesting to compare the fourteenth-century experience in England and Germany in two ways; the historiography and the actual process. Both have been attributed to individuals: the Parlers for Germany; a court mason (William Ramsey or Thomas of Canterbury) working at Gloucester for England. The achievements of the Parlers at Gmund and Prague were great but they were at best producing fine examples of trends already established and even assembled elsewhere. The only reason for identifying the designer of Gloucester as a court

90 Winchester nave north wall

mason is that it is considered that the designer of such a building, the origin of a style which was to dominate English building for 200 years, must have come from London, the hub of all style, just as the Parlers can be associated with a great cathedral commissioned by the emperor. Underlying both stories is the assumption that innovation in church style arises at the centre of power. In England there is a second example of the result of a zeal for attribution; much of the later fourteenth-century work is attributed to Henry Yevele. His name has emerged because of his royal commissions – royal work is well recorded – and then a sort of balling process has occurred. Works are attributed to him, sometimes on dubious grounds, but this establishes his reputation as an important player; other works are then associated with him, and so his reputation grows, pulling in more attributions. In terms of the process of development, in Germany the new style combined ideas already in existence and took at least a generation to be settled. In England, where the Perpendicular was essentially an aesthetic reaction to the Decorated manner, it is possible to identify the time and place where the new principles were put in place. Combining the disparate techniques and elements of the German late Gothic style was a much more complex process to accept and implement than a set of aesthetic ideas.

Both late German Gothic and English Perpendicular show parallels in the history after the late fourteenth century. The most striking is the lack of any change in the features of the buildings through time. As in Germany, the fifteenth century in England is marked by a shift in the sort of churches being built; the great cathedrals and abbeys saw little work during the period, while the parish and collegiate churches dominated. On the positive side, there is a shared enthusiasm for towers. In the great churches of England the transepts continued to be separated from the rest of the church and consequently the crossing was also important. Crossings were stressed in a series of cathedral crossing towers from the fourteenth to the sixteenth centuries, such as: Wells (1315-22), Worcester (1357-74) York (early fifteenth century), Durham (1465-75), Bristol (1466-71), Norwich spire (late fifteenth century) and Canterbury (1490-1503). To these may be added west towers at Wells (1385-95), Beverley (1380-1430), the south-west tower at York (after 1431) and Canterbury (also the south-west – 1423-34). Uniquely, Fountains abbey received a tower at the north end of the north transept, probably because the crossing was judged to be too weak to support one on its pier, between 1495 and 1526. Towers are a theme which connects the other main churches of the Perpendicular. Western towers mark out many of the major parish churches and are also found in colleges. In these last, the pattern developed where the tower was built over the entrance to the quadrangular space of the college and commonly housed the warden or master of it, so that he could monitor who was coming in and out.

Parishes were a very powerful facet of late medieval life (*3, 97, 98* and *99*). The focus of building in their churches was often the nave: the domain of the laity rather then the body, usually monastic, who appointed the priest and managed the chancel. The rich towns saw the construction of fine parish churches. Some were great churches, as big as small cathedrals, which indeed some of them became in post-medieval times, such as Nottingham or Manchester, while the grandeur of St Mary Redcliffe stands as a reminder of the wealth of Bristol merchants. The same could be found in a city such as York where the ancient parishes had proliferated. Here the smaller parish churches were the recipients of the burghers' benefactions, not the more aristocratic Minster; at All Saint, Pavement, the result was an innovative tower with an open-work octagonal upper stage (99). Rural wealth was also reflected in the churches. The space may not have been as overtly open and unified as the German hall-church but the Perpendicular manner was well suited to the parish church also. The high narrow piers of the arcades opened out the space, while the rows of repeated windows lit it splendidly; the four-centred arch commonly used for the arcades raised the arch higher then the thirteenth-century designs.

The English parish churches in particular show a strong tendency towards regional designs. In some cases this is due to the nature of local building resources, just as the brick Gothic is common in the north and east of Europe where good building stone is rare. Hence we find ornamental flint work mostly in the similarly stone-poor east of England, as opposed to the splendid display of stone churches along the Oolite belt from the south-west to the East Midlands. The patterns of towers also vary regionally: the spires of the East Midlands contrasting with towers in the south-west. Within the latter, the towers of Gloucestershire are different from those of Somerset, themselves different from those of Devon and, likewise, of Cornwall. A number of contracts survive in which the patrons specify to the masons, either that they shall view other churches before settling on a design, or that the new work shall be as good as (or better than) a named church. In these cases the places named are almost always quite near the new site, reinforcing the local character. Parish churches rarely had the resources for vaulting the nave, but in the late Middle Ages this necessity was made into a virtue by the marvellous series of decorative timber roofs, especially in eastern England.

The idea of the college is very typical of the late medieval church and covered a much wider spectrum of purpose than the educational, with which we now associate them. The key was personal charity; they replaced the monasteries of the twelfth century and the friaries of the thirteenth as the most popular recipient of benefactions. At their heart lay the practice of saying masses for the souls of the patron and his family but other functions were grafted on. Broadly speaking these were either the provision of accommodation for some group judged to be in need and worthy of it and the patronage of education, whether at school or university. In each case the college required one or more ranges of lodgings for accommodation, along with a common chapel for worship and a hall for food, to emphasise the communal nature of their life. They took as their overall model the idea of the monastic cloister, setting the buildings around a formal courtyard, entry to which was usually confined to the one gate. The individual lodgings related to those provided for the retainers in a late medieval castle or for minor officials such as the vicars choral who deputised for the grander canons of the cathedral.

An excellent example, combining many of the functions usually separated, is to be found at Ewelme in Oxfordshire, founded by the De la Pole Earls of Suffolk. The parish church was rebuilt between about 1432 and c.1450; it provides a large, light space for both the parishioners and the chapel for the almshouse attached. This was built a little later, from c.1437 to 1442, brick and timber houses around a small cloistered court with a well at the centre, to accommodate 13 poor men, presumably former servants of the De la Poles, and two priests. One of these was the master of the college, the other taught in the school which forms the third unit in the complex. The old men, along with the priests, were required to pray daily for the souls of the De la Poles in the chapel.

Colleges varied greatly in their elaboration and the resources spent on them, as well as in their purposes. At one end were the magnificent royal educational foundations such as Eton and King's College, Cambridge. In Oxford, following New College, founded by Bishop Wykeham, the college design, such as at All Souls or Magdalen (1474-90), favoured a formal square enclosure with a tower over the gate for the master, the hall and chapel on one side and rooms for the fellows and scholars around the other three sides. The main expenditure went into the chapels; the one at Merton receiving a central tower from 1448-52; Magdalen had two towers, the traditional one at the entrance to the quadrangle and the bell tower built around 1500. At the other end of the spectrum were the smaller colleges and almshouses founded by merchants for the sick, poor and elderly of their towns.

The colleges in the wider sense were the churches where the last phase of the English grand medieval church building is to be found. England saw a burst of elaborate decoration in the decades around 1500, like Germany, and also focused on the decorative possibilities of vaults. The choir of Sherborne abbey saw the first surviving building, in progress by 1437 and finished by 1459, of a fan vault wide enough to span the central vessel of the choir; a more elaborate example spanned the choir in the last quarter of the fifteenth century. This may have sparked off an interest in the decorative qualities of the design, which centred on the ornament of the cones of the vault and on the means of infilling the flat spaces between them. By their nature, the fan vaults did not need arches across the width of the space to be vaulted because they relied on the stability of the cones and the stones wedged between them, but this conflicted with the traditional division of the bays. In 1423, the University of Oxford started to construct a building for teaching, the Divinity School (91).

In 1444 they decided to raise this to a two-storey building by adding a library to accommodate Duke Humphrey of Gloucester's gift of books. This was still not finished in 1479 when a major gift of money prompted the University to change the scheme again; they decided to insert a vault over the ground floor Divinity School. This was a difficult task: it had to be fitted around the existing windows and made extremely flat so as not to encroach on the space of the library above, but William Orchard accomplished it. He both blended in his new work with the old and produced an elaborate vault decorated by large carved stones springing

91 Oxford, the Divinity School; the east side showing the panelling on the buttresses, omitted on the west side to save money

from the voussoirs of the cross arches, from which rise the cones of a fan vault, and which are also carried down to form pendant structures decorated with figures. A similar vault crowns the space of the chapel which Henry VII willed to replace the thirteenth-century Lady Chapel at Westminster abbey in 1507. Here the cross arches are made to seemingly disappear behind the pendant fans which arise from them and the whole is carved in elaborate detail. The elaboration in the church is reflected in the elaboration of the bay windows of Thornbury castle, also of the early sixteenth century.

FRANCE

The change to German late Gothic or to the Perpendicular manner in England was a more drastic one then we can see in France during the fourteenth century. Here, there was a change, to the Flamboyant, but this is even more a question of changes in elements of the decoration of the elevation alone. The core of this new manner was the adoption, as in Germany, of the curvilinear tracery for windows developed in England by the beginning of the fourteenth century; the term Flamboyant refers to the flame-like patterns developed and commonly used, but not exclusively so. Along with this went a number of other individual features: the

92 Villefranche de Rouergue, Carthusian monastery cloister; fifteenth-century cloister windows

practice of eliminating the capitals at the springing of arch and vault shafts so that they seemed to simply grow out of the pier; the elaboration of wall surfaces with niches and plastic ornament, and new forms of arch, base and shaft mouldings. They were not accompanied by changes in either the structure or the plan of the churches; in the terms outlined it is a classic change of manner rather than style.

One of the consequences of this is that it is difficult to pin down precisely what constitutes a church built in this manner and, in particular, to chart its origins. The south transept of Amiens cathedral has a fine rose window of the earlier fourteenth century, with a display of curvilinear tracery, based on the use of the ogee curve and the lights of the window below have the same. It has not, strictly speaking, the narrow flame-like Flamboyant forms, but it stands in contrast to the geometric tracery on the wall of the gabled balustrade below it; does this qualify as Flamboyant, at least a variant of it or should we think of it as separate? The small cloister of the Carthusian abbey at Villefranche de Rouergue, founded in 1451 has fine tracery but it is curvilinear rather than Flamboyant (92).

The practice of omitting the capitals at the springing of arch mouldings, another of the elements of Flamboyant, can be seen by c.1300 at Narbonne cathedral. The elaborate display of niches, sculpture and porch gables rising in front of the west front of the cathedral of Toul, from 1460 an example of the sort of surface decoration which we associate with the manner. On the other hand, the walls of the side of the Lady Chapel at Lisieux cathedral added by Bishop Cauchon (the prosecutor of Joan of Arc) in the 1430s are totally plain, as are the surfaces of the west front of Béziers cathedral of the end of the fifteenth century. This is not just a case of a choice made at different periods or because of different resources. When faced with a manner which consists of a number of individual features, it is always possible for the builders to pick and choose among them. The question of origins is further compounded by the vicissitudes of France during the second half of the fourteenth century, caused not only by the plague but also by the destruction caused by the fighting of the Hundred Years' War, especially during the 1350s and 1360s. We lack the churches built in the period to assess its crucial opening phase.

The late Gothic period in France was not a great time for grand cathedral or abbey projects; such as were undertaken proceeded slowly and were often uncompleted. The nave of Nantes cathedral was started in 1434 as part of the ambitions of the Duke of Brittany for his principal city; the transepts and choir were only finished in the nineteenth century. The structure and general design, internally a tripartite elevation with a triforium, is traditional although the triforium is composed of triple ogee arches. The manner is expressed in the mouldings of the arcade piers and arches, in the lack of capitals for the shafts. Toul lies at the frontier of France with the Empire; its west façade was started in 1460. Again the overall design, with three portals and two towers flanking the central vessel, which has a grand rose window below the gable, is traditional. The Flamboyant manner contributes the flowing tracery in the openings, an elaborate ogee gable over the central porch and a second high one over the rose, the form of the towers (square below, octagonal above) and the pinnacles, lesser gables and the open tracery of the balustrades, which decorate the whole surface. Around 1500 the cathedral chapter of Beauvais embarked on the completion of their cathedral, which consisted since the 1330s of the choir alone. They had only managed to build the two transepts and the first bay of the nave, needed to support the crossing arches, when work stopped in the middle of the century. The design inevitably was based on the high choir to which it was joined and the main effort went in to the façades. The wall surface of the main transept and the angle turrets was panelled and decorated, while the main façade was composed of glass, dominated by a rose window with flowing tracery. The rest of the tracery is made up of rows of lancets divided by three balustrades; the tracery is flowing but the overall pattern of lancets makes the composition very traditional in effect.

For complete churches we have to turn to ones of lesser institutional status. The main church of the town of Caudebec in Normandy was started in 1426 but its western façade was not completed until the end of the century, held up no doubt by the English occupation of the province and its re-conquest (98). It provides a large interior well lit in the traditional way by a high clerestory; unlike the Germans and English, the French seem to have felt no need to improve on their tradition to provide a more open space. The plan has an eastern apse and omits a transept, in a pattern stretching back to the late twelfth century. Midway along the south side (the common position in late Gothic German churches) is a high tower, topped by a spire. The west front is an elaborate composition of gables, traceried openings and balustrades and statue niches. The church of La Trinité at Vendome dates from after *c*.1485; the abbey church of Notre Dame at Alencon is not dated but is likely to be of a very similar date of *c*.1500. Both have traditional aisled structures with three-storey internal elevations. The tracery is truly Flamboyant, with many narrow vertical, curved motifs all pointing upward like the flames of a fire. Internally the arcades are not high, preserving the traditional equality of proportion with the clerestory; the arch mouldings spring without capitals from the piers. Uncommonly, neither of the vaults are simply quadripartite; at Alencon tierceron ribs which spring slightly apart from the three main ones are added to the design along with odd niches for statues along them. At Vendome there are hints of bosses rather in the English manner. The western front of Alencon has a three-arched porch in front of the main wall. Above the arches is a riot of gables and balustrades pierced with curvilinear tracery and statues. These portray the Crucifixion; the lesser figures are set below the cross with their backs to the viewer in a striking composition.

Elaborate porches and façades were a prominent feature of the French late Gothic manner, like the five porches set in a gentle curve at the west end of the church of St Maclou at Rouen or the porch of Albi cathedral. Transept façades were a means of display, as at Sens or the wildly elaborated Senlis, both decorated with rose windows and ogee-gabled porches. Like the twin-towered western façades at Auxerre or Troyes cathedrals, both of *c*.1500, and the one at Toul earlier, they preserve traditional overall design, only changing the decorative features. Towers in France as elsewhere saw the addition of spires. The one at the relatively small cathedral of Autun was quite plain when it was added after 1462. The north-western tower of Chartres received a higher and more elaborate example, started in 1507, with open work and pinnacles which masked the transition from the square tower to the octagon of the spire itself. The early sixteenth-century church at Mortagne gives us an example of the eclecticism possible in the French late Gothic manner. The windows along the north side have tracery which would pass for early fourteenth century in England, while the interior is dominated by a vault with tierceron and ridge ribs which are both decorated themselves with pendants from the voussoirs and have bosses at the junctions.

THE NETHERLANDS

The area of the Low Countries covered a number of boundaries. Politically they were united to the Duchy of Burgundy, initially by marriage between Margaret of Flanders and Philip the Bold, created Duke of Burgundy in 1364 by his father, King John II of France. This union crossed the old, and moribund, border of the Empire and the kingdom of France but the difference arose again after 1477 when the last Duke's heiress, Mary, married Maximilian of Hapsburg. As the consequence of this further dynastic marriage the Imperial counties of her father came to the Emperor Charles V while Burgundy and the lands facing Flanders went to the French king. These were simply transfers of sovereignty among the rulers but they occurred because the Netherlands were at the junction of the powers of France and the German states; the individual provinces were very much separate units with a local liberty which they guarded fiercely. They were divided, as they are now, by language; French to the south-east, ancestral Dutch to the north-west. In the Burgundian regime, French may have had primacy but the administration was always to a large extent formally bilingual and the individual provinces and communities protected their own language. Rich, divided and placed between two or three different styles of building, the Netherlands may be expected to illustrate the cross currents of Europe in the late Gothic period.

The Netherlands were also divided in terms of resources. To the north, especially in Holland, there was no good building stone and this part, like the northern plain of Germany, used brick. In towns such as Amsterdam, Haarlem and Leiden the churches survive from the period. The nave of St Bavo's, Haarlem, dates from the first half of the fifteenth century (*93*). Because the structure was in brick, the builders thickened up the piers of the arcade and, especially, the piers of the crossing. The internal elevation is of two storeys, but is awkward because the clerestory is not carried down to the arcade top, leaving a blank area of walling between. This is compounded by the way the windows of the clerestory are narrower than the bays, again leaving a blank area of wall surface. St Pancras at Leiden shows a similar result of using brick in its thick, round crossing piers which contrasts with the thin tracery of stone in the windows. A further consequence of the use of brick is that the main vertical mullions in windows are often thickened also.

The general pattern of churches follows that of France in that it does not involve a radical change in plan or structure. Traditional, French-derived chevet plans continue, as does the three-storey internal elevation with arcade, triforium and clerestory. As with Germany and France, the capitals were often omitted from the point of the springing of vaults or the mouldings of the arcade arches, which were made to spring directly from the piers and columns. The practice of having the clerestory narrower than the bay, seen at Haarlem, is found in the Meuse region at the beginning of the fourteenth century. Blank walling is often decorated with panelled arcading. The main decoration is provided by the tracery in the windows and along the line of the triforium. As in France or Germany it derives from the curvilinear pattern developed at the start of the fourteenth century and it is often related to the French Flamboyant. Strictly speaking, this is inaccurate, for the designs do not show the narrow vertical forms of the French manner, but are more horizontal in design, often based on circles (commonly filled with whirling patterns of commas) or loops. The tracery of balustrades or façades could become extremely elaborate, as in the south porch of the cathedral of Shertogenbosch (Bois-le-Duc). Here each of the two openings of the porch is surmounted by an

93 St Bavo's church Haarlem

ogee, intersected by a hanging semicircular line. Behind, the transept window is divided by a vertical mullion and surrounded by carved panelling.

The rivalry of the great cities, again as was common elsewhere, resulted in a proliferation of high towers surmounted by stone spires. Following the German pattern, these were usually set singly at the west end of the churches. Towers were also an important part of the pomp of the city and market halls and the array of them which confronted, and still confronts, the visitor after entering the city walls was an effect dear to the medieval consciousness since the ninth century.

The church of Brou, at the extreme south of Burgundy, can stand for much of the Burgundian achievement when linked to the Netherlands. It was founded as a personal act, in completion of a vow made by her mother, by Margaret of Austria, daughter of Emperor Maximilian, grand daughter of the last Duke of Burgundy, who ruled the Netherlands in the name of her nephew, the Emperor Charles V, with great skill. Its primary purpose was to be a mausoleum for the tombs of Margaret and her immediate family and to celebrate her wealth and taste; the tombs are superb examples of early Renaissance motifs applied to a late medieval monument, while the church is the work of a master from Brabant. The plans, of the tombs especially, were prepared in the two years before 1513 when the foundations were laid. It proceeded quickly with Margaret's resources behind it; she died in 1530, two years before its completion. In plan it is traditional, a cruciform basilica with a short nave and a polygonal apse. The two-storey internal elevation is straightforward also, an arcade rising without capitals from the moulded piers, surmounted by a low balustrade for the triforium. This provides the background to the decoration lavished on the rood screen, the windows (tracery and glass), the tower at the south east and the west façade. The rood screen in particular is a mass of intricate tracery covering the three arches and the balustrade above; there is miniature vault of great complexity behind the arches.

SCOTLAND AND IRELAND: THE BOUNDARIES OF PERPENDICULAR

For 150 years before 1300, the buildings of these two countries had depended on England for masons and ideas. At the end of the thirteenth century the wars began which saw Scotland repel English power and assert a greater independence than before. These wars, combined with the Black Death in the middle of the fourteenth century, ensured that there was little major church building in Scotland until the end of the century. In 1385 the English burned the Cistercian abbey of Melrose, which was then rebuilt from 1389, in part with English compensation money. The tracery of the east window and the eastern parts of the choir shows a variant of the Perpendicular manner, implying an English mason, while an inscription records John Morow, who was born in Paris, as master; this probably reflects a shortage of Scottish masons at the time. If this was the case, the fifteenth century saw this rectified under the stimulus of a whole series of new projects. The patrons for these were some of the old cathedrals and abbeys, but more often the aristocracy who, as elsewhere in Europe, founded a number of colleges to pray for their families, while the Scottish towns also saw burgher parish churches erected in the period.

The plans of the churches were often different from the thirteenth century. The most obvious sign of this is at the east end where polygonal apses are common. Colleges such as Seton, abbeys such as Crossraguel and borough churches such as Linlithgow erected these, presumably in imitation of European models. However, at the same time, colleges, Lincluden or Roslin, and borough churches at Edinburgh or Haddington put up the more traditional square east ends. The latter had the advantage of providing for a fine display in an east window. Again in common with other European examples, the popularity of altars and chapels is very obvious in the additions at St Giles' in Edinburgh or in the expanded transepts at Melrose or Jedburgh. Another plan element was the tower. Some were constructed over the crossing but these tended to be unimpressive; the usual place for this display was a single tower at the west end. Here, as in Germany or the Low Countries, it was normally placed centrally, but a variation, found at Dunkeld cathedral or at King's College, Aberdeen, was to place it to one side, possibly in the hope of adding a second later, as was started at Glasgow.

Two aspects of the structure of the churches stand out. One is the internal elevation design. The cathedral of Dunkeld and Paisley abbey both have versions

94 Dunkeld cathedral: the nave from the south-east

of the traditional three-storey framework. Dunkeld triforium is a remarkable piece of work, consisting of a nearly continuous series of semicircular arches, almost as wide as the arcades below them, each divided by a Y-shaped mullion (*94*). The semicircular arches of the triforium and the very blunt points of the arcade are strongly reminiscent of Romanesque work and the whole looks like a conscious recalling of the past.

Paisley abbey triforium is less reminiscent of the past, with segmental arches divided by cusped mullions, and the clerestory is much larger and also traceried, so the whole effect is less archaic. Apart from these, elevations were normally of two storeys. The other major structural development was in the field of vaulting. Around 1400 the nave aisle of St Giles' in Edinburgh received a vault which both sprang all along the wall and omitted the wall arches; in effect it was a barrel vault with ribs applied. The same was built at Seton College at the end of the fifteenth century, a barrel vault with ribs stuck on at the east end; other churches had straightforward pointed barrel vaults without any ribs. Again the effect is archaic, but the reason for them is probably the popularity of barrel vaults in the tower houses of the period; the hybrid of barrel vault with ribs is found at the same time in Dundonald castle as the experiment in St Giles' Edinburgh. These are not the only vault types however. Quadripartite vaults are also fairly usual, and more complex star patterns are found over such centralised spaces as the chapter house of Elgin cathedral.

The main concentration of decoration was in the grand façades, whether at the east or west ends of the churches or of the transepts. These were usually

95 The south transept of Seton College church; the window has the wide central division also seen in brick churches of the Netherlands

dominated by large traceried windows, but the west end of Aberdeen cathedral has a row of seven lancets. The Scottish late Gothic tracery patterns are ultimately derived from the curvilinear tracery of the early fourteenth century, but they developed along the path of the circles and loops, more in line with those of the Netherlands than anywhere else. Some, like the west windows of Haddington church or King's College, Aberdeen, were divided by the sort of thick central mullion used in the brick churches of Holland (95). As with the east window at Melrose, or at Carnwath, there were some examples of the vertical emphasis of Perpendicular manner tracery, but this is very much in the minority. We can see the Scots following the French in abandoning cusping in their looping tracery at the end of the fifteenth century. As with the bulk of the tracery patterns, the Scots' late Gothic fondness for round piers or columns in their arcades probably derives from the Netherlands. On the other hand the prominent crowned steeples of Edinburgh or Aberdeen derive from one at Newcastle-upon-Tyne.

The evidence points to a Scottish industry at the end of the fourteenth century having very largely to reconstruct itself. It did so, inevitably, through an eclectic approach, possibly inspired by immigrant masons from England, France and the Netherlands. The result was very different from the Perpendicular manner. With innovations in plan, structure and elevation of their churches, the Scots had the makings of a whole new style, like that of Germany. What is missing, perhaps, is a sense of the repeated and coherent use of these distinctive elements; there are as many examples of variant plans, vaults or elevations.

IRELAND

Ireland had a different history in the fourteenth century from Scotland. The wars were not as destructive and the English crown continued to exercise some authority in the east, while claiming (ineffectively) sovereignty over the whole island. On the other hand, the dangers posed directly by the Scots and the attractions of fighting in France meant that England neglected Ireland. Some of the families of English lords died out, some retreated back to England while others prospered during the period. Particularly in the western half of the island land changed hands, some to rising English families such as the Butlers, some to fragments of English ones whose leaders had gone, like the De Burghs who became the Connacht Burkes and some to resurgent Irish ones like the O'Brians. The power of the English king was the biggest loser, shrinking increasingly to the land around Dublin, the Pale; his civil servants bewailed the loss of their power and privilege, describing the result as calamity and degeneration.

The patronage of church building in Ireland from the middle of the fourteenth century is different from that of the rest of Europe. Work on cathedrals was largely limited to repairs, not new parts, there are no great town churches and colleges such as those of Slane or Howth are rare. The new lords of the fourteenth century founded churches to celebrate or consolidate their status, usually in the lands they had taken over, and their patronage followed more traditional routes. Cistercian abbeys were the mainstay of Irish monasticism since the twelfth century and they continued to receive building work; the abbey of Holy Cross in particular was completely rebuilt on the initiative of the Butler lords who had taken over rich lands around the abbey, in south Tipperary and Kilkenny. The great winners were the Orders of Friars. In Europe generally throughout the Middle Ages and in Ireland before 1350, they were a feature of the urban scene. The Irish foundations after 1350 were overwhelmingly rural and in the western half of the island, in the lands of the new lordships of the region.

As a result of this there was more continuity of building in Ireland than in Scotland during the fourteenth century. The number of foundations of friaries fell to zero in the generation after the Black Death of 1348 but there was work on the buildings of those founded before the plague and some large projects such as repairs to the Dublin cathedrals. During the first half of the century, the patterns of curvilinear tracery had become established in Ireland. In 1347, two years before the Plague struck Kilkenny, the Franciscan friars there had started to raise money and build a new bell tower. This is the present tower and is the earliest dated example of what was to become a major element in the late Gothic buildings of Ireland. It is tall and slim in its proportions and set (as was common in friary churches elsewhere) at the junction of the nave and the choir that had just been extended.

Continuity from the buildings of the early fourteenth century is the main feature of the subsequent two centuries of church building in Ireland. The plans of the Cistercian abbeys were followed, a feature being their embellishment with low crossing towers. The friaries are the main examples of new plans, again following the earlier pattern with square-ended choirs, naves and transepts, opportunities for large windows. The cloisters were usually to the north of the church, leaving room for an enlarged south transept or aisle to provide the extra chapels that late medieval religious practice demanded. A major feature in the southern two thirds of the island is the greatly increased use of the hard limestone of the region for carved stone. This had not been used before, perhaps because of a lack of technique, more probably because in the fourteenth century steel tools became harder and sharper. This stone is very resistant to weathering so that many of the details of Irish churches, although they are roofless, are as crisp as when they were cut. Simplicity of construction is another hallmark. The walls are usually of rubble with only the arches, windows and furnishings such as altars, tombs or sedilia made of cut stone. Vaults are unusual, and in the towers are often simple barrels; as with Scotland this reflects practice found in the contemporary tower houses of the gentry and lords. One of the few elaborate vaults covers the choir of Holy Cross abbey, an elegant composition with ridge and tierceron ribs.

Window tracery makes up the great majority of the decoration. The general pattern of the forms continues that of the smaller Decorated Gothic windows of early fourteenth-century England. They follow neither the Perpendicular manner of England, nor the French Flamboyant or the circles and loops of the Netherlands and Scotland but continue with basic geometrical and curvilinear designs with strong cusping stressing the sharp lines of the shapes. One feature does follow practice elsewhere. As in France and Scotland, at the end of the fifteenth century masons omitted the cusping, giving a stronger impression of looping designs to the windows. A study of all the friary buildings of Connacht in the west found that there was no difference in plan or details between the buildings of the various orders of Friars: the only variations could be attributed to the amount of resources put into them. A study of the distribution of window tracery patterns showed a tendency towards regional distinctions. The windows of north Leinster were more elaborate than those of north Munster, where the simple switchline tracery predominated. One form was based on a stem and flower pattern, either with the 'leaves' spreading outwards or else rising upwards. The latter form appears to have been popularised at Holy Cross; it is found in its immediate hinterland in Co. Tipperary but also in two abbeys north-west of Galway. The other version with spreading leaves is to be found by contrast in Co. Meath in north Leinster and in Co. Limerick but also in Connacht. The same pattern of local variation can be seen among the tower houses of the time. It would appear that the patrons in Ireland were given little choice of what they got for their money; the masons produced the local standard tower, friary or window.

96 Rosserk friary; the central tower seen through the south transept window; note the small head carved on the left window jamb

The story of Irish late Gothic can be summed up by two places. The friary of Rosserk in Co. Mayo was founded before 1441 for the Third Order regular of Franciscans, an order which started as an association of laymen linked to the Franciscans and became more popular in Ireland than elsewhere. The site is now isolated and the buildings, although roofless (they were burned during the Tudor wars in 1590) are well preserved. The main decorative features are the east window of the nave and the south window of the south transept with their tracery and the tower over the crossing (96). As well as these there are, equally typically, small carvings such as the one on the west side of the south transept window (but not on the east), apparently added at the whim of the mason.

The hill of Slane was the site of a barony held by the Fleming family from the twelfth century and is marked as such by a motte castle. The church is often, but wrongly, identified as that of a friary but is in fact the parish church, poorly preserved but retaining its tower, which has a traceried west window, at the west end. Near it is the college for four priests, four clerks and four choristers, founded by a Fleming in 1512. Its domestic range for the four priests is well preserved; unfortunately the hall and chapel range, which would have shown us the decorative elements, is not. Their sites are very different: Rosserk friary apparently in the open country in a Gaelic part of the west, Slane parish church and college at the centre of an English barony in the east and set in a township – unusual for Ireland. Their architecture unites them, the towers and the window tracery which are the hallmarks of the late Gothic in Ireland.

SUMMARY

During the thirteenth century the church buildings of Europe were dominated by ideas coming out of France. Even if, like England and eastern Germany, this was a matter of adapting rather than imitating them, the builders continually referred to France and brought in new ideas, such as tracery. After 1300 this changed, although the beginnings of Prague cathedral show the continued prestige of France. The origins of many of the ideas of the fourteenth century come from the patterned vaults and curvilinear tracery of England. This has led to a certain amount of nationalistic debate, identifying this as an 'English' style – contrasted with the 'Frenchness' of early Gothic – which has generated more heat than light. Apart from the general fallacy of such 'national' identifications for the Middle Ages, it is not where the ideas originated but the use that was made of them which is interesting. Here the histories are quite distinct. As we would expect there is a period of assimilation of the ideas by the masons and the industry. The length of this period depends on the amount of change required: for Germany where they developed a new style this was much longer than France or Ireland where there were only new decorative elements to be incorporated into the traditional scheme of church building. In Germany, the plan and structure of hall-churches was combined with the new vault patterns and the decoration; it took a half century, starting just before 1300, for the elements to be combined into a coherent style. In England the Perpendicular manner required no new plan types and little change to the structural systems which the masons knew; after its development in Gloucester in the late 1330s and 1340s, it spread relatively rapidly. In Scotland, where the new developments also meant new plans and structural systems (even if, like the barrel vault, they were a revival of a past and simple technology) political and economic factors delayed this until the half century on either side of 1400. In France and the Netherlands it is difficult to identify the period of assimilation because it consisted simply of the adoption of tracery forms and mouldings. The origin can be put back to c.1300 at Narbonne with the omission of capitals or about 1325 with the curvilinear tracery of the Amiens south rose window, or else delayed until we see these being used together. In Ireland the absorption of new tracery forms and a type of tower was very quickly achieved.

What all these regions have in common, however, is a similar later history. After the builders had decided on the style or manner which they liked, they changed it very little change for at least a century. It is often quite difficult to tell from the appearance of the church whether it was constructed in 1420 or 1480. This stasis of design aligns well with a second feature of the time. In numbers of cases, projects started in the thirteenth century remained incomplete into the fourteenth and fifteenth just as, indeed, many of the fifteenth-century ones did. Continuing work on old projects presented the builders with a problem of fashion: did they carry on the (now out-dated) earlier design in the name of uniformity or did they change it in the name of modernity. In the thirteenth century there was very little pressure for continuity; Romanesque buildings were targeted for replacement simply because they were old fashioned and dark. During the fourteenth century there were a number of high-profile examples of the reverse. When King Richard II decided to complete the Westminster abbey church started by his predecessor Henry III it was done in conscious imitation of the earlier work. The monks of St Ouen in Rouen carried on their new church whose choir dated from 1318; they did so into the fifteenth century: only the window tracery in the nave reflects the late date. The lack of change in design which prevailed for much of the century broke up at the end. In Germany we see the almost baroque development of the patterns of shafts and vault ribs: in England the austerity of the Perpendicular changed into the developments of pendant vaults and elaborate additional decoration. In the Netherlands the elaboration of design has been well termed 'Florid'.

The period is also marked by an upheaval in the pattern of patronage. The thirteenth century was dominated by the projects of the great lords, bishops and abbeys with royal wealth always behind them. Cathedrals and great abbeys were the centres of work. As always the later Gothic there were foundations of great churches to further the ambitions of powerful men: secular lords patronised the construction of Prague, Vienna and Nantes cathedrals. During the fourteenth century the emphasis shifted, colleges and urban parishes were as important as the older churches. Three churches are examples of the new patronage: Schmalkalde in Germany (97), Caudebec in France (98) and Lavenham in England (3).

97 Schmalkalde parish church, typical of a German town church, set beside the market place

98 Caudebec: a French late medieval town church

99 York, the church of All Saints Pavement; the tower is a characteristic elaboration for a town church set on a cramped site

All are the parish churches of what are now small towns but were prosperous in the fifteenth century when they were built; all three face their market place. They are very different in appearance; each belongs to its own region. They share major similarities, however. Each has a large, open nave, although the masons who constructed the hall-church at Schmalkalde and the array of glass windows of Perpendicular Lavenham had the better designs to deliver this. All three have side chapels for the private patronage. The two prominent aspects of late medieval Western Christianity, the increased participation of the parish congregation and private devotions, are reflected in the buildings. They also celebrate the wealth of their communities, especially in the towers at Caudebec and Lavenham.

Lavenham tower in particular records the finances behind this; it has the arms of the De Vere Earls of Oxford and the merchant's mark of Thomas Spring, old money and new, carved on its base (4). The Springs prospered and acquired arms later; their private chapel is smothered in them, celebrating the replacing of their earlier merchant's mark. In the larger cities, parish churches such as St Merri in Paris or Holy Trinity Goodramgate in York contrive to provide the same combination in a cramped site, decorated by glass and carving (99).

These churches are clearly responding to the needs of the patrons, and the designs are reflecting these too in a general way. There are also examples from the period of patrons influencing not simply the fact of construction or a general pattern but specifics of design. The most obvious, if general, example of this is the whole question of the Perpendicular manner. This had its origins in a twin track: the aesthetic move away from elaborate curvilinear tracery, seen in London, and the need for the mason designing the new south transept at Gloucester to work to a tight budget. Aesthetics and parsimony came together, resulting in the new manner of decorating churches in reaction to the elaboration of the Decorated. There are also documented examples of the patron issuing specific instructions about design. These include a common formula, stipulating that the new work should be like, or better than, a similar work at a specified place. In many cases, either the original or the later work has gone and it is impossible to study the process and meaning of the stipulation in detail but it may be noted that in a number of cases the model was too recent to have been finished. In these cases we may be looking at a simple, generalised requirement that it be bigger, costlier (or the reverse) or as well decorated.

It seems most probable that completing the naves of Westminster or St Ouen in Rouen in a style consonant with the earlier work rather than modern fashion, was a decision at the very least influenced by the patron. The nave of Dunkeld cathedral in Scotland has a triforium which gives a prominent place to round arches, apparently recalling the Romanesque style of the past in the fifteenth century. This has been linked to the possibility that this was Dunkeld asserting its ancient prestige as a shrine of Columba and Scottish pride and antiquity (in the Middle Ages the two went together); associated work is described by a contemporary as 'in the Scottish manner'. The building of the new teaching block for the University of Oxford, the Divinity School, provides a well-documented example of specific interference by the patrons in the details of the design. The project was started in 1423; by 1439 progress had been so slow that the University assembled a commission of 'magnates and other wise men' to advise them on how to complete it. They recommended that all 'supervacuous curiosity' be eliminated as irrelevant and expensive. Their words were heeded: the buttresses on the north side have blank arcading, those on the south side have not; complex mouldings are stopped a third of the way up windows and niches are omitted (*91*).

These examples raise again, for this period, the question of the means of communication of ideas and the respective roles of patrons and craftsmen. There is an impressive degree of parallel development in these histories which we may compare with the synchronous developments of Romanesque and the Gothic styles. These could be distinguished because the elements which spread were either non-technical or attributable to patrons (Romanesque) or the reverse, technical and attributable to craftsmen (Gothic). Here the messages are mixed. The changes required by the religious practices of the patrons, such as in the individual cases quoted, or the spread of such ideas as curvilinear patterns of tracery point to communication among them regarding design features. Against this is the evidence for the delivery of the styles and manners used in the churches. The components of such a style as the late German Gothic were clearly the responsibility of the masons who understood the structural consequences of a hall-church or a stellar vault. The differences visible between the designs prevailing in different regions have been attributed to politics and a nascent nationalism. The case of Scotland illustrates this well: the masons' use of the Netherlands and France as a source of ideas is likely to have been at least influenced by a desire to differentiate their work and themselves from England; this must be nationalism at work. On the other hand both eastern Ireland and Gascony in France were happy, even eager, to assert their loyalty to the English Crown yet in neither did the masons copy the ideas of Perpendicular. We might expect the linguistic differences of the Netherlands to be reflected in the culture of building but they are not.

The Middle Ages after the Black Death were more complex than the periods before. Communications between regions increased as the economic boom of the thirteenth century, when each region produced as much of everything it could, was replaced by a regime of specialisation and exchange. As well as the traditional connections of war and marriage between aristocrats and royalty, this was the era of the Hanse merchants and the development of shipping so that fishermen could routinely go to Iceland for cod. The old thirteenth-century simplicity of society and communications was gone.

9

THE END OF MEDIEVAL CHURCH BUILDING

The early sixteenth century saw the medieval church building industry in a healthy state. The stagnation of the fifteenth century, when designs had shown little invention or originality, had been replaced across Northern Europe by a phase of elaboration and decoration. Money and ideas were apparently abundant but two major upheavals combined to bring about the end of medieval church building: an aesthetic and a religious one. The aesthetic change involved the revival of Classical fashions which started in fifteenth-century Italy and has become known as the Renaissance. The other was the religious revolution of the Reformation, with its origins in the 1520s, which struck more directly at the Church and its buildings. Not only did the Reformation challenge the whole basis for the Church and its many of its churches (notably monasteries) but it sparked off a century and a half of religious wars throughout Europe, immensely damaging to the settled economy required to build. The two issues intertwined, however, as can be seen in the different chronologies and processes visible in France and England from the 1520s onwards.

The first difference is in their political history. In the first half of the sixteenth century France was much the richer country and more closely in contact with the Italian ideas. After the 1560s it spiralled down into religious civil war, only recovering its position in the earlier seventeenth century. During even the period of the worst of the war, the king and the central elite remained Roman Catholic; it was only by conversion that the Protestant Henry IV could make good his claim to the throne and end the wars. In England, Henry VIII embarked on a course of religious reform, replacing the pope with himself as king. His power and that of his children, Edward VI, Mary and Elizabeth, was often challenged but never successfully limited. They were now responsible for the religious attitudes of the country and they swung backwards and forwards in their views: Protestant Edward, Roman Catholic Mary and Elizabeth reluctantly but decisively Protestant. In the seventeenth century the Stuart kings also tried to continue their hold on

100 St Pierre, Caen: ambulatory chapel windows. The two on the left are Flamboyant Gothic, the one on the right has sixteenth-century Renaissance tracery

power and the Church; it was his failure to control his subjects' religion as much as anything that brought Charles I to his death. In France Protestantism was always outside the State, warring with it. In England the religious tension and debate was contained within the structure of the State Church until the explosion of the Civil War in 1641.

During the earlier part of the sixteenth century, French builders made a series of attempts to reconcile the new fashion for Classical motifs with the traditional medieval Gothic church structures. A number of chapels were added to the ambulatory of the church of St Pierre in Caen, of the same plan and proportions as the earlier Gothic ones beside them (*100*). The windows are round-headed, however, with simple cuspless tracery while the piers between them and the frieze above them are decorated with Classical motifs. The west front of St Michel in Dijon, started in 1537, is more ambitious. The basic design is the traditional medieval one of twin towers flanking the central space and fronted by three porches, into the nave and two aisles. The three porches are quite successfully combined into a Classical three-bay portico with round arches; the decoration is also Classical. The towers were more of a problem for, instead of medieval shafts, it was decorated with Classical columns whose proportions required the towers to be broken into four storeys piled on top of each other. The buttressing also clashed with the Classical features and proportions. The central space lost its great medieval window, replaced by two round-headed windows which only reached a little over half way up. Above this is a muddle of a balustrade and frieze.

The real problems of combining the two systems were well exposed at the church of St Eustache in Paris, started in 1532. It has a traditional plan, of a double aisle and outer ring of chapels. This requires the traditional proportions of a high central part and lower sides to give any light to the interior. The central vessel, choir and nave, has an elaborate rib vault, decorated with heavy, vaguely Classical

101 St Eustache, Paris: a Gothic scheme but Classical details. The shafts and capitals on the piers and arches show up the impossibility of combining the proportions of the two styles

pendants; to support it the church had to have flying buttresses. The builders tried to combine this essentially medieval building with Classical motifs and aesthetic (*101*). The transept façade on the exterior was, like the west façade at Dijon, partly successful, although the height was too great for the Classical proportions of the elements so that it had to be broken into three storeys which integrate poorly. The interior, with a traditional three-storey bay structure, was worse. The triforium could be made into a Classical blank arcade but the proportions of the main arcade (of round arches) and the clerestory were too high for the Classical formula. The medieval vault and the Classical canon demanded that the piers be decorated with vertical shafts. These were made to look like applied Classical half columns or pilasters, but the proportions of these demanded that they be lower than the heights of the arcade and clerestory, so intermediate capitals were inserted.

In secular architecture, at a château such as Chambord, the basic frame of corner towers to a square façade could be adapted to accept Classical features; in the interior the medieval layout of rooms could be continued while the rooms themselves received the new fashion in décor. A medieval castle or country house did not have to be high to be a successful design. Classical proportions and decoration could easily be adapted to a medieval castle house façade and make it a country house; the interior rooms could then be organised in a traditional plan but given Renaissance ornament. Classical design had been developed for regular spaces, usually with a simple wooden roof and relatively low proportions. Medieval church design, especially in France, had been directed at height for the 500 years before 1500, ever since the towers of the First Romanesque. What the experiments of the earlier sixteenth century in France had shown was that only the basilican plan was compatible between medieval churches and Classical buildings. When French building resumed in the seventeenth century, after the wars of religion, the Classical style, merging into the Baroque, held complete sway.

One of the key acts of the English Reformation was the Dissolution of the Monasteries in the 1540s; no movement with a main programme like this was going to be fertile ground for much grand church building. To English people of the later sixteenth century, the problem must have been seen as one of a surplus of great churches, not a need for more; certainly none were built. At the same time the fashion for the decorative motifs of the Renaissance was accepted as eagerly in England as in France, although somewhat at second hand. The great Elizabethan and early Jacobean country houses of the aristocracy were all equipped with the same trappings; just as, behind the façades, the planning of the rooms and the life they served was almost entirely medieval in nature. These same great houses also served to divert resources, of men and money, away from church building.

Under Elizabeth, the second half of the sixteenth century, there was some church building but it was in general small-scale and unambitious in design. Much of it was the inevitable matter of repairs to existing fabric, usually carried out in the idiom of the original and entirely directed at parish churches. There were some new ones; the largest of these at Denbigh, started by Elizabeth's favourite Leicester in 1578 but never finished, which was to be a model of a new Protestant preaching church. It was a simple rectangle in plan, with a nave and two aisles but no structural chancel. The windows had a simple version of Perpendicular tracery and the surviving door is Tudor Gothic but the nave arcade arches seem to have been carried on Tuscan columns. In Lancashire the church of Standish attempted a combination of styles; the arcade of the otherwise Perpendicular nave was also carried on Tuscan columns. As in France, Classical and medieval styles could be combined but only if the space was simple and regular and the proportions low. The main effort of the time went into the internal fittings of the church, in part as result of the requirements of Protestant worship such as the fixed pews which followed sermons. Tombs were an eternal need and the new aristocrats and gentry were enthusiastic builders of them. They embraced the new style for them eagerly. The parish church at Framlingham gives a good illustration of the new attitude: in the 1550s the Duke of Norfolk rebuilt the chancel to house his family tombs. These are in fine early Renaissance style, but the chancel is in late Perpendicular. Nothing typifies the new style more than the ugliness of Leicester's Renaissance tomb of 1589, all squat Classical columns and cherubs, smashed into the beautiful early fifteenth-century chapel of the Beauchamp earls at Warwick.

The early seventeenth century saw more activity, although there were still few, if any, great projects. Bishop Montagu of Bath and Wells finished the cathedral at Bath, started in the early sixteenth century and including a major fan vault, doing it so carefully that it is difficult to tell the two periods apart. The University and colleges in Oxford provided larger projects than the parish churches, the nearest thing to the large medieval church projects of medieval times, both in scale and being not continuations but new builds. During the 1610s there were four large projects going on simultaneously there: the creation and extension of the Bodleian Library, the Schools quadrangle linked to it, new work at Merton College and the new foundation of Wadham College. All were basically stone masonry in a late Perpendicular manner; Renaissance elements were added extras: timber screens or the tower displaying the five Classical Orders which formed the centrepiece of the Schools quadrangle. Wadham may stand for them all. It was built quickly, in four building seasons from 1610 to 1613, to a strictly formal version of the quadrangular plan pioneered by William of Wykeham's New College. Most of the details are of late Perpendicular character; the windows of the chapel in particular are fine examples of tracery which could have been erected two hundred years earlier. There is Renaissance work also: the screen in the chapel, the window tracery in the hall and the frontispiece of the door to the hall (*102*). The stone is local, quarried from sites bought or rented for the job in the traditional way. The workmen were mostly from the founder's County of Somerset. The demand for labour at Oxford at the time seems to have drawn in many craftsmen from across England; the Schools quadrangle was the work of Yorkshire masters. Clearly there was a reserve of men who worked in the traditional way while being able to carve new details if required. The final effort of their work before the English Civil War

102 Wadham College, Oxford, quadrangle. The basic design is Gothic but the windows of the hall and ante-chapel have bizarre tracery and there is a Classical frontispiece over the entry to the hall

was the magnificent fan-vaulted staircase to the hall of Christ Church, although it is recorded as being to the design of a London mason.

This reserve of workmen was responsible for the contemporary building of parish churches. During the first half of the century, a small number of them was constructed from new, not just repaired or extended. The church of St John in Leeds, built in 1632-4, reflected the same priorities as Wadham College. The main structure and the stonework, such as the window tracery, were in the Perpendicular manner but the woodwork, such as the screens, was an exercise in Jacobean Renaissance. Later than this, started and substantially built during Cromwell's Commonwealth in 1653-65, is the parish church of Staunton Harold, complete with an inscription recording the unrepentant Anglicanism of its patron, Sir Robert Shirley. Apart from being higher for its length than would have been usual before, this is a church which has changed little from those of the fifteenth century. In Devon we can see the local design of window tracery used from the early sixteenth century into the early seventeenth. It is a very much simplified Perpendicular of three or four lights, where the central one carries on up to the apex of the arch without a separate arch, used mostly in the south of the County, in South Hams. The commonest of the medieval features are the towers, given the absence of towers in the Classical style they had to be medieval. Some are overtly copied from medieval examples, such as Christow in Devon of the 1630s, copied from the nearby tower of Throwleigh of *c.*1500. The

103 Derry cathedral. Early seventeenth-century Perpendicular built by an English mason working for the London companies in Ulster

only thoroughly Renaissance or Classical churches in England before the Civil War and the Restoration are the work of Inigo Jones in London. One of these was the chapel built for Charles I's Roman Catholic Queen; the other St Paul's, Covent Garden. This is a Classical temple on the exterior, with a portico of columns facing the street.

A curious footnote to these churches is provided in Ulster. After 1610 the land was planted with Protestant English and Scottish settlers who found a country where the churches were mostly destroyed. Many of the local landlords set about building a number of new ones as part of their overtly colonising project in the Protestant interest. Their plans reflected the modesty of their resources but also their religious programme, particularly in their omission of separate chancels. The transepts were usually more related to the Scottish, Presbyterian, practice of adding a separate wing to act as a lord's pew over their burial vault; the very English Lord Deputy of Ireland, Arthur Chichester, added such a transept to Carrickfergus church. The City of London was responsible for the town of Derry (hence Londonderry) which was the seat of the bishopric. The Londoners built the grandest church project of the Plantation, a new cathedral between 1628 and 1633. The mason was an Englishman called William Parratt and the church is an exercise in late Perpendicular (*103*). The east window (the present one is a later copy of the original) is a fine composition of Perpendicular tracery; the aisle windows examples of the South Hams tracery from Devon.

The parish churches were inevitably more modest, although Derry cathedral is only the size of a reasonable English parish church. Their main decoration lies in the windows, where the predominant forms are the square-headed windows seen in the lesser windows of Oxford or versions of simple intersecting tracery, as at Staunton Harold aisles. The church of Castle Caulfield (Co. Tyrone), built in the 1680s, has more elaborate tracery, based on the Perpendicular but with bizarre additions of circle motifs. Classical design is confined to porches, most elaborately in the frontispiece added to the medieval church of Newtownards. Internally, the Church of Ireland authorities tried to introduce the internal furnishings of Anglican worship, most notably the altar rails which would distinguish the church from a Presbyterian one. The complexities of the messages the styles of the buildings conveyed in early seventeenth-century Ulster had to take into account not only religious differences but also the rival building traditions of England, Scotland and Ireland for the lords were drawn from all three. The Renaissance porch added to a medieval building is a sign of secular civility seen at churches built by lords of all three nationalities. Three buildings exemplify the architectural sensibilities of the situation. The cathedral of Derry is one, as we have seen the expression of English building par excellence. Its mason was almost certainly also responsible, however, for the grand new hall that Randal MacDonnell, first earl of Antrim, built at his castle of Dunluce. This has the bay windows and Classical features of a contemporary English great house as suited his position as a newly created Earl, loyal to James VI and I. But Randal was also a Roman Catholic Highlander and as part of his ambitions to revive MacDonald lordship there he financed a Franciscan mission to the Highlands, based at Bonamargy in north Antrim. Randal rebuilt it but not in Anglican Perpendicular but using the late Gothic of Ireland; for his family's vault and chapel attached to the south of the chancel, however, he used a Scottish Presbyterian idea (like the Anglican Chichester) with Lowland Scottish mouldings but English brick.

The problem of church style in England between 1550 and 1650 was much more complex than the purely aesthetic one which the French had confronted. Architectural styles were loaded with symbolism, with the period after 1600 aligning the Renaissance not only with modernity but also with France and the Mediterranean. These were the heart of the Roman Catholic powers and the Counter-Reformation, so that inevitably for some people the style and the ideas were linked. At the same time the Church of England was increasingly assailed by people with Calvinist ideals, so that the religious establishment, from the time of Elizabeth onwards, tended to see themselves as being in a middle position between Rome and Geneva. Conservatism (medieval style) could, in the middle of the sixteenth century, mean Rome; by the earlier seventeenth century, as the Church of England became ever more firmly rooted in Protestantism, it meant opposition to Rome. At Oxford and in the parish churches of England and Ulster (led by the Londoners' cathedral of Derry) there was a consensus by the beginning of the seventeenth century. The patrons were well aware of Renaissance buildings; they erected and lived in them. They did not, however, like them for their churches;

the Renaissance style was confined to fittings or tombs. Porches might be in the new style, just as the tower of the Schools quadrangle was, or the hall entrance to Wadham College and the window tracery of its hall, but the chapel tracery was Perpendicular. Medieval building style, in particular the Perpendicular manner, had become associated with the Anglican Church.

After the Restoration in England in 1660, building of churches in the Perpendicular manner continued. The grandest was perhaps the work of Bishop Cosin of Durham in the 1660s. He repaired his cathedral in medieval style and rebuilt the chapel of his palace at Bishop's Auckland as a medieval hall. He restored the fourteenth-century tracery of the aisles and added a new clerestory with three-light versions of Decorated tracery in round arches. The year 1665 struck a serious blow to this. The Great Fire of London meant that a whole series of churches had to be replaced at the one time. The churches of Christopher Wren were brilliant examples of late Renaissance (or restrained Baroque) style; they were also particularly successful in solving the problem of Classical towers and spires. This was style which not only squared the circle between the overall impression of a medieval church with Classical style, but also provided exactly the restrained and dignified setting for the Anglican compromise. From then on, in London and wherever the court interest was dominant, late Gothic was no longer deemed suitable for church building. It did not die immediately, of course. Dynasties and individual masons carried on the tradition of medieval masonry down into the eighteenth century, such as the Sumsions of Colerne in Wiltshire or the Woodwards of Chipping Campden. Three things are significant about their work. They were no more original in their designs than the builders of the sixteenth or earlier seventeenth centuries. In the 1730s Thomas Sumsion modelled the new tower at Sherston in Wiltshire on his own parish church tower of Colerne built in the fifteenth. They were centred on the area of the best building stone of England, in the Cotswolds, where demand for good masonry would be strong and most easily satisfied. Even though they and their kind carried on their work down to the time of the Gothick revival of the later eighteenth century, they played no part in it, for this remained a matter for the intellectual pursuit of the elite.

The decline of the medieval building industry and style, in the sense of its practising innovation, started in the early sixteenth century but it was not inevitable. Particularly for Protestants, there were a number of medieval models which would have served their ideas. The churches of the Friars were designed to give large open spaces for preaching; both the hall-churches and Perpendicular ones could also do so. Additionally, the Perpendicular manner could be easily stripped down to be very acceptable to them. Simple churches could combine the two styles, late Gothic and Classical, as Denbigh and Standish showed. The experiments of the French in the sixteenth century, however, showed the impossibility of combining the Classical and the medieval styles in churches of any pretension. In England, although the medieval style continued to be the acceptable style for a church, it ceased to be the subject of any development. It was a cultural inheritance, important for the messages of conservatism and decent

Protestantism and therefore for its existence not its innovation. When a suitable alternative was found, which conveyed the same messages, the medieval building tradition was relegated to the world of the rural backwater and traditional crafts.

The patrons exacerbated the decline by shifting away from great churches to great houses from the 1530s onwards. This principally concerned the masters and designers; there would be no demand for the complex high vaults or buttressing of the medieval church. Neither Inigo Jones nor Christopher Wren were trained as masons and the focus on secular buildings encouraged patrons to become involved in design, a movement greatly increased for both them and the masters, by the arrival of printed pattern books. This would lead to an increasing concern with academically correct Classical style rather than innovation. The medieval building community was thus broken up. The patrons and the masters were no longer concerned with designing ever more ambitious churches in the tradition of the last 500 years. The industry which had conceived and delivered the great medieval churches was dismantled in favour of different principles of design and structure. These trends left the sub-contractor level alone; as the buildings of Oxford showed clearly, the same craftsmen could produce both medieval tracery and Classical motifs. They became the mason dynasties and the last remnant of the craft training and tradition of the Middle Ages, the 'provincial' builders of the time.

Neither the faith nor the pride was ended, for they are still with us, nor were many of the individual skills. It was the way in which they were combined, by patrons and craftsmen working together, that was lost with the Middle Ages. We may regret, along with Morris and Ruskin, the loss of the community which had connected all these levels together into the one industry, based on the handicraft skill of the masons. This is futile, for the social and economic world which had sustained the industry had gone and it cannot be recreated. What it has left, however, are many of its products. It is no wonder that so many have survived, compared to the other traces of the Middle Ages, partly because they were often very well built. More importantly it was only in the eighteenth century that they have ever been seriously disparaged. Ever since then they have been appreciated both as direct points of contact with the period that produced them and as buildings of great beauty which can still inspire and astound us.

BIBLIOGRAPHY

Very obviously this is simply a list of the principal sources used in the writing of this book, not in any way a complete bibliography of all the articles used, let alone of the subject. It omits many of the articles on individual churches, or aspects of them, found in journals, especially the *Antiquaries Journal, Architectural Journal, Journal of the British Archaeological Association* (and note particularly the series of their *Conference Transactions* studying individual major churches, published individually), or the *Journal of the Society of Architectural Historians*. That the weight of the bibliography is on the earlier chapters reflects merely that the remains of these are more fragmentary, or found through excavation, so that they cannot be simply visited and observed so much and, also, that there are fewer general studies of them.

GENERAL

A number of books cover more than one chapter, collected here to avoid repetition:

Conant, K.J. *Carolingian and Romanesque architecture*, Penguin, 1966
Fawcett, R. *Scottish medieval churches*, Tempus, 2002
Frankl, P. *Gothic architecture*, Penguin, 1962
Greene, J.P. *Medieval monasteries*, Leicester, 1992
Grodecki, L. *Gothic Architecture*, H.N. Abrams, 1977
Harvey, J. *The Gothic world*, Batsford, 1950
Morris, R. *Cathedrals and abbeys of England and Wales*, Dent, 1979
Nussbaum, N. *German Gothic architecture*, Yale University Press, 2000
Stalley, R.A. *Early medieval architecture*, Oxford University Press, 1999
Webb, G. *Architecture in Britain; the middle ages*, Penguin, 1965
Wilson, C. *The Gothic cathedral*, Thames and Hudson, 1996

I INTRODUCTION

The account of the financing of churches comes from:

Colvin, H.M. *The building accounts of Henry III*, Oxford University Press, 1971

Colvin, H.M., Brown, R.A. and Taylor, A.J. The history of the King's works, HMSO, 1963

James, J. What price the cathedrals, in *Ancient Monuments Society Transactions*, 19, 1972, 47–65

Kraus, H. *Gold was the mortar*, Routledge Keegan Paul, 1979

For the organisation and trades involved in the building of a church:

Binding, G. *Medieval building techniques*, Tempus, 2004

Harvey, J. *Medieval craftsmen*, Batsford, 1975

Harvey, J. *Henry Yevele*, Batsford, 1944; for which see also McLees, D.A. Henry Yevele, disposer of the King's works of masonry, in *Journal of the British Archaeological Association*, Third series, 36, 1973, 52–71

Salzman, L.F. *Building in England down to 1540*, Oxford University Press, 1952, chapter 3 (for the two Williams)

2 THE FIRST ROMANESQUE

Blockley, K., Sparks, M. and Tatton-Brown, T. *Canterbury Cathedral nave*, Canterbury Archaeological Trust, 1997

Cambridge, E. and Williams, A. Hexham abbey; a review of recent work and its implications, in *Archaeologia Aeliana*, Fifth series, 1995, 23, 51–138

Cramp, R. Monkwearmouth and Jarrow in their European context, in Painter, K., *Churches built in ancient times; recent studies in early Christian Archaeology*, Society of Antiquaries occasional papers 16, 1994, 279–94

Fernie, E. *The architecture of the Anglo-Saxons*, Batsford, 1983

Gem, R.D.H. A B C: How should we periodize Anglo-Saxon architecture? In Butler, L.A.S. and Morris, R.K. (eds) *The Anglo-Saxon church*, C.B.A. Research Report 60, 1986, 146–55

Gem, R.D.H. Tenth-century architecture in England, in *Settimane di Studio del centro Italiano di Studi sull'Alto Medioevo*, 1991, 38, 803–36

Gem, R.D.H. Architecture of the Anglo-Saxon Church, 735 to 870; from Archbishop Ecgberht to Archbishop Ceolnoth, in *Journal of the British Archaeological Association*, 1993, 146, 29–66

Gibb, J.H.P. and Gem, R.D.H. The Anglo-Saxon cathedral at Sherborne, in *Archaeological Journal*, 132, 1975, 71–110

Oswald, F., Schaefer, L. and Sennhauser, H.R. *Vorromanischer kircher*, Prestel-Verlag, 1966

Ottaway, J. Traditions architecturales dans le nord de la France pendant le premier millénaire, in *Cahiers de Civilisation Médiévale*, 23, 1980, 141–239

Rigold, S.E. The distribution of early Romanesque towers to minor churches, in *Archaeological Journal*, 1979, 136, 109–17

Taylor, H.M. and Taylor, H.J. *Anglo-Saxon Architecture*, vols 1-2 (1965), vol. 3 (1978),
    Cambridge University Press
Taylor, H.M. 1987, St Wystan's church, Repton, Derbyshire, in *Archaeological Journal*, 144,
    205-45
Wilkinson, D. and McWhirr, A. 1998, *Cirencester Anglo-Saxon church and medieval Abbey*,
    Cotswold Archaeological Trust

3 SECOND ROMANESQUE: THE GREAT CHURCH ACHIEVED

Blockley, K., Sparks, M. and Tatton-Brown, T. *Canterbury Cathedral nave*, Canterbury
    Archaeological Trust, 1997
Gem, R.D.H. Lincoln Minster: ecclesia pulchra, ecclesia fortis, in the *Conference
    Transactions of the British Archaeological Association for 1982*, 1986, 9-28
Gem, R.D.H. England and the resistance to Romanesque architecture, in Harper-Bill,
    C. *et al.* (eds), *Studies in medieval history presented to R. Allen Brown*, Boydell, 1989,
    129-39
Jarrett, M.G. and Mason, H. Greater and more splendid; some aspects of Durham
    cathedral, in *Antiquaries Journal*, 75, 1995, 189-234
Kaiser, W. Romanesque architecture in Germany, in Toman, R. (ed.), *Romanesque*,
    Konemann, 1997, 32-73
Royal Commission of the Historical Monuments of England, Excavations at York
    Minster, vol. 2, HMSO, 1985
Stalley, R.A. *The Cistercian monasteries of Ireland*, Yale University Press, 1987
Stalley, R.A. Three Irish buildings with West Country origins, in the *Conference
    Transactions of the British Archaeological Association for 1981*, 1981, 62-80
Wilson, C. Abbot Serlo's church at Gloucester, in the *Conference Transactions of the British
    Archaeological Association for 1985*, 1985, 52-83

4 EXCURSUS: ARCHES, VAULTS AND BUTTRESSES

Mark, R. Structural analysis of Gothic cathedrals, in *Scientific American*, no. 251, 1984, 89-9

5 THE DEVELOPMENT OF THE GOTHIC STYLE:
THE FRENCH KINGDOM 1125-1225

Clark, W.W. Spatial innovations in the chevet of St Germain-des-Prés, in *Journal of the
    Society of Architectural Historians*, 38, 1979, 348-65
Crosby, S.M. *The royal abbey of St Denis*, Yale University Press, 1987
James, J. Flying buttresses before 1180, in *Journal of the Society of Architectural Historians*, 51,
    1992, 61-87
von Simson, O. *The Gothic cathedral*, Bollingen Foundation, 1962

6 THE EARLY SPREAD OF GOTHIC STYLE

Bony, J. The resistance to Chartres in early 13th century architecture, in *Journal of the British Archaeological Association*, Third series, 20-21, 1957-8, 35-52

Brakspear, H.A. West Country school of masons, in *Archaeologia*, 81, 1931, 1-18

Colchester, L.S. and Harvey, J. Wells cathedral, in *Archaeological Journal*, 131, 1974, 202-14

Kidson, P. St Hugh's choir, in the *Conference Transactions of the British Archaeological Association for 1982*, 1986, 29-42

Leask, H.G. *Irish churches and monastic buildings*, vol. 2, Dundealgan Press, 1962

Stalley, R.A. The architecture of St David's cathedral, in *Antiquaries Journal*, 82, 2002, 13-45

Woodman, F. *The architectural history of Canterbury cathedral*, Routledge Keegan Paul, 1981

7 CLASSIC GOTHIC: 1200-1330

Bony, J. *The English decorated style*, Phaidon, 1975

Coldstream, N. *The Decorated style*, British Museum Press, 1994

8 LATE GOTHIC

Ashwell, B.J. Gloucester cathedral south transept: a fourteenth century conservation project, in *Antiquaries Journal*, 65, 1985, 112-20

Harvey, J. *The Perpendicular style 1330-1485*, Batsford, 1978

Fawcett, R. Re-living bygone glories? The revival of earlier architectural forms in Scottish late medieval churches, in *Journal of the British Archaeological Association*, Third series, 45, 2003, 104-37

9 THE END OF MEDIEVAL CHURCH BUILDING

Colvin, H.M. *Essays in English architectural history*, Yale University Press, 1999, chapters 3 and 13

Roulston, W. *The provision, building and architecture of the Anglican churches in the North of Ireland*, unpublished Ph.D. thesis, Queen's University of Belfast, 203

GLOSSARY OF ARCHITECTURAL TERMS

Italic words are found in other entries

Aisle – A narrower space to the side of the *nave* of a church, separated from it by an
    arcade

Ambulatory – A space for circulation between the high altar and the chapels at the east
    end

Apse – A projecting part of the building, semicircular in plan (hence apsidal). Apse
    echelon is when the central apse of three or five projects more than those to the
    south and north

Arcade – A continuous row of arches

Arch – Arches may be classified/described according to their shape, usually made by
    compass arcs from points or centres. They are made up of wedge-shaped stones
    (voussoirs), and supported by piers or columns; the arch and the support are usually
    separated by an impost (pier or walling) or a *capital* (column)

Base – The decorated plinth on which a column sits

Bay – A vertical division of a wall; in the nave of a church usually defined by the arches
    of the main *arcade*. When two bays are linked together, they make up a double-bay
    system

Buttress – A pier of masonry projecting from the line of a wall to provide support to
    the wall or the vault it carries

Capital – A decorated stone at the top of a column or shaft, which separates it from the
    arch above

Chancel – East end of a church; in bigger churches divided into *choir* and *presbytery*

Chapter House – The room in a monastery (normally in the east *range* of the cloister)
    where the community met to hear a chapter of the Rule read out and to discuss
    business

Chevet – The east end of church with a semicircular (or apsidal) *ambulatory* of which are set a ring of chapels

Choir – The part of the east end of a large church reserved for the clergy singing during services

Clerestory (Clearstory) – The upper stage of the nave wall of a church, above the top of the aisle roof, providing a line of windows

Moulding – A projecting strip of masonry (often around an arch) carved into a continuous, shaped profile

Mural tower – A tower set along a wall

Nave – The main space in a church west of the transepts and crossing; the most public part

Pilaster strip – A vertical strip of masonry projecting from the wall face; decorative rather than structural, like a *buttress*

Presbytery – The part of the east end of a large church, housing the main altar

Quoin – Corner stone

Range – A row of rooms or buildings, often used when they run down the side of an enclosed space, such as a cloister

Shaft – A narrow column, usually attached to a wall, pier or larger column

Transept – The arms of a church, projecting north or south of the crossing

Triforium – The middle stage of the internal elevation of a church, between the main *arcade* and the *clerestory*, covering the roof of the *aisle*: it may be opened out to be a gallery

Tympanum – The semicircular space between an arch and the top of a rectangular door frame, or smaller arch, set within it

Vault – A stone covering over a building, below the roof. The main systems are: barrel, groin and rib vaults

INDEX

If you are interested in purchasing other books published by Tempus,
or in case you have difficulty finding any Tempus books in your local bookshop,
you can also place orders directly through our website

www.tempus-publishing.com